THE HAPPY DESIGN TOOLKIT

Architecture for Better Mental Wellbeing

RIBA Publishing

BEN CHANNON

© RIBA Publishing 2022

Published by RIBA Publishing, 66 Portland Place, London, W1B 1AD

ISBN 978 1 85946 986 6

The right of Ben Channon to be identified as the Author of this Work has been asserted in accordance with the Copyright, Designs and Patents Act 1988 sections 77 and 78.

All rights reserved. No part of this publication may be reproduced, stored in a retrieval system, or transmitted, in any form or by any means, electronic, mechanical, photocopying, recording or otherwise, without prior permission of the copyright owner.

British Library Cataloguing-in-Publication Data
A catalogue record for this book is available from the British Library.

Commissioning Editor: Ginny Mills

Assistant Editor: Scarlet Furness

Production: Sarah-Louise Deazley

Designed and typeset by Mercer Design, London

Printed and bound by Short Run Press, Exeter

Cover illustration: Ben Channon

While every effort has been made to check the accuracy and quality of the information given in this publication, neither the Author nor the Publisher accept any responsibility for the subsequent use of this information, for any errors or omissions that it may contain, or for any misunderstandings arising from it.

www.ribapublishing.com

Contents

Acknowledgements IV
About the author V

Introduction 1

1. Light, natural and artificial 4

2. Comfort and materials 30

3. Control and autonomy 60

4. Nature and biophilia 92

5. Aesthetics and legibility 130

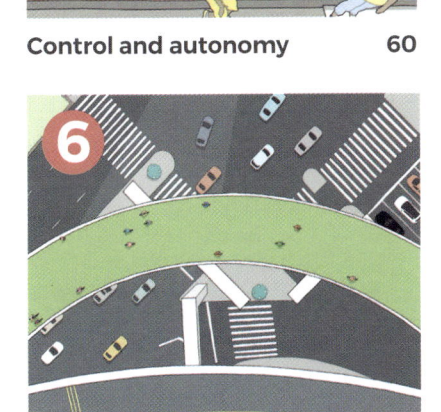

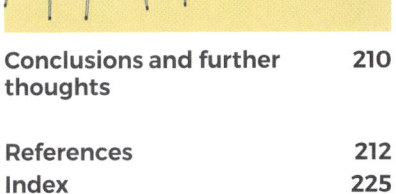

6. Activity and exercise 154

7. Social interaction, community and sense of place 180

Conclusions and further thoughts 210

References 212
Index 225
Image Credits 234

Acknowledgements

There are several people without whom this book wouldn't have happened, and I'd like to take the opportunity here to thank them.

First, thank you to my old colleagues at Assael Architecture for supporting me on my quest to better understand what makes buildings truly healthy, for giving me opportunities to explore and research this topic and for championing my work for many years.

Thanks also to the amazing team at Ekkist for helping me to take my understanding of designing healthy buildings even further, for their ongoing support, and their continual enthusiasm around this subject.

Thank you to my family for pushing me on the good days and being there on the bad ones – I'm very lucky to have you and very proud of every one of you.

Biggest thanks of all to my incredible wife, Alex, for putting up with all the weekends I've spent at my laptop and for getting through a year of lockdown with me in our tiny flat. Let's hope for all our sakes we never have to do that again.

About the author

Ben Channon is an architect who has specialised in designing healthy buildings. He is a director at the design-for-wellbeing consultancy Ekkist, where he advises clients and design teams on how to create healthier places, and researches how buildings and urban design can have an impact on how we feel.

He developed an interest in design for mental health, wellbeing and happiness after suffering with anxiety problems in his mid-twenties. This led him to research the relationship between buildings and happiness, which formed the basis of his first book, *Happy by Design: A Guide to Architecture and Mental Wellbeing*. Ben now speaks on this subject to businesses and universities around the world.

Ben became a WELL Accredited Professional in 2019, broadening his knowledge to encompass design for physical wellbeing. He now sits on the WELL Mind Advisory panel, using his expertise to raise the bar for healthy buildings worldwide.

In 2017, Ben co-founded the Architects' Mental Wellbeing Forum, which is focused on improving mental health within the industry. He is also an accredited mindfulness practitioner with the Mindfulness Association and is interested in how buildings can help us to be more mindful and present every day.

Introduction

> 'Architecture is an act of optimism.'
> – NICOLAI OUROUSSOFF, ARCHITECTURE CRITIC

Figure 0.0: John Morden Centre, London, UK, by Mæ

Growing up, I didn't think much about mental health. While I certainly had my ups and downs, it wasn't something which I ever really thought I would need to give much attention. However, this all changed in my mid-twenties.

I was working at a large architecture practice and putting in long hours to try to impress those above me with my work ethic. Like many people at that age, I had the sense that in some ways I was almost indestructible. I soon discovered, though, that doing 70-hour weeks interspersed with nights out at the weekends was not as sustainable as I had first thought.

My problems initially took the form of physical health issues – coughs or colds that wouldn't budge, for example. After numerous trips to the doctor, my GP suspected something else was going on and asked me about my mental health.

It quickly became clear that I wasn't as indestructible as I had believed, and that to all extents and purposes I had completely burned myself out. Without realising it, I had become a very anxious person and my mental resilience to dealing with problems had almost completely disappeared. Fortunately, I was able to access some support in the form of CBT sessions, and I began meditating on a daily basis – something that I try to maintain today. I also reassessed my working habits and began to cultivate a philosophy of working smart and focusing on output rather than hours at the desk.

As a result of these lifestyle changes, I am pleased to say I made a return to full health, but as I continued designing homes for people every day, I began to think about the ways in which the buildings I was designing were affecting people psychologically. I became acutely aware that in spite of going to an excellent architecture school, the implications of architectural design on mental wellbeing were something we were never taught.

I started to research the subject and discovered there was a vast wealth of knowledge and research being generated by a fascinating group of people called 'environmental psychologists' about the ways in which space affects how we think and feel. However, for some reason this knowledge wasn't always making its way to the people who design spaces, meaning that much of this valuable research never had the opportunity to inform the buildings that people use every day. This prompted me to write my first book, *Happy by Design: A Guide to Architecture and Mental Wellbeing*.

Happy by Design was an exploration of the ways in which buildings can have an impact on how we feel, for better or for worse, and through the book I hoped to provide a conceptual overview of the subject. Since this book was published, the same questions kept cropping up after I gave lectures or talks: 'How can we bring this knowledge into our buildings?' and 'What does it look like?' This book seeks to answer exactly those questions.

In a way, this book can be considered a big brother or sister to *Happy by Design*. While that book can be seen more as a conceptual overview of the relationship between our environment and our mental wellbeing, this is more of a practical guide or a set of tools to help people integrate those concepts and philosophies into real-life projects.

When I began my own mission to learn more about how buildings affect our mental wellbeing, very few people within the architecture industry were talking about the subject. This mirrored a wider societal problem that – even in the early 2010s – mental health was still a taboo subject that was largely ignored or brushed under the carpet. However, in recent years we have witnessed a change in mindset around this issue, which has been felt within the construction industry too.

I now speak to developers almost every day who want to know how they can make their buildings healthier places for the people who use them, and the perception of healthy buildings is gradually shifting from a 'nice thing to have' to an essential component of any new project. Globally, the percentage of both retail and institutional investors that apply environmental, social, and governance (ESG) principles to at least a quarter of their portfolios jumped from 48% in 2017 to 75% in 2019,[1] demonstrating that ethical construction has become more important than ever, while surveys suggest that healthy buildings are becoming ever-more important to consumers too.[2] This book is therefore meant to help not only designers, but developers in their quest to create healthier places and fund managers seeking to identify buildings that have been designed with health and wellbeing in mind.

I wrote this book during the COVID-19 pandemic, and while I was keen for this not to dominate its content, it has been impossible not to reflect in some way upon the impact the pandemic has had on us and our relationship with the built environment. One of the few positives to come out of the situation is, I believe, that the numerous lockdowns have caused us all to think more deeply about our homes and the psychological impact their design has had on us, with a survey by the Royal Institute of British Architects discovering that 70% of people felt the design of their home affected their mental wellbeing during the pandemic.[3]

While many have discovered that the buildings they use every day perhaps do not suit their psychological needs as well as they may have thought pre-pandemic, we have seen a spirit of optimism emerge over the last year. Rather than focus on the failings of the built environment around us, there has been a call by many to see this as an opportunity to 'build back better' and to learn lessons from the situation so that we may keep improving the built environment.[4]

Before we can consider the different tools that we can use to design buildings that support good mental wellbeing, it is important for us to outline exactly what we mean by this term. The *Oxford English Dictionary* describes wellbeing as: 'The state of being or doing well in life; happy, healthy, or prosperous condition.' Psychologists talk of two forms of mental wellbeing: eudaemonic, which is associated with a sense of purpose or a meaning in life, and hedonic, which can be thought of as a form of happiness in response to a stimulus or behaviour.[5]

A building that is designed with our mental wellbeing in mind should consider all these issues, thereby making our lives easier and happier. It should allow us to live and work productively, form and maintain positive relationships, and support a sense of purpose and personal pride in our lives. It should also create a simple but often overlooked phenomenon: joy!

Joy and happiness may sometimes be seen as frivolous or unimportant, but in fact research shows that they play a critical role in our quality of life.[6] Not only do happier people perform at a higher level in the workplace and as a result tend to achieve greater career success,[7] research from Harvard University shows that happy, positive people are likely to live longer too.[8] Optimists have been found to have a reduced risk of heart disease, stroke, early death from cancer and decline in lung performance as they age. This means that if we can create buildings that make people feel happier than they are currently, the potential benefits to both individuals and society as a whole could be enormous.

It is important to distinguish between mental wellbeing and mental health. While good mental wellbeing and good mental health may have many similarities, I am not arguing in this book that we can use design to 'cure' serious mental health problems such as schizophrenia or psychosis. However, it is also important to explain that just as we all have physical health (be it good or bad), we also all have mental health. Like our physical health, this can fluctuate from one day to the next, but as with many things both tend to be distributed across a bell curve, with the majority of people having neither terrible nor exceptional physical or mental health at any given time.

While the design of places around us may not be able to tackle serious mental health crises, these often occur as the result of an accumulation of many factors.[9] This could include problems with sleeping, physical health, social isolation or discrimination, for example – all of which are factors that we can address and improve through the built environment. This means that (along with other strategies) buildings could, in fact, play an important role in preventing problems with our mental health before they spiral out of control, by shifting everybody a few percentile points up on the bell curve.

There are a few final points I would like to make before we dive into the toolkit itself. The first is the importance of research and data in writing both this book and *Happy by Design*. I firmly believe that evidence and scientific data should play a vital role in the designs we are creating today. That is not to say that artistic merit and creativity do not have their place, as the work of countless architects from Michelangelo to Gaudí clearly illustrate. However, if we are claiming to make design interventions that will have a positive impact on the people who use them (particularly if it will also affect, say, build cost or design programme), we must be able to back up our argument with evidence.

Designing and constructing buildings of any type requires a broad knowledge base, but if we are prepared to use data within our designs and engage the services of experts such as environmental psychologists and neuroscientists, we can strengthen our case for high-quality design.

I also wanted to touch upon a key theme that is repeated within this book: the importance and value of diversity in both cities and design teams, be this in regard to gender, age, race, sexuality, disability or socioeconomic background. As we all write from a specific cultural and biological starting position, I have tried my best to consult with a diverse range of people in the researching and writing process. I hope that this comes across and that no parts of the book seem narrow-minded in their approach; if this is the case, I can only apologise in advance and would welcome hearing readers' differing perspectives on some of the book's themes. While many of the tools will be of benefit to the majority of the population, it is important to consider the ways in which design decisions will affect everybody – a raised window sill may offer benefits to some, but if it is too high it could prevent views out for a wheelchair user, for example.

Designing buildings for mental wellbeing can be viewed as a simple goal that unfortunately cannot always be achieved, usually as a result of other obstacles that get in the way, be they cost, time or lack of expertise. It is about creating places and cities that act as a supportive backdrop to people's lives and allow them to thrive. This book offers tools to help anybody working on a building to do exactly that, whether you are an experienced architect or a first-time homeowner who wants to improve how your new house makes you feel every day. The tools span a range of scales and building types, so not all may be suitable for every site, but I would encourage you to find the ones that are the best fit for your goals and consider how you could integrate them into your project. The most important thing is that people set out with the intention to create better places and I hope this book helps you to achieve exactly that.

How to use this book

The book is organised into seven chapters, which I hope are fairly self-explanatory. These key themes emerged from the research process and connect back to the concepts I explored in my first book, *Happy by Design*. This research process was a combination of reviewing existing literature from environmental psychology, neuroscience and architecture, alongside conversations with experts in each of these fields and my ongoing work at Ekkist, where we continually research ways in which to improve the health and wellbeing of the people who use our clients' buildings.

Each chapter contains a series of 'design tools' or building features, which can be utilised across a range of project types from homes to schools, workplaces to community hubs, or allotments to sprawling parks. As these vary in terms of both scale and cost, they have been labelled as S, M, L and XL, to quickly give readers a sense of what size of project and budget they might be suited to. There is an additional category for tools which are conceptual rather than physical, such as 'Personal Space Bubbles' (see Chapter 3) – such tools have been labelled with a '⌘' symbol.

S **M** **XL** **L** **⌘**

While the design tools have been sorted into their most relevant chapters, there is unsurprisingly a great deal of overlap between the various themes. As an example, something as simple as a well-designed window can have benefits in terms of our sleep, thermal comfort, air quality, privacy, nature-connectedness and the creation of joy. Each design tool, therefore, also includes a summary of the potential mental wellbeing benefits it offers, along with some of the likely considerations or issues that one may need to be aware of when including such a feature in a built project.

CHAPTER 1
Light, natural and artificial

> 'Light belongs to the heart and spirit. Light attracts people, it shows the way, and when we see it in the distance, we follow it.' – RICARDO LEGORRETA, ARCHITECT

Figure 1.0: In Praise of Shadows house, Tel Aviv-Yafo, Israel, by Pitsou Kedem Architects

It is not an exaggeration to say that without light, we simply would not exist. The sun's light is responsible for sustaining almost all life on earth, with the exception of the animals who receive their energy from hydrothermal vents on the ocean floor. Without light there would be no plant life, destroying food chains and the planet's supply of oxygen.

The other obvious way in which light helps us, of course, is in allowing us to see things. It is easy to forget that when we look at buildings, we are not actually seeing the bricks or timbers themselves, but the electromagnetic radiation that bounces back off them. Even if we could somehow survive without light, daily life would undoubtedly become a much more challenging experience, forcing us to rely on our other senses to navigate the world around us.

Despite this, for the most part we take light for granted, with most of us having access to electric light at the push of a button – although our forebears would have been all too aware of what a world without light felt like. As Bill Bryson explained: 'We forget just how painfully dim the world was before electricity. A candle, a good candle, provides barely a hundredth of the illumination of a single 100-watt light bulb.'[1] Before we harnessed the power of electricity to light spaces in the nineteenth century, even with candles, gas lamps and oil lamps, humanity was immeasurably more dependent on the sun's light than we are today.

While we might not think about its existence that much, three and a half billion years of evolution on a planet abundant with the sun's light has unsurprisingly resulted in daylight being rather beneficial for us as a species. Most of us are aware of its connection to vitamin D – when our skin is exposed to sunlight, our bodies produce the vitamin using energy from cholesterol. The production of vitamin D is vital for good physical and mental health, helping to regulate our calcium and phosphate levels. Without it, we can develop problems with our bones, teeth and muscles, and it can lead to fatigue and depression.

Exposure to daylight plays a key role in supporting our mental health in other ways too, with a key example being our circadian rhythms. Circadian rhythms are the physical, mental and behavioural changes that all our bodies undertake every day, from waking and sleeping to releasing hormones, and even when we eat or use the toilet.[2] The body naturally manages these rhythms itself through a 'master clock' in a part of the brain called the hypothalamus, but this is highly sensitive to the colour – and most importantly quantity – of light (sometimes called Equivalent Melanopic Lux or EML) to which our eyes are exposed.

Every morning, as we are exposed to high quantities of blue morning light, our body temperature starts to increase and chemicals are released that make us feel more awake.[3] As this light changes throughout the day, becoming 'warmer' on the colour spectrum, our bodies release melatonin and we start to get sleepy. For this reason, a good amount of morning daylight exposure – particularly within the first hour of waking – is connected to getting a better night's sleep. As anybody who has read Matthew Walker's excellent book, *Why We Sleep*, will know, regularly losing even just a couple of hours sleep a night can have a significant impact on both our physical and mental health.[4]

Studies have also demonstrated that the rate of production of serotonin by the brain is directly related to the quantity of bright sunlight available at a given time.[5] Serotonin is a hormone which affects our mood and appetite (as well as our sleep). This can result in low mood and even symptoms of depression, and when this happens as a result of reduced exposure to light in winter it is known as seasonal affective disorder (or SAD).

Historically, architects have generally championed the importance of light. Le Corbusier stated: 'Architecture is a learned game, correct and magnificent, of forms assembled in the light.'[6] This poetic dialogue between light and physical forms seems to have fascinated architects since the ancient Greeks at the very least, although in a sense this is very logical – without light, we could not experience their visual compositions, and indeed there could be no 'beauty' as we know it.

It is certainly true that visual experiences, be it a vibrant colour or the play of light across a surface, can create a feeling of uplifting joy in us. However, bringing light into buildings can create problems for designers. Solar gains can result in overheating, whereas too much glass in the wrong orientation can cause heat loss. If handled badly, light can cause glare, resulting in discomfort, distraction, headaches and even damage to the eyes. It is up to designers to therefore harness the power of light in a positive way, avoiding these issues while maximising the positive benefits it has to offer.

A welcoming window seat

> 'Your desire to be near a window is your desire to be close to life!'
> – MEHMET MURAT ILDAN, AUTHOR

Figure 1.1: A window seat can be a cosy place to relax and socialise

Potential mental wellbeing benefits

- Improved sleep
- Feel-good chemical release
- Nature interaction
- Sense of privacy
- Mindfulness opportunity

Potential issues and considerations

- Space requirements
- Impact on layouts

I got the idea for writing this book when sitting on a window seat at my family home, so it seems fitting that it should be the first feature in this book. The window seat in question is something between a bench and a bed, with soft cushions and a beautiful view along a green Devonshire valley. As I sat there reading, I realised just how many positive psychological benefits were provided by such a simple design feature.

First, due to their inherent proximity to glazing, window seats offer more daylight than perhaps any other form of internal furniture. Not only does this light offer all those unseen benefits – such as supporting our circadian rhythms – but as the sun falls on skin it can provide a gentle warmth, giving us an instant sense of pleasure and positivity, as well as engaging our senses.

I am aware that in the introduction to this book I explained that it is vital for us to support all our design decisions with a strong base of evidence and that this might feel fairly anecdotal, but studies show this feeling of pleasure I experienced from the sunlight on my skin is fairly universal across humans. One such study found that people had higher serotonin levels on sunny days than on cloudy ones, which may have caused that feeling of positivity, as it correlates with better mood, feelings of satisfaction and calmness.[7] There was certainly an element of being more mindful and more in touch with my senses too – something we will come on to explore later in this book.

Being in close proximity to the window also allowed me to experience how the light, sky and weather changed throughout the morning, providing a gentle reference to the passing of time. These dynamics of light and shadow are an element of biophilia – or love of nature – which we will also explore the benefits of later.[8] Window seats can offer other biophilic interactions, too, such as the view on to trees, hedges and animals I was afforded in this instance. With the seat located snugly inside a nook, I was fortunate enough to have both a view out over the countryside and a good view back into the room itself, giving me a psychological sense of safety and a reassurance of my privacy.

Furthermore, when the sun's heat became too much, I was able to easily open the window and benefit from a cooling breeze, giving me an instant level of control over my personal thermal comfort. Added advantages of this were the pleasant smells that drifted in from the garden, along with the sound of birds, engaging two more of my senses with further biophilic elements.

As you continue reading this book, I encourage you to come back to the humble window seat, as it addresses many of the chapters: light, comfort, control and nature in particular, with social and aesthetic benefits too, if designed in the right way. While it may seem like a small element of a building, in a sense the window seat encapsulates everything this book is about: using design moves or features that are often seemingly simple to create better places for the people who use them every day. By doing so, we can create moments of joy in the lives of our buildings' occupants and support better mental health throughout the population.

Design tips

1. Look to integrate other concepts from this book into a window seat; for example, by addressing human comfort through the materials specified, control by giving users autonomy over the thermal environment, or nature by locating it in the position with the best natural views.

2. Window seats can offer chances for storage within them too, reducing clutter and improving the internal appearance of a space. Where possible, consider how storage opportunities can be maximised in the design of any built-in furniture.

3. Explore how a window seat could encourage social interactions too; for example, by creating a space for two or more people, or using a larger nook to create facing seats or even a table within the recess.

Windows with raised sills

> 'Daylight reveals colour; artificial light drains it.'
> – HELENA RUBINSTEIN, ENTREPRENEUR

Figure 1.2: House in Kentish Town, London, UK, by TAK Architecture / Design

Potential mental wellbeing benefits

- Sense of privacy
- Greater adaptability
- Personalisation opportunities
- Nature interaction
- Physical comfort

Potential issues and considerations

- Aesthetic challenges (external)
- Use by all

The earliest 'windows' were little more than openings in walls or roofs, created to allow smoke and smells out as much as to let in light. As time went on these evolved, initially through being covered by animal skins or other materials to protect internal spaces from the elements, but this had the unfortunate result of blocking most or all the light from entering the interiors.

These simple openings developed differently around the world. In ancient China, Korea and Japan, for example, paper windows were commonplace.[9] While these would let in some light, they still did not offer views out when closed. Glass windows are first believed to have been used by the ancient Romans around AD 100, although these would have been very different to our windows, with poor optical quality due to the challenges of the manufacturing process.[10]

These disappeared (in Britain, at least) with the collapse of the Roman empire and did not reappear until the early seventeenth century.[11] However, it was not until experiments with automated manufacturing and float glass in the 1800s that window panes were able to expand beyond the split sashes common in the Georgian era – and the floor-to-ceiling height windows we are familiar with today were not possible until the invention of laminated glass in 1903.

As a result of this, traditional housing typologies (in the western world at least) generally feature smaller windows which do not run the full height of rooms, more in line with traditional Renaissance or Georgian sash windows. Nevertheless, floor-to-ceiling windows are often seen as the standard design approach for modern apartment buildings, begging the question: Why would apartments need different windows to houses?

At first glance, these big windows are an easy win, as they let in more light than 'house windows' with raised sills and have a larger openable area, allowing for better ventilation. However, like many aspects of design, the benefits and drawbacks are more complex than that. For example, thermal and daylight modelling tends to show that below 850mm lighting gains are minimal, but there is still a significant impact in terms of thermal gain, contributing to overheating. This effectively means that the bottom portion of the window is negatively impacting our thermal comfort without offering a great benefit in a daylight sense.

We must therefore conclude that this trend for full-height windows is an aesthetic decision only, rather than one based on any real science or health benefits. Before researching this subject thoroughly, I designed a number of apartment buildings with full-height glazing, having never questioned it as a design philosophy. Interestingly, when we reject it as an approach, we find that windows with raised sills offer further benefits to our wellbeing.

Firstly, they boast a greatly increased sense of privacy – it is much harder for somebody to look into an upper-floor bedroom from the street if its window has a raised sill. Full-height windows are also restrictive in a layout sense, as many furniture items can't be placed in front of them. By raising the bottom of the window, we allow homes to become more flexible and adaptable, giving residents greater choice and control over how they use them. Finally, raised sills create opportunities for decoration, personalisation, and the introduction of objects such as plants – all of which can better support our mental wellbeing.

Design tips

1. If designing a building with full-height windows, step back and question why these have been specified. If it is simply for external aesthetics, can another solution be used, such as ventilation panels below the window to create the sense of a taller opening?

2. Seek ways to give your window sills more functionality, such as a form of seating, a place for people to stop and talk in an office, or an opportunity for storage or ornamentation.

3. Use sills as an opportunity to bring natural or tactile materials, such as timber, into your design. Be aware of which materials are going into other parts of the window, such as sealants, as these can include toxic materials which can release harmful Volatile Organic Compounds (VOCs) into the air.

4. Be aware of the potential impact on wheelchair users and children – ensure views out are not restricted and that windows can still be opened from a seated position.

Deck access

> 'Any engineer can quantify light by which to read a book. But what about the poetic dimension of natural light: the changing nature of an overcast sky, the discovery of shade, the lightness of a patch of sunlight?' – NORMAN FOSTER, ARCHITECT

Figure 1.3: Freiburg Town Hall, Freiburg, Germany, by ingenhoven architects

Potential mental wellbeing benefits
- Improved sleep
- Nature interaction
- Physical comfort
- Social opportunities

Potential issues and considerations
- Protection from elements
- Safety
- Maintenance

Deck access is a simple concept: rather than bury your circulation space in the centre of a building where it has no daylight or reference to the outside world, you move it to the periphery. It is an approach that architects in the UK have tried to employ since the 1960s, when Alison and Peter Smithson proposed what they called 'streets in the sky'.

The Smithsons used this strategy for their design of Robin Hood Gardens, a social housing scheme in East London, envisaging their streets in the sky as social places where neighbours could meet and chat. Unfortunately, the scheme faced numerous problems, as did many similar ones. In the words of architectural critic Edwin Heathcote, 'what was built did not reach those techno-utopian heights. Instead, poorly maintained, ill-lit, urine-soaked routes often came to a dead end while half-hearted walkways became dark and uninviting.'[12] Heathcote identifies three of the major problems with such strategies, particularly when used in the setting of 1970s council housing: maintenance, safety and a distinct lack of legibility – all of which have their own issues when it comes to the mental wellbeing of people using those buildings and spaces.

However, deck access and versions of 'streets in the sky' have been employed with great success elsewhere in the world, suggesting that perhaps it is not the approach itself that is flawed but instead how it is designed and managed. It has been especially successful in east Asia, with Singapore and China in particular embracing this model, as seen in projects such as Zaha Hadid's Galaxy SOHO which feature both decks and sky bridges. When it is done well, the benefits of deck access for both physical and mental wellbeing are substantial.

The quality of the access itself is dramatically improved – provided, of course, that it improves upon the less successful examples above. Rather than a windowless, featureless corridor, residents benefit from a daylit journey, with potential for pleasant views of natural elements. Overheating is a significant comfort issue in many corridors, too, as they often have no way to ventilate their heat and even in the UK can exceed temperatures of 35°C (95°F) in winter months.

This is, of course, not an issue with deck access – although the cold and wet present other challenges. It is therefore important to consider local climate when using this approach and ensuring adequate protection from the weather is designed-in. Artificial lighting in such spaces is also key, to ensure they are safe and pleasant to use at night. If these issues are considered, deck access can indeed become valuable social space, with wider decks often being appropriated by residents playing cards, having a cup of tea or just stopping for a short chat.

Deck access can also offer significant benefits to the spaces they serve. They can allow a whole block of residential apartments to become dual aspect, as they do not back on to an internal corridor space. This not only allows for light to permeate both facades of the apartments, but it also enables cross ventilation, improving resident comfort. However, it is important that we consider privacy of such spaces if people are allowed to walk right past windows into spaces such as bedrooms.

While deck access may have earned itself a bad reputation in the twentieth century, on balance this seems unjustified. If used correctly, it can enhance not just the access route itself, but the quality of the accommodation it serves and ultimately the lives of the people who live (or work) in the building. It deserves another chance.

Design tips

1. Explore a deck access strategy early in the design process, even just as a quick study; it may offer more benefits than you initially anticipated.

2. Consider which side of the building would be best suited for deck access; this will depend on the character and function of the access route itself, as well as the surrounding context.

3. If designing a shared access space which is generous and intended to be used by residents for social interaction, look first to place it on the 'more pleasant' aspect. However, it could also be used as a glazed buffer to a noisy road to protect housing and provide acoustic benefits; every site will be different.

4. Consider local fire regulations when it comes to planning uses on your access routes – these may be restrictive and you may need to consider ways to manage this issue.

Roof lights, light tubes and sawtooth roofs

> 'Light, God's eldest daughter, is a principal beauty in a building.'
> – THOMAS FULLER, ARCHITECT

Figure 1.4: Office building, Zwartsluis, the Netherlands, by Arnoud Olie, B+O Architecten

Potential mental wellbeing benefits

- Improved sleep
- Physical comfort
- Environmental benefits
- Spatial benefits
- Greater adaptability

Potential issues and considerations

- Maintenance
- Loss of views
- Detailing

The idea of placing a hole in a building's roof is not a new one. In ninth-century Norway, Viking longhouses often featured openings in their ceilings to let light in and smoke out.[13] The traditional Mongolian yurt (or *ger*) generally included an openable section of felt above the centre of the structure which could serve much the same purpose. Today the need for such openings to remove smoke and dust is rarer, but we still employ them for their powerful ability to bring light into spaces.

There are a wide range of strategies to bring light in from above, depending on the constraints of the space and the desired outcomes. For example, a light tube or 'sun tunnel' can be an effective way to bring light into a space that is buried deep within a building or a natural structure like an earth mound or cave. However, the only reference it will offer to the outside world is the type of light that enters, as generally no real views are afforded by these devices.

The design and profile of the roof itself can also bring light into a space, such as through a sawtooth roof, which typically features a series of vertical glazed faces connected by diagonal 'roof' elements. Historically these were used in industrial spaces to bring daylight into large, deep-span buildings, where perimeter windows would have left the centre of the space insufficiently lit. Today, however, they are frequently used in art galleries or museums to prevent direct sunlight damaging delicate pieces. A further benefit is that the south-facing diagonal roof elements offer a great opportunity for solar panels, reducing a building's carbon footprint.

By far the most common approach, however, is the traditional roof light (or skylight). These offer a number of benefits to our wellbeing, not least the sheer amount of light they bring into a space. Tests by Velux have shown that roof windows provide at least twice as much light as vertical windows of the same size, and more than three times that of equally sized dormers.[14] Roof lanterns, which project upwards from the roof itself, can bring in even greater quantities of light and they also add height to rooms, giving us a greater sense of space and the associated feeling of psychological freedom (mentioned in *Happy by Design*[15]). However, they can generally only be used on flat roofs.

Roof lights can also help to ventilate spaces and offer instant control over occupant thermal comfort. As hot air rises to the top of rooms, opening a roof light is an even more effective way of cooling a space than opening a window.[16] However, they do have their downsides.

One of the main sacrifices of using a roof light instead of a window is the offer of views out, which can often be reduced or compromised. Even if we are in a position to see out of the opening, Pythagoras' theorem tells us that a piece of angled glass offers us much less of a vertical component than a window of the same size. Another issue to consider is glare, which can be significant if the location of roof lights is not carefully considered and tested during the design process. Nevertheless, openings in the roofs of buildings can offer significant benefits to both the lighting and thermal comfort aspects of a space – and while they are not a direct substitute for a window, they can play an important role in improving the quality of almost all building typologies.

Design tips

1. If a roof light doesn't offer views out, do not see it as a direct substitute for a window. These views are important to us psychologically in several ways and should be provided where possible.

2. Integrate roof lights into your wider ventilation strategy. Ensure they are openable where practical and consider modelling air flows to inform best positions.

3. Proprietary roof light products will be cheaper than bespoke ones. Explore 'off the shelf' options and use these as a starting point if you are keen to maximise your light and ventilation benefits on a tight budget.

4. Direct sunlight on to a workspace or seating area can be unpleasant in a sense of overheating or glare, so consider this when positioning roof lights.

Circadian lighting

> 'The best bridge between despair and hope is a good night's sleep.'
> – E. JOSEPH COSSMAN, ENTREPRENEUR AND AUTHOR

Figure 1.5: Living Lab experimental work environment, London, UK, features a circadian lighting system, by DaeWha Kang Design

Potential mental wellbeing benefits

- Improved sleep
- Increased productivity
- Physical comfort
- Increased autonomy

Potential issues and considerations

- Build cost
- Specialist input useful

Sleep is undoubtedly one of the biggest factors in our mental and physical health. In fact, Matthew Walker, author of Why We Sleep, argues that it is the underlying foundation on which all other pillars of health are built.[17] Sleep deprivation has been shown to increase a person's risk of cardiovascular disease by 45%,[18] with another study showing that people who averaged six or less hours of sleep a night were five times more likely to have a cardiac arrest, even when accounting for other factors.[19]

A lack of sleep impacts on our awareness and reactions as well, potentially making us more dangerous to those around us. Research shows that after 19 hours without sleep, people perform as badly on concentration tests as those who would be legally deemed over the alcohol limit to drive. Unsurprisingly, when we are in this state of sleep deficit, our mental health suffers too, with cortisol levels increasing and the rates of almost all common mental health problems rising.[20] Chronic sleep problems affect 50–80% of patients in a typical US psychiatric practice,[21] compared with 10–18% of adults in the general population. Given that between 50 and 70 million Americans are estimated to suffer from sleep-related problems (around 15–20% of the population), this is a major concern.[22]

While circadian rhythms vary from person to person (which is why some people are early risers and others are night owls), they are essential to a good night's sleep, and their main driver is light.[23] While it may seem that we all get significant exposure to light, typical indoor electric light levels often do not come close to the outdoor daylight equivalent, as most electric lighting does not provide the Equivalent Melanopic Lux (EML) levels we need to support our circadian rhythms on their own.[24]

As we will explore later, our circadian rhythms are also sensitive to the colour temperature of light (although quantity is the most important factor), as our brains associate bluer light with the morning sunrise and warmer light with the evening. With modern use of screens day and night, our natural rhythms are thrown further out of sync, potentially exacerbating sleep problems even further.

There is some good news, however: artificial lighting systems are now available that respond to and cater for our circadian rhythms. These can work in a number of ways, but essentially they mimic the pattern of light seen from sunrise to sunset, moving from warm colours (below 3,000K) at dawn through to the higher levels of brighter, cooler light we need at mid-morning (around 6,500K), before returning back to dimmer, warmer light as evening approaches.[25] While not all researchers agree on the effectiveness of this approach, numerous studies suggest that it can improve alertness and wellbeing across a range of building types, and major research bodies such as WELL are strongly in support of such systems.

What is clear is the vital role that sleep plays in relation to our mental health, and at present our relationships with the world around us seem to be magnifying this problem. If we want to improve our relationship with sleep, it will require lifestyle changes such as getting outside more and being more active, and the ways in which we design the built environment can play a key role as well. It is essential that we bring as much natural light as possible into buildings, but when we are reliant on artificial lighting it should be sympathetic to our bodies' needs and support a healthy relationship with sleep.

Design tips

1. Good light levels are especially important in the early and middle parts of the day. Consult a lighting specialist about how to achieve appropriate EML levels during these hours (a target of at least 150 EML at eye level is a good starting point).

2. When designing spaces that will be used in the evenings, consider the colour temperature of the lighting you are specifying: colder light (5000K and above) may have a negative impact on circadian rhythms

3. Where possible, design-in systems that allow users control over the brightness and temperature of the lighting themselves. We all respond to light slightly differently based on factors such as age and chronotype (how we sleep), so it makes sense to give people greater control over their own environments (see Chapter 3 for more information).

Atria, courtyards and double-height spaces   Ⓛ

❝ We are born of light. The seasons are felt through light. We only know the world as it is evoked by light.' – LOUIS KAHN, ARCHITECT

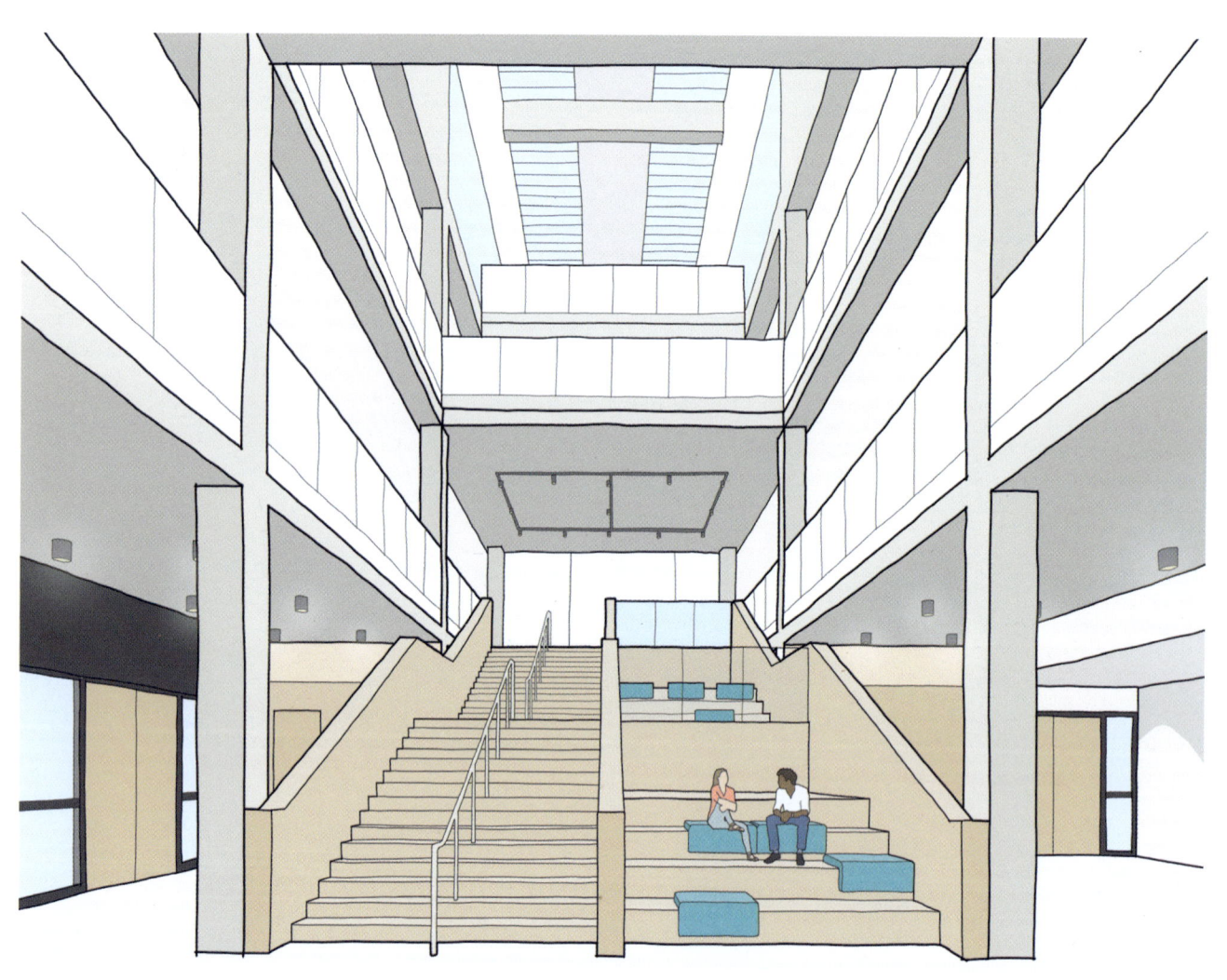

Figure 1.6: Moss House, University College Birmingham, UK, by Glenn Howells Architects

Potential mental wellbeing benefits

- Improved sleep
- Social opportunities
- Spatial benefits
- Nature interaction
- Moments of joy / awe

Potential issues and considerations

- Comfort issues
- Space / layout requirements
- Build cost

Typically, as designers we look to outside spaces to find light. However, it is possible to bring light deeper into a plan through other means such as an atrium or a courtyard. These architectural tools have been used for millennia, from the atria of the Roman *domus*, to the courtyard gardens or *tsuboniwa* of Japanese *machiya*, or the riads of Morocco and Andalusia. Modern construction techniques, with the large structural spans and expansive areas of glazing, have made the inclusion of increasingly impressive atria possible.

The primary benefit of atria is to bring light into a dense floor plan, which is typically achieved in two ways. The first approach is the creation of a central atrium, which offers light to all spaces around its perimeter and is generally the most effective at maximising the built footprint on a site. It can also be used for a series of buildings, such as individual houses, allowing for very dense typologies while still ensuring all spaces benefit from good levels of daylight – although in this example we might refer to it as a courtyard rather than an atrium.

Further wellbeing benefits of this approach include the inevitable creation of a quiet, fairly private central space which can easily become a peaceful garden or an area for socialising; as well as opportunities for visual connections, say between different office spaces gathered around the same atrium. This, of course, can generate privacy issues, depending on the dimensions of the atrium or courtyard.

The second common use of atria takes the form of a large entrance volume, around which secondary rooms may be arranged. This can be the full height of the building, allowing light in from the top, but similar benefits can be achieved on a smaller scale with double- or triple-height spaces, which still allow sunlight to permeate deeper into a room and can achieve a similar sense of space above us as we enter.

As well as the additional light brought into spaces, this sense of 'awe' is one of the other key psychological benefits of this approach and is perhaps why it was commonly used in the design of Byzantine churches and of many mosques around the world. High ceilings and a sense of space above us has been seen to inspire feelings of psychological freedom, and research also shows that a 'sense of awe' can be beneficial for our state of mind.[26]

Studies show that when we experience awe – either physically or even through being shown an awe-inspiring picture or being told an amazing story – we report greater life satisfaction and improved wellbeing, showing reduced symptoms of stress up to a week later.[27] While it may seem strangely intangible, we have all experienced awe through the world around us, and as designers it can be another tool in our armoury to help improve people's state of mind.

There are, of course, obstacles around using atria. When designed well, they can be useful tools in natural ventilation strategies; however any large internal volume can present challenges around thermal comfort, so input from a thermal design expert is important. It is also important to remember that a window on to an atrium will be unlikely to receive as much daylight as an external one, so modelling studies may be required to check spaces actually receive enough daylight. Finally, it is important to ensure the outlook on to an atrium is still a pleasant one, so explore bringing plants, art or colour into these spaces.

Design tips

1. The dimensions of an atria or courtyard can vary, depending on the building's use type. While they will need to be generous for a large office complex or shopping mall, they can be effective at quite narrow widths in a single home.

2. Building height will also have a significant impact on the appropriate width of an atrium, so remember that the dimensions of these will need to increase as the surrounding buildings get taller.

3. Atria and courtyards can often be some of the most expensive parts of buildings, so ensure you are maximising the value they offer, whether this is through using them as a social space, an opportunity to integrate nature or as a quiet place for relaxation and restoration.

Cloisters and daylit circulation

> 'All truly great thoughts are conceived by walking.'
> – FRIEDRICH NIETZSCHE, PHILOSOPHER

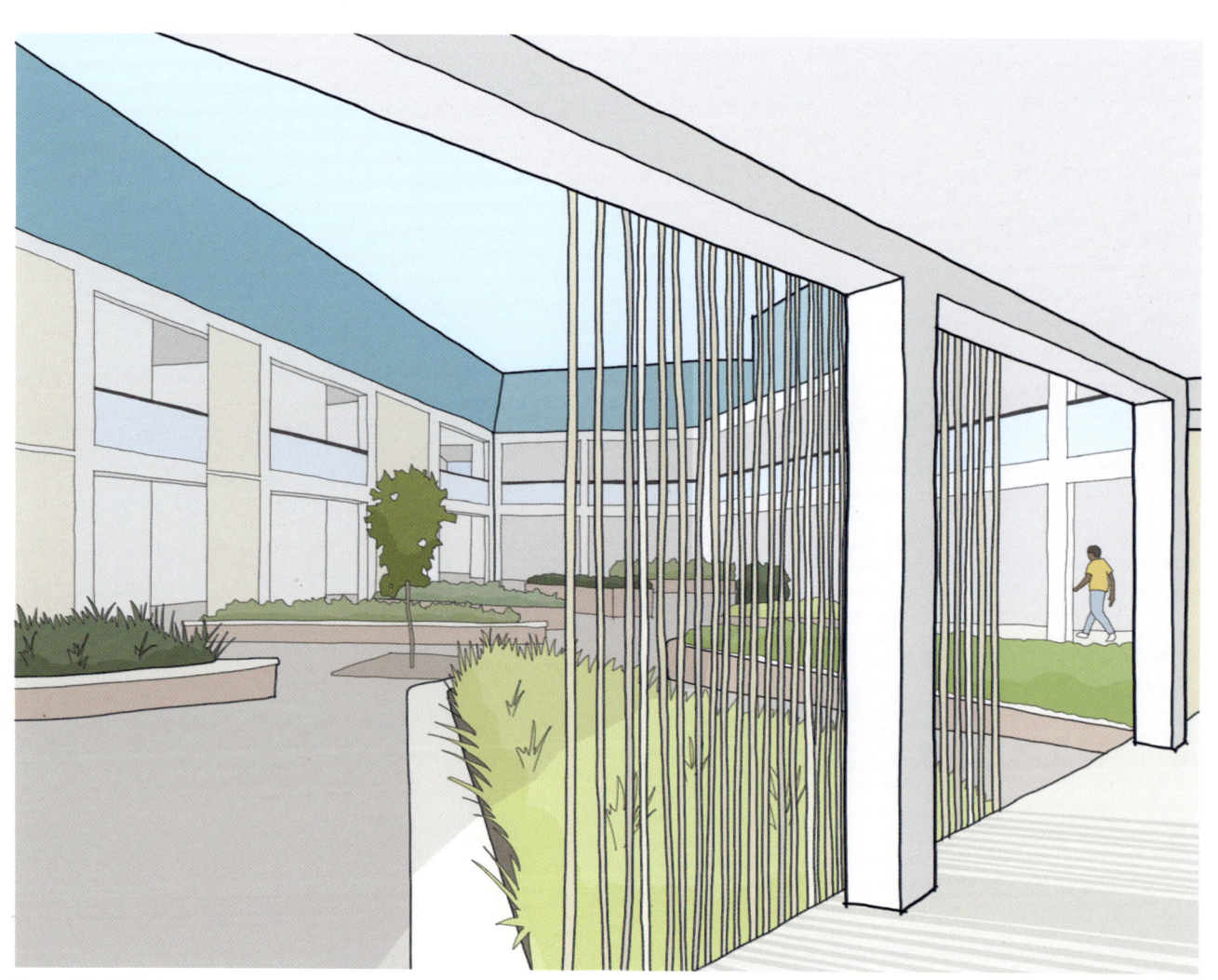

Figure 1.7: GHESKIO Tuberculosis Hospital, Port-au-Prince, Haiti, by MASS Design Group

Potential mental wellbeing benefits

- Increased activity
- Nature interaction
- Moments of joy / awe
- Physical comfort

Potential issues and considerations

- Protection from elements
- Space / layout requirements

Circulation space can often be one of the least-considered parts of a building. When designed poorly, it can simply become the way we get from one important space to another, with little thought given to the journey itself or the emotions people experience as they move around the building. It is not always the fault of the architect or interior designer, as circulation space is frequently viewed as unglamorous or unexciting by clients, and as a result often has very little budget allocated to it.

However, these spaces are important, be they corridors, stairwells, atriums or decks. These are very often the places in buildings where people have chance interactions with their neighbours or colleagues. They are where we experience the building with no tasks to carry out other than to walk and to look around us, and as such they can have a significant impact on how people remember a place. And they are possibly the only parts of a building that are guaranteed to be used every day – without them people simply couldn't move from space to space.

Historically, there seems to have been an understanding of the importance of these spaces, as a walk through the corridors of any Renaissance building will show you. Thankfully, as our understanding of the dangers of a sedentary lifestyle increases, more emphasis is being put on improving these spaces again, as we will come to investigate further in Chapter 6. We are now seeing a push towards wider corridors, with daylight, art, nature and stopping places, and I think we can all unite in the hope that narrow, white-painted plasterboard corridors will soon be a thing of the past.

Cloisters, like a deck access, are a fantastic way to bring many of these elements into a circulation space. The word 'cloister' actually has a variety of meanings, derived from monasteries and convents. It can be used to describe these places themselves or the central courtyards that they often feature, but in this instance we are using the word to refer to 'a covered passage on the side of a court usually having one side walled and the other an open arcade or colonnade'.[28]

Despite their history of use in religious buildings, cloisters are an excellent design tool for almost any use class, from schools to apartment buildings, particularly if we are already designing atria or courtyards into buildings. Arranging circulation to run alongside them can be a simple strategy to turn an uninspiring journey around a building into one that puts us in contact with light, nature and air.

By doing so we can give users views out on to natural elements, and it was common for traditional monastery cloister courtyards to include planting or ponds within them. We can even go a step further and open them up along one side, bringing in fresh air and blurring the lines between inside and out, creating even stronger connections with natural elements.

However, perhaps most importantly, cloisters offer the chance to bring in a lot of light. Instead of walking along a corridor with artificial lighting, occupants experience a space that feels partly inside, partly outside, where they can feel the warmth of the sun and see the play of shadows across its volume, and where it is pleasant to stop and have a conversation with fellow building users.

Design tips

1. Take inspiration from Roman or Renaissance cloisters: integrate colour, detail, art and views into a garden to make the experience of moving around your building special.

2. Traditionally, these spaces were used to separate monks from common people, allowing a 'cloistered' life, but now we should look to these spaces as opportunities to encourage social interaction, providing stopping places or chances to sit.

3. Where possible, maximise the light that these spaces receive to further encourage their use. If it is possible to add width or make them double height, this will further increase the sense of space and openness.

Windows positioned based on use

> 'The structure of life I have described in buildings — the structure which I believe to be objective — is deeply and inextricably connected with the human person, and with the innermost nature of human feeling.' – CHRISTOPHER ALEXANDER, ARCHITECT

Figure 1.8: Starter Home Adaptive Reuse Housing, No. 4-15, New Orleans, Louisiana, USA, by OJT

Potential mental wellbeing benefits

- Improved sleep
- Nature interaction
- Improved liveability
- Greater adaptability
- Physical comfort

Potential issues and considerations

- Aesthetic challenges (external)
- Design programme / budget
- Specialist input useful

For many, a successful building is judged largely on how it looks from the outside. It seems reasonable to assume that external appearance has played a role since the very earliest buildings were designed. Even the oldest building remains in the world, Göbekli Tepe in Turkey (dating back to the tenth millennium BC) includes decorative features. In the comparatively recent times of the Roman empire, Vitruvius established his three essential principles of good architecture: stability, utility and beauty.[29]

This idea of 'beauty' is one that endures to this day, and in fact has dominated the British architectural press in recent years in the so-called 'style wars'. To the dismay of many architects, the government-commissioned 'Living with Beauty' report was published in 2019, followed by a draft national design code which looked to 'stamp out ugliness', forgetting, of course, that what is deemed beautiful to government advisors may not be seen as beautiful to everybody else.[30]

While it may seem strange to argue that creating 'beautiful' buildings shouldn't be our top priority as architects, there is a case for this. Core to the classical principles of beauty, revived in Renaissance and Georgian architecture, are symmetry, proportion, regularity and geometry. This approach posits that it is far more important for a window to align with others in the facade than to be positioned based on the impact it will have on the internal space.

By its very nature this approach therefore seems to suggest that the outside of buildings is more important than the inside, despite the fact that we now spend over 90% of our time indoors.[31] If we become obsessed with designing buildings from the outside inwards, we are not actually focusing on the most important element of architecture: the people who use it.

The alternative approach, of course, is to design from the inside and work outwards, beginning with details and elements people will use every day and considering what impact these will have on their experience of space. Architect Christopher Alexander has argued, for example, that windows should be individually sized and located to suit the shape and proportions of a room and its requirements.[32]

With most of us now spending so much time inside, this is a compelling argument. Why should we spend our waking hours in a space where the amount of light is determined by the appearance of the facade? The likely outcome is that windows will be either too small or too large for many of the internal spaces, which in turn will either become dark and melancholy or too hot and unpleasant in which to spend time. Another potential issue resulting from this approach is that windows will be in entirely impractical positions – perhaps preventing optimal furniture layouts and having an impact on how the space can be used, or facing in the wrong direction to maximise the best views.

This is not to say that architecture which begins with the human experience needs be ugly. There are many ways to design buildings that allow for well-considered, attractively proportioned facades, while still creating freedom in the potential positions of windows. One frequently used and effective approach is to place windows within a larger grid system, with the freedom to move around within each portion of the grid. However you decide to tackle this issue, be certain that you have considered how window positions will impact on people on both sides of your building's facades.

Design tips

1. When designing a space, consider all the issues that window position and size might create, including amount and quality of light, views out and potential impacts on the internal layout of the room itself.

2. Be aware of a room's specific location within a building and the impact that has on the internal space. An identical room on the fifth floor might need smaller windows than one on the first, as it will likely receive more daylight.

3. Remember to keep switching between both external and internal appearance when designing. Much like we create external elevations and visualisations, it can be helpful to do the same internally, even for smaller rooms.

High-quality task lighting

> 'Live in rooms full of light.'
> – AULUS CORNELIUS CELSUS, ROMAN DOCTOR

Figure 1.9: Dyson Lightcycle Morph, which automatically adjusts its brightness and light temperature throughout the day to reduce eye strain

Potential mental wellbeing benefits

- Increased productivity
- Greater adaptability
- Physical comfort
- Increased autonomy

Potential issues and considerations

- Specialist input useful

In the last 300 years or so, the type of work the average person engages in has changed enormously. At the start of the eighteenth century, for example, agriculture was the biggest source of employment in Britain, but over the next 150 years this shifted dramatically and by 1850 Britain had the smallest proportion of its population engaged in farming of any country in the world, at just 22%.[33] This was the result of industrialisation and farming increased yields, which meant that much less of the population needed to work the land. Instead, the population saw a move towards indoor work, often featuring close concentration tasks such as manufacture or writing, which was reflected in literacy levels during this period. In 1800, around 40% of men and 60% of women in England were illiterate; by 1900 this had fallen to around 3% for both sexes.[34]

This pattern has continued, with the UK literacy rate now at around 99% and the number of people doing 'close concentration' jobs still on the rise. The most common form of employment in the UK today is that classed as 'professional', at around 21% of all workers, while just 1% now work in agriculture, forestry and fishing.[35] As a result, it is vital that workplaces – and with the increase in remote working, homes – support people working on close, visual tasks.

One of the key elements in supporting this is good lighting. Without appropriate task lighting, people can suffer from eye strain, headaches and migraines. While all of these are fairly certain to make you feel less happy in the moment, perhaps more interesting to us is the fact that adequate lighting has been shown to have a positive impact on mood and cognitive performance, while lighting environments that are customised by individuals have been shown to improve satisfaction levels.[36]

Part of the reason for this is that what is deemed an adequate level of light varies from person to person, based on a number of factors. For example, as we age the amount of light that can pass through our lenses is reduced, meaning that individuals over 65 can require up to twice the light levels of their 25-year-old counterparts. This is obviously challenging to achieve with uniform light levels across, say, an office space, so providing staff with individual, adjustable desk lamps can be a far more effective approach. An alternative approach is to use what is known as a 'free address' strategy, allowing staff to work wherever they like in a space and splitting it into lighting 'zones' which can be adjusted based on occupant requirements.

As well as the quantity of light provided, it is also important to bear in mind its quality, with issues such as glare, flicker and low colour rendering becoming potential problem areas. Where possible, consult with a lighting specialist to ensure task lighting is designed to consider these aspects.

Like many other tools in this book, people tend to feel better when they have control over the lighting of their immediate environment. There are many solutions to this challenge, but ultimately the people using your buildings will feel greater satisfaction if the lighting design empowers them to tailor their space to their own personal needs.

Design tips

1. List the daily tasks likely to be undertaken by people in any space you are designing and explore ways in which lighting can support them in these, not just in regards of brightness and temperature, but also in terms of adaptability.

2. Explore the possibility of breaking a building or floorplate down into different 'lighting zones' – perhaps some could be used to encourage social interaction while others could be better suited to reading a report.

3. Be aware of other wellbeing issues related to lighting, such as glare, flicker and colour rendering, and consult with a specialist lighting designer to help avoid these issues.

Phone lockers

> 'Technology can be our best friend, and technology can also be the biggest party pooper of our lives. It interrupts our own story, interrupts our ability to have a thought or a daydream, to imagine something wonderful.' – STEVEN SPIELBERG, FILM DIRECTOR

Figure 1.10: The Italian Building co-living, London, UK, by Mason & Fifth

Potential mental wellbeing benefits
- Improved sleep
- Physical health

Potential issues and considerations
- Possible social impacts

The amount of time that people spend looking at screens has rocketed in recent years. Even pre-COVID-19, the average person in the UK was spending nearly three and a half hours a day – or 50 days each year – looking at screens.[37] If you're brave enough now, why not open your device, go into your settings and see how much screen time you've accumulated in the last week?

This isn't all our fault, however. Strategies such as push notifications, red bubbles on apps that we feel we have to 'resolve' and infinite scrolling feeds are all designed-in so that we struggle to put down our phones. When our brains feel rewarded (for example, when we clear a notification or receive a 'like' on social media), they release the feel-good chemical dopamine, of which app designers are all too aware. While it may feel good at first, this dopamine hit can be highly addictive and in the long run it doesn't always make us happy.[38] 39% of people who have attempted a digital detox said they felt better as a result, while 11% of people said that the amount they used their phone made them feel anxious.

Much of this screen time takes place in our bedrooms too, with 55% of people reporting that they use their phones in bed and 79% stating that they spend time looking at their phones before going to sleep. Unfortunately, these habits can have a significant impact on our quality of sleep, in part due to the impact that blue light can have on our circadian rhythms, but also because the sorts of activities we do on our phones – reading emails, using social media or checking the news – can keep our minds engaged and 'fired up' just before try to go to sleep.

The impacts of mobile phone use around bedtime have been proven in numerous studies, to the extent that The National Sleep Foundation now recommends we should stop using all electronic devices at least 30 minutes before we go to sleep, instead suggesting activities such as reading.[39] Even keeping a phone near our pillows has been shown to correlate with sleep disturbances, increased sleep latency (how long it takes us to fall asleep after turning the lights off) and daytime sleepiness.

However, there are ways in which designers can encourage a healthier relationship with our phones and promote 'digital detoxing' – perhaps the most effective of these being 'digital lockers'. Companies such as 'Unplugged' are now offering weekend breaks in relaxation cabins – with the first rule being that on arrival you lock your phone away, where it will stay for the duration of your holiday, allowing you to truly unplug and relax.

We can also use similar strategies in homes, such as at the Italian Building by co-living provider Mason & Fifth, where residents have cupboards by beds (complete with openings for charging cables) in which to store their phones at night. While they might still be within reach, the simple step of putting the phone away for the evening is intended to create a psychological barrier to using them during the night.

Design tips

1. Provide places for people to store their phones when doing 'relaxing' activities. This could be during sleeping, on holiday, during activities such as yoga or playing sport, or simply just during lunch hours.

2. Make the lockers or cupboards more appealing to use, by allowing for phone charging within them.

Staggered balconies

> 'Anyone's life truly lived consists of work, sunshine, exercise, soap, plenty of fresh air and a happy contented spirit.' – LILLIE LANGTRY, ACTRESS AND SOCIALITE

Figure 1.11: Ocean Estate, Tower Hamlets, London, UK, by Levitt Bernstein

Potential mental wellbeing benefits

- Improved sleep
- Improved liveability
- Moments of joy / awe
- Physical comfort

Potential issues and considerations

- Structural issues
- Aesthetic challenges (external)
- Space / layout requirements
- Design programme / budget

When setting out balconies on the facades of residential buildings, the initial temptation is usually to align them vertically. After all, since the Renaissance the perceived wisdom within architectural design was that features or openings look better when lined up with those above them. Similarly, when we lay out apartments, we are taught to stack elements. By placing quiet spaces above one another we can reduce potential acoustic issues, efficiently stack services and reduce the amount of design work required with repetition across floors.

However, by aligning projecting balconies above each other we effectively guarantee they are all in shadow, which – although sometimes providing useful shading to the outdoor spaces themselves – can significantly reduce the amount of daylight they (and subsequently the rooms behind them) receive. Lighting experts speak of the 'vertical sky component' of each window, which is essentially a measure of how much of the sky is visible from the centre point of a window – for reference, a window that achieves 27% is deemed to provide good levels of light.[40] As you can imagine, a pair of double-glazed doors that sit below a deep, wide balcony can easily fall short of that figure, particularly if the building is already in a dense urban area.

Private amenity spaces are highly valuable to those living in cities. However, when stacked vertically they can also have significant negative impacts to the quality and quantity of light received by spaces below them. When designing residential buildings, we therefore have a responsibility to consider the impacts of the balconies.

One of the most effective ways to reduce the impact on flats below is to return to the vertical sky component, by ensuring that we increase the area of visible sky from each window as much as possible (unless, of course, we are deliberately shading them for other reasons, such as part of an overheating strategy). One way to achieve this is through staggering balconies by alternating their position up and down a building to prevent them from sitting directly above windows below.

It is possible to achieve this without losing all the aforementioned benefits of stacked apartments. For example, flats can remain identical to those above and below them, but the door positions can move within each living space so that on one floor it is at the far right-hand-side, while on the floor below it is at the far left, and so on.

If this is deemed to be too costly or challenging, then balcony doors can even stay in the same position up and down the building. Simply moving the balconies to the alternating ends of those doors will allow for more daylight to reach the rooms behind them, as well as the balconies themselves. A further benefit of this is that it does not even result in new flat types that need to be designed, minimising the amount of extra design resource required.

To those who argue that vertically stacked balconies are more attractive, we can counter that this is simply a personal view, and likely a result of being taught to think in such a way. We know that humans tend to enjoy some level of pattern and visual interest, both of which can be created if designers become a little more playful with the setting out of balconies.

Design tips

1. Think about structure from an early stage. It is important to ensure that a straight line of vertical structure can be provided even if windows and balconies are moving around.

2. Explore ways in which balconies can be alternated without significant changes to the spaces they serve.

3. Use balconies as an opportunity to create movement, visual interest or joy in a facade.

4. Consider implications on privacy, as those above may be able to look down on to lower balconies with such an approach.

Sinks next to windows

❝ Even the mundane task of washing dishes by hand is an example of the small tasks and personal activities that once filled people's daily lives with a sense of achievement.'
– B.F. SKINNER, PSYCHOLOGIST

Figure 1.12: Penthouse kitchen, The Rye apartments, London, UK, by Tikari Works

Potential mental wellbeing benefits

- Mindfulness opportunity
- Nature interaction
- Personalisation opportunities
- Moments of joy / awe
- Improved liveability

Potential issues and considerations

- Space / layout requirements

According to a 2015 report, the average American spends around 13 minutes a day washing-up and cleaning the kitchen after meals.[41] This equates to around an hour and a half a week, and nearly 80 hours (or just over three days) every year. While dishwasher use is on the rise, with roughly half of British homes now owning one, using the sink to wash-up certain items is still unavoidable, be it at home or in the workplace.[42]

However, we needn't always see this chore in a negative way. Doing the washing-up can be a satisfying task, in the sense that we are making an immediate improvement to our environment and also as a way to experience a few moments of mindfulness. Buddhist monk Thích Nhất Hạnh, for example, talks about how we can use everyday tasks such as washing-up to practice mindfulness.[43] Hạnh describes the process of taking his time with each dish, being aware of what his hands are doing and savouring the sensation of the water on his skin, arguing that this practice can change the task from something we dread to a pleasant experience.[44] Research supports this argument, as a 2015 study discovered that people who read Hạnh's passage on mindful washing-up felt more inspired and less nervous after washing a bowl full of dishes.

Even for those who don't have an interest in mindfulness or meditation, the fact that the washing-up forces us to spend time away from phones, screens and other distractions while engaging many of our senses, means that this simple chore can still be a pleasant moment of respite if approached in the right way.

A simple strategy that designers can use to enhance this everyday task and make it more enjoyable is placing the home or office kitchen sink in front of a window. This has a number of benefits to the pot-washer – not least the exposure to natural light that we know to be so positive for our state of mind. It can also afford this person views out on to nature and the opportunity for a fresh, cooling breeze if the kitchen gets too hot.

This may all seem like common sense, but like most of the features in this book it's included because it is so often overlooked. With the current move towards apartment typologies, kitchens in UK homes are often placed at the back of layouts in a combined living-kitchen-dining room. This is especially strange, as so many of us now see the kitchen as the 'heart of the home', and although architects and developers are aware of the importance of daylight, they do not seem to question the logic of placing this 'heart' in the most light-starved part of the flat.

It is worth noting that this is not the accepted approach in many European countries, particularly those with warmer Mediterranean climates. In part because of the importance of eating outdoors in these areas, kitchens are generally placed on the outer face of apartments, adjacent to the balcony or terrace. To many people from Italy or Spain, the idea of a kitchen without a window would simply not be acceptable. Perhaps, then, we can learn from our Mediterranean cousins and re-assess how we lay out our homes in other parts of the world.

Design tips

1. Kitchens, whether in homes or workplaces, should ideally be placed on an external wall of a building to create the opportunity for daylight, views and ventilation.

2. This can be challenging with modern, deep-plan, single-aspect apartments, so challenge the paradigm and explore opportunities for dual-aspect layouts.

3. Integrate other ways to make everyday tasks like washing-up more enjoyable through strategies such as materiality, texture or views.

CHAPTER 2
Comfort and materials

> 'Recognising the need is the primary condition for design.'
> – CHARLES EAMES, ARCHITECT AND DESIGNER

Figure 2.0: Villa Wienberg, Aarhus, Denmark, by Mette and Martin Wienberg, Wienberg Arketekter

When we think about comfort, the first thing that comes to mind might be a large, warm bed, a soft sofa that swallows up anyone who sits on it, or perhaps the way clothes feel when we put them on. Despite this, the issue of comfort in buildings is far more wide-reaching than an ergonomic desk chair or designer furniture. It encompasses everything that creates an optimal environment that is pleasant for all the senses – from acoustic issues to overheating – not to mention how psychologically comfortable we feel in a space. Almost every decision that designers make can have some impact on the comfort levels of occupants, whether it is the insulation they specify, where they place windows on a facade, or where in the building they decide to place bedrooms. This is also innately connected to how we service and manage buildings, such as the ways in which we ventilate and heat spaces.

It may seem like an obvious statement, but it is vitally important that buildings meet their occupants' basic physical needs, and that those occupants are comfortable within them. Yet many of today's buildings are failing to achieve this goal, as was discovered in recent UK Government research which highlighted overheating in homes as a significant problem.[1] The very word 'comfort' conveys a sense of contentment with our situation, and when people are uncomfortable it can have a significant impact on both immediate mood and longer-term physical and psychological health if sustained.

Today we can design with a wider range of building materials than ever before, and these can all have different ramifications on us based on a wide range of factors, including how they look, feel and smell, how they affect air quality or sound, and even the psychological associations they may provoke in us. As designers we are taught to choose materials based on a certain set of parameters, such as their strength, insulative quality and, of course, their appearance. However, there are many more qualities to materials that we aren't always taught about at design schools, such as whether they are emitting potentially harmful chemicals into the environment or the physical and psychological responses they can evoke in us.

This chapter also explores the ways in which buildings and their materials can promote physical interaction and engagement with our senses, in turn encouraging occupants to be more mindful. Research, including fMRI (functional magnetic resonance imaging) scans, suggests that 'rumination' – where we dwell on or overthink specific ideas, often repeatedly – is associated with depression.[2] A major issue with ruminating is that we don't often realise we are doing it until we have been lost in thought for some time. As one of my mindfulness teachers once put it, 'it is as if we are standing by a river of our thoughts – when we see a juicy one, we jump in, and it is not until much later that we let go of that thought and are surprised to discover we are a long way downstream by the time we climb out'.

One way that we can avoid slipping into such thought patterns is through a more mindful approach, with research showing that people who practise mindfulness demonstrate less 'mind wandering' and repetitive negative thinking,[3] with some studies even showing that it can cut recurrence of depression by up to 50%.[4] It is no surprise, therefore, that over 30% of GPs now prescribe 'mindfulness-based cognitive therapy' to patients with recurrent depression.[5] If we can design buildings which use materials and strategies to encourage people to engage mindfully with their senses and the immediate moment, supporting a more mindful approach, we can in turn support better mental wellbeing.[6]

Today we have amazing tools to predict how a building will behave long before a spade has even been put in the ground. Simply from a set of drawings we can calculate how many hours of daylight a given space is likely to receive each year, how wind will move around proposed buildings or how a building will perform thermally. Yet, despite all this modelling software, many buildings today are still struggling with the issue of comfort. Homes are overheating, offices are too noisy and in many cases our sense of touch seems to have been an afterthought or forgotten entirely. In this chapter we will explore some of the causes of these problems and provide some tools that we can all use to help avoid them.

Materials that connect us with nature and our senses

> 'I work a little bit like a sculptor. When I start, my first idea for a building is with the material. I believe architecture is about that. It's not about paper, it's not about forms. It's about space and material.' – PETER ZUMTHOR, ARCHITECT

Figure 2.1: Mourners' shelter, North Watford Cemetery, Hertfordshire, UK, by John Puttick Associates

Potential mental wellbeing benefits

- Nature interaction
- Mindfulness opportunity
- Environmental benefits
- Moments of joy / awe
- Improved air quality

Potential issues and considerations

- Hygiene
- Detailing
- Build cost

Since the construction of the very earliest buildings, their creators have had to consider which materials to use. For builders even a few hundred years ago this was often a simple choice, as they had a very limited palette of materials to hand. This is one of the reasons that we see such distinct vernacular styles in different parts of the world, from the Neolithic stone dwellings at Skara Brae on the Scottish Orkney Islands to the rammed earth and bamboo Tulou homes of the Hakka people in China.[7]

In contrast, architects today have an almost limitless range of materials available to them. Modern transportation allows them to specify materials from anywhere in the world – even the UK, with its rich history of brick production, imported 12.5% of its bricks in 2017.[8] We can design and engineer new materials to meet our exact requirements, from self-cleaning glass to self-healing concrete, or homeostatic facades which change in response to external conditions.[9]

When specifying materials, architects generally have three key attributes in mind: sustainability, performance and safety. Today, more than ever, materials must be sustainably sourced and have as small an impact on the planet as possible, both in terms of their initial carbon footprint and their overall lifespan. They must also do the job they are specified to do: what Vitruvius termed *utilitas*. Insulation must keep us warm, glass must let light through and flooring must be hard-wearing. And, of course, buildings and their materials must be safe – sadly, we have all seen far too many examples of what can happen when they are not.

However, what seems to be missing from many contemporary buildings is an understanding of the psychological, emotional and physical impact of the materials within them. How many architects can say that they understand how specifying timber over plastic flooring will affect an occupant's heart rate or blood pressure? Using natural materials such as wood has indeed been shown to have a positive impact on both these measures of health when compared with 'control' finishes such as concrete or steel, as well as reducing cortisol levels and making spaces seem more appealing[10] – yet these lessons are rarely shared from the world of research with architectural practices.

Research seems to indicate that the introduction of natural materials into buildings activates our parasympathetic nervous system, which acts to reduce stress levels and promote healing and recovery functions in the body. The reasons for this are still up for debate, but considering all we know about biophilia (the inherent human need to interact with nature), it is fairly unsurprising. Having spent billions of years evolving from single-celled organisms with nothing around us but natural materials, it is logical that we would still find them comforting.

Natural materials can also be a positive way to engage our senses and encourage us to be more mindful, which in turn is also shown to reduce stress and have a positive impact on the activity (and even the shape) of our brains.[11] While a white painted wall does little to engage our sense of touch, a stone or even natural fabric material can be pleasant to interact with and – even if only for a brief moment – inspire us to focus on physical sensations instead of being caught up in what psychologists (and indeed Buddhists) would call 'the ego': the conscious part of our minds that reflects on our thoughts, feelings and actions.

Design tips

1. Integrate natural materials and finishes into projects where possible. Understand the value these add to people who use your buildings and use this data to justify their inclusion.

2. It is generally not practical to use natural finishes everywhere, so pick locations or uses where they can have the biggest impact. Research shows that people prefer rooms with around 45% natural finishes rather than 90% natural, so it isn't necessary to avoid other materials entirely.

3. Be aware of users' sense of touch when specifying materials and aim to design tactile, physically engaging spaces.

Low Volatile Organic Compound (VOC) products and ingredients lists

'There's so much pollution in the air now that if it weren't for our lungs there'd be no place to put it all.' – ROBERT ORBEN, AUTHOR

Figure 2.2: EDGE Technologies HQ, Amsterdam, the Netherlands, by Fokkema & Partners

Potential mental wellbeing benefits
- Improved air quality
- Physical health improvements
- Sense of safety
- Increased autonomy
- Environmental benefits

Potential issues and considerations
- Build cost
- Design programme / budget

The average human takes about 17,000 breaths a day. By the time we reach 50, we have taken well over 300 million breaths, which works out at roughly 150 million litres of air – the equivalent volume of 60 Olympic swimming pools. We breathe not only to absorb oxygen into our bodies, but to also rid them of carbon dioxide. Unfortunately for us, we can also breathe in some fairly nasty chemicals without meaning to do so. Data from the World Health Organization shows that nine out of 10 people worldwide breathe air containing high levels of pollutants, including Volatile Organic Compounds (VOCs). This can not only affect our lung health but that of our wider bodies,[12] and can lead to a number of chronic physical conditions that can also take a significant toll on our mental health.

Researchers in Denmark and the US have found that people who grew up in more polluted areas were more likely to develop depression, bipolar disorder, schizophrenia or personality disorder – although, as with many issues, other factors such as income and reduced access to green space may also have played a part.[13] However, other studies have also linked concentration in particulate matter (tiny pollutant particles in the air often known as PM2.5 or PM10, depending on how small they are) and nitric oxide levels to increased likelihood of mental health problems like depression, and even increased risk of Emergency Department visits for depressive episodes, suggesting there may indeed be a connection between air quality and mental health.[14]

We often think of air pollution as being generated from cars or factories, but many sources exist within our homes and workplaces too. Log burners, ovens, printers and other machinery can all be contributors, but even many common building materials can 'off-gas' harmful VOCs. Insulation, paints, wood coatings, adhesives, furniture, composite wood products and flooring materials can all be responsible for the emission of these VOCs, which makes it extremely important that we review the 'ingredients' that go into our buildings.[15] We now live in a world where everything we come into contact with is under a huge amount of scrutiny, so it is strange that many of us have no idea what our homes are really made of, or which chemicals they are releasing into the air that we and our families breathe every day. As Harry Knibb of Oxford Properties has said, 'most people now know more about what goes into their sandwiches than their homes'.[16]

Some developers and product suppliers are now addressing this issue of what the WELL Standard calls Material Transparency, by introducing 'materials ingredients lists', setting out what goes into different building elements. There are also a number of 'disclosure organisations', such as Cradle-to-Cradle Certified or the Declare Label, which identify where products come from, what they are made of and where they can go at the end of their life cycle. While low VOC products and material transparency labels used to be rare, they are now growing in popularity and are becoming much more affordable and attainable.

Such strategies are not only effective ways to ensure that we are using healthy building materials, but they can also help communicate to building occupants that they are not being slowly poisoned by the building around them. This can be reassuring to building users and they address fears around toxic materials and air quality, which only look set to increase as public awareness of this issue continues to rise.

Design tips

1. Research the common sources of indoor VOCs (the above list is a good place to start) and consider these when specifying building materials or furniture.

2. Use healthy alternatives where available, such as low VOC paints or carpets.

3. Compile a materials ingredients list for building occupiers, to give them reassurance of the safety of their building and to champion the hard work you have done in creating a healthy building!

Upcycled finishes

' There is no such thing as "away". When we throw anything away it must go somewhere.'
— ANNIE LEONARD, CO-EXECUTIVE DIRECTOR FOR GREENPEACE USA

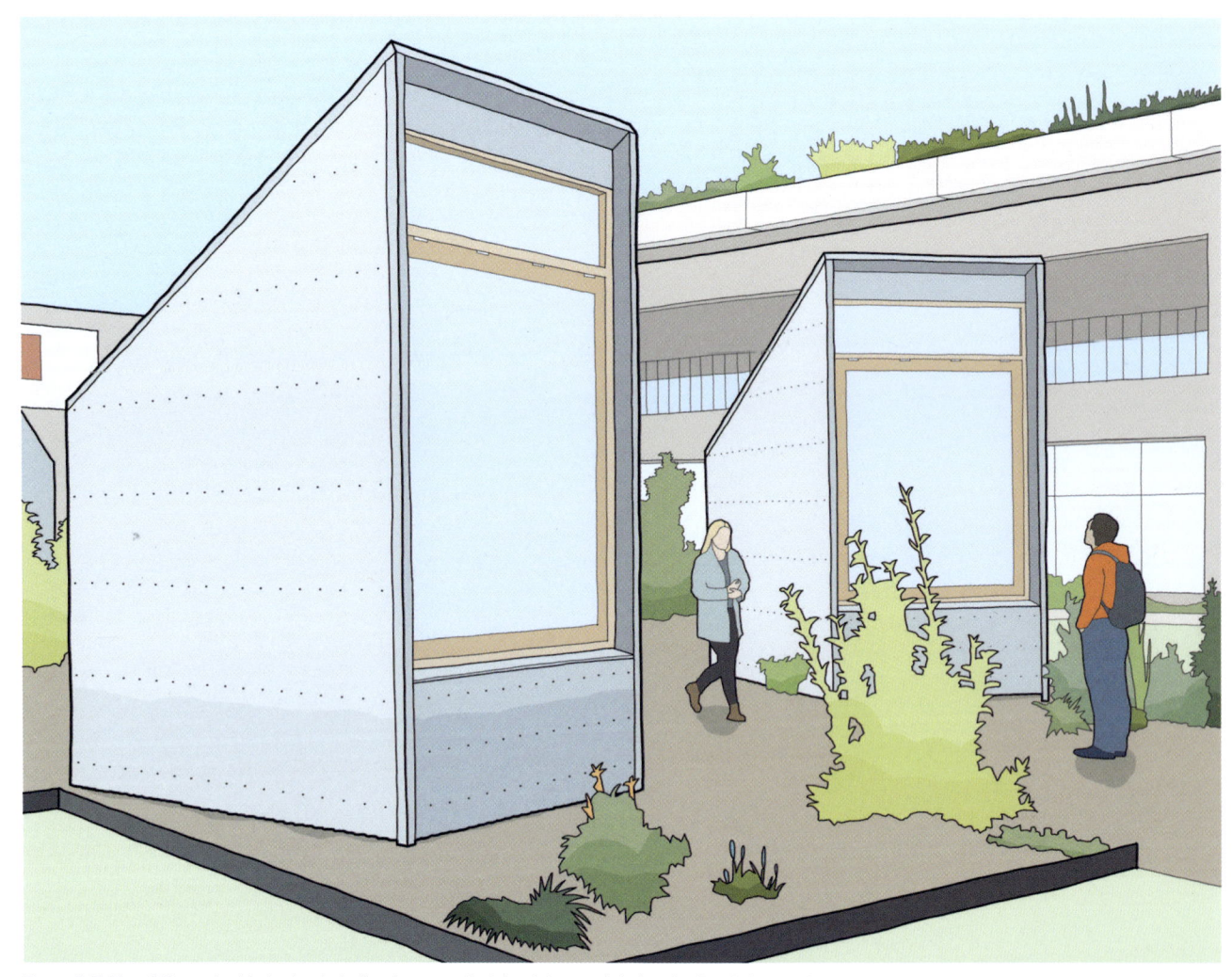

Figure 2.3: Tiny Offices, the Netherlands, built using upcycled aluminium and timber, by Dutch Invertuals

Potential mental wellbeing benefits

- Mindfulness opportunity
- Environmental benefits
- Moments of joy / awe
- Improved air quality

Potential issues and considerations

- Hygiene
- Detailing
- Structural issues

The concept of upcycling is simple: take something of little worth and reuse it in a creative way to increase its value or become part of something larger. For this reason, upcycling is also often known as 'creative reuse'. Upcycling has a strong history in art, fashion and industry, but in the last few decades has gathered momentum within architecture as well. Practices such as Superuse Studios have even specialised in this area, building walls from discarded carpet tiles and creating cladding shingles from old mooring posts.

There are certainly enormous environmental benefits to this approach. For every building component that we upcycle, it is one more that does not need to be manufactured. Across an entire building the impact on total embodied carbon can be significant, and we are also giving an object a second life instead of sending it to landfill.

This can be powerful for occupants' mental health. Eco-anxiety, caused by worries about the environment and the future of our planet, is a very real problem that impacts an enormous number of people – and research says that this number is growing. According to a 2018 survey, almost 70% of people in the USA are worried about climate change, and over half feel 'helpless' about the issue.[17]

As we understand more about the environmental challenges we face, it is perhaps not surprising that so many people find this has a negative impact on their state of mind. One 2018 paper on climate collapse, known as 'Deep Adaptation', went viral, being downloaded over 110,000 times, and was so worrying that many people have since shared that it sent them into a spiral of depression.[18] When creating buildings, it is therefore vitally important that we not only take an environmentally friendly approach, but also signal this approach to people to help reassure them and feel less daily guilt and worry about the impact on the planet of the buildings they use. Upcycling is a clear way to send a message to occupants that steps have been taken to minimise the damage their building might be doing.

There are also further benefits to upcycling. We have already discussed the impact of VOCs on air quality and the damage this can do to our health, but generally upcycled materials or furniture did their worst off-gassing some time ago. We do still need to be aware of the toxicity of certain materials, however: simply because something is recycled from another building does not automatically make it safe.

Upcycled materials are also another way to introduce texture and tactile materials into a building, with the associated benefits we've previously seen. They can also create visual interest, perhaps in the slight variation between elements that has occurred as part of the object's patina. Humans like to see variation with some level of pattern and we find it visually comforting.

Upcycling can also provide an opportunity for references to the surrounding context or the history of a site, which can enrich our experience of a space and generate local pride. It can even stimulate intellectual interest through the intrigue of a material taking on another meaning, like Marcel Duchamp elevating a urinal to become a piece of art. Through such strategies we can become playful with upcycling, and it can become a helpful strategy in our toolkit to bring joy, humour or pleasure to buildings.

Design tips

1. At an early stage, explore what local waste streams might exist that you can utilise: perhaps a local tile factory throws away surplus or 'defective' goods, or a nearby demolition site or car breaker's yard is looking to get rid of elements.

2. Think creatively about how items could take on an entirely different life. Old pallets might become furniture or discarded gutters could be turned into cladding shingles.[19]

3. Research building supply companies that use upcycling in their process, allowing you to purchase 'off the shelf' upcycled bricks, tiling or furniture.

Ergonomic and adaptable furniture

> 'Real comfort, visual and physical, is vital to every room.'
> – MARK HAMPTON, INTERIOR DESIGNER

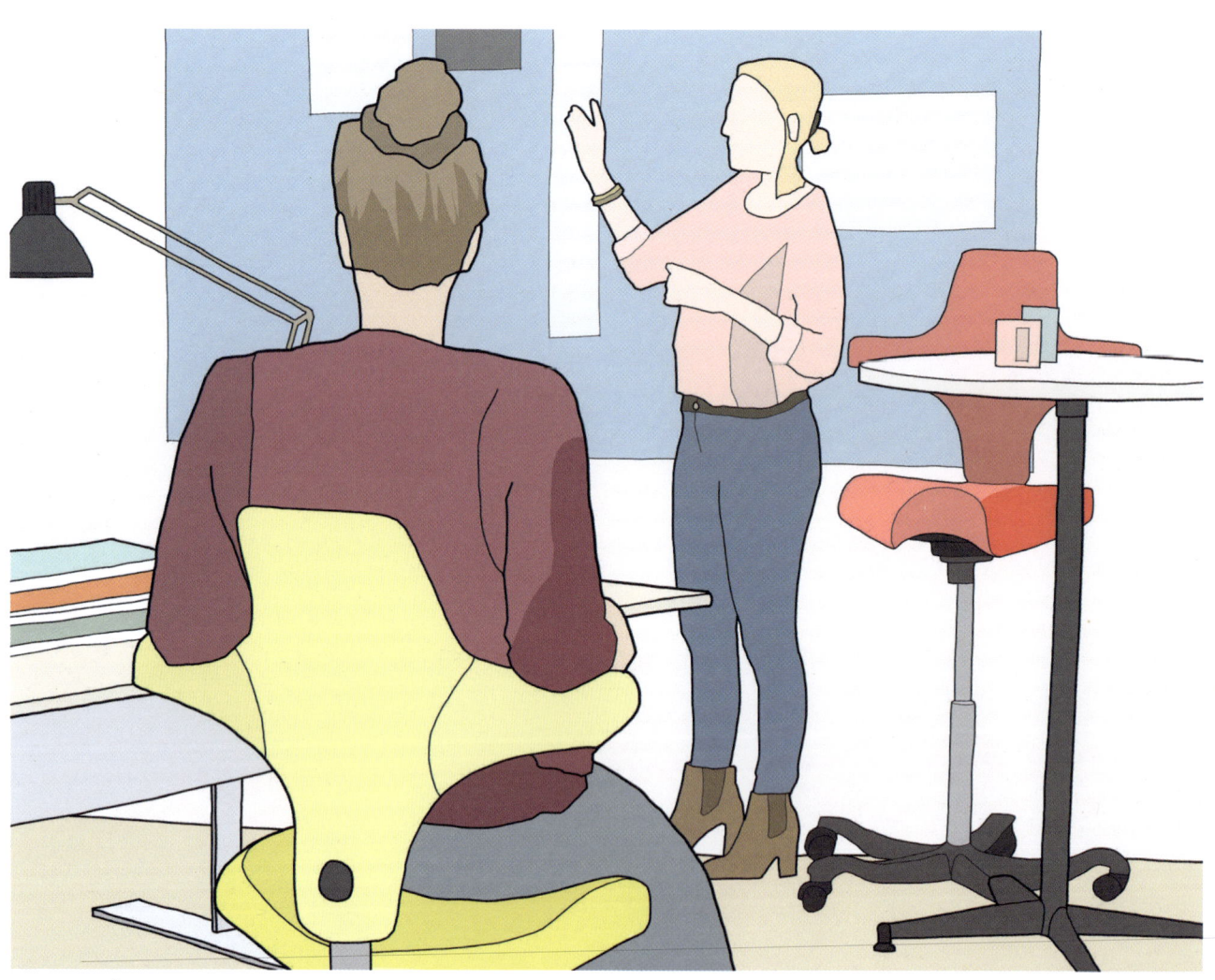

Figure 2.4: HÅG Capisco ergonomic office chair

Potential mental wellbeing benefits

- Physical health improvements
- Physical comfort
- Greater equity
- Improved sleep
- Increased autonomy

Potential issues and considerations

- Fitout cost
- Specialist input useful

Engaging mindfully with our bodies and surroundings can have significant benefits for our mental health. It doesn't simply change our state of mind, it can affect the production of chemicals in our brains, shrink our amygdalas (which are closely related to stress) and thicken up our pre-frontal cortex, which is responsible for planning, problem-solving and controlling our emotions.[20] However, people are unlikely to engage with their environments in a physical sense if they are uncomfortable or unpleasant.

We now spend more time than ever using furniture, particularly seating and desks. As a result of an increasing number of office jobs, car travel and seated leisure activities such as watching television, adults in England now sit for around nine and a half hours a day, a figure that increases further as we enter retirement.[21]

This creates its own problems, being linked to higher rates of diabetes, heart disease, mental health problems and overall mortality, and this can cause even more issues if our chairs and desks are poorly designed. In 2016, musculoskeletal disorders were one of the top causes of global disability, and they are also one of the most common causes of reduced work time, absenteeism and low productivity.[22] Unsurprisingly, therefore, in Savills' 2019 'What Workers Want' survey, workplace comfort was the most important factor for participants, while the aspect respondents most wanted to change about their office was the design of their personal workspace.[23] What is clear is that we need to provide better furniture for both our physical and mental health, and at present there is a shortfall in this provision. But what does 'better' look like?

Firstly, our chairs, desks, and sofas need to be designed with the body in mind. This sounds obvious, almost to the point of stupidity, but a quick scroll through many interior design websites shows that this isn't always the case. With the present-day focus on 'Instagrammability', a large amount of furniture is designed to be visually striking rather than providing good support for our backs or at a good height for us to work.

As well as supporting our bodies in the right ways, furniture should be adjustable and adaptable. We should be able to change a seat's height and depth, the angle of our backrest, the height of any lumbar support and the position of armrests. Ideally, work surfaces should also be adjustable in height, as we are not all the average 1.8m-tall man that many of these pieces of furniture have been designed by and for.

If we can consider all these issues when designing or providing furniture, we will be able to reduce rates of chronic musculoskeletal problems, which can have a huge impact on people's daily mental wellbeing. More than this, however, we will create environments in which people feel happy and comfortable spending time, and in which they will enjoy engaging with their physical experience – rather than shutting off to their bodies' sensations – encouraging a more mindful way of life.

Design tips

1. Carry out an early review of how spaces are likely to be used, and how furniture can support those activities in a physical sense.

2. Don't select furniture based solely on its visual appearance: request information on its ergonomic features and how it will support the human body.

3. Where possible, make individual pieces of furniture adaptable. We are all different shapes and sizes, so it is not possible to design one piece of furniture that is suited to everyone.

4. If providing standing desks, consider what support might be needed for users. This could include anti-fatigue mats, impact-reducing flooring, enough foot space or the potential for something to lean on.

Thermal mass and underfloor heating

> 'And forget not that the earth delights to feel your bare feet and the winds long to play with your hair.' – KAHLIL GIBRAN, AUTHOR

Figure 2.5: Centre for Creative Learning, Francis Holland School, London, UK, by BDP

Potential mental wellbeing benefits

- Physical comfort
- Spatial benefits
- Greater adaptability
- Mindfulness opportunity
- Moments of joy / awe

Potential issues and considerations

- Build cost

Another way in which we can engage our human senses and encourage people to be more mindful of physical sensations is through the use of temperature within building materials, particularly those with which we are frequently in contact.

Small variations in temperature, particularly warming sensations such as getting into a hot bath, have been observed in clinical settings to elevate our mood.[24] We have probably all experienced the pleasant feeling of stepping out of a shower on to a warm floor at some point, and the enjoyment of this seems to be relatively universal to us humans. This can therefore have an impact on us psychologically in two ways: the emotional boost that seems to be demonstrated by this sensation of warmth, and the promotion of engaging mindfully with our bodies.

Of course, there are many ways to heat a space, from log burners to radiant heating systems, but one surface that we will almost always be in contact with in some way is the floor. As a result of this, by utilising underfloor heating systems we can create maximum opportunity for people to enjoy this warming sensation, especially on colder days. It is not surprising that most estate agents agree that underfloor heating adds value to a home.[25]

Another approach to heating (and cooling) a building that can engage our sense of touch is through the use of thermal mass. This is where high-density materials, such as stone, brick or rammed earth – which take a lot of energy and time to heat up, are used throughout a building, acting as a 'thermal battery'. If designed well they can achieve a 12-hour 'thermal lag', meaning they absorb heat in the day and release it by night, helping to keep a space cooler when outdoor temperatures are hot and vice versa – often reducing or eliminating the need for insulation as well.[26] This is why you may have felt the pleasant sensation of touching a cool wall inside a church or cathedral on a hot summer's day, or of being surprised by how warm a concrete surface might be on a cool evening.

As well as these sensation benefits, there are other advantages to these approaches. If designed well, both underfloor heating and thermal mass systems can be more energy efficient (again addressing eco-anxieties while also offsetting initial construction costs) and can heat a space more evenly, helping to avoid cold spots. They can also remove the need for radiators, which has two benefits: increased space and adaptability of layouts, which can empower a building's occupants and increase livability, and ease of cleaning a space. Radiators are notorious dust-gatherers and a build-up of these small particles can quickly affect air quality as well as increasing the amount of time we spend each week cleaning.

We can even use these approaches to encourage certain types of activity or behaviour. A lovely example of this is at the Francis Holland School by BDP, which won the New London Architecture Award for wellbeing. In the school's library, the architects included a heated floor to incentivise children to sit on the floor and read books. Not only does this encourage learning and activate much more of the space, but it also makes the occasion a pleasure for the senses through a warming, comforting and relaxing experience.

Design tips

1. Become well-versed on the various benefits of thermal mass and underfloor heating approaches, and communicate them to the client at an early stage. They may not be aware of these wellbeing benefits or the potential long-term cost savings.

2. Even if a client is keen to stick to a traditional heating strategy, thermal mass can still play a role and improve thermal comfort or create a moment of joy. Look for opportunities to use dense (but sustainable) materials where possible.

3. If only used in select instances, aim to put them in places where people will experience the variation in temperature they produce, such as on a floor designed for sitting or a low wall people will run their hand along.

4. Be aware of the balance between using thermal mass and achieving flexibility in buildings – use a combination of dense and lightweight materials to obtain the benefits of both.

High-quality sleeping environments

> 'Sleep deprivation is an illegal torture method outlawed by the Geneva Convention and international courts, but most of us do it to ourselves.' – RYAN HURD, AUTHOR

Figure 2.6: JapoNeza Retreat House, Atlangatepec, Mexico, by Fausto Terán

Potential mental wellbeing benefits

- Improved sleep
- Physical health improvements
- Physical comfort
- Increased productivity

Potential issues and considerations

- Fitout cost
- Environmental impacts
- Impact on layouts

Sleep plays an incredibly important role in our health. While our sleep can be affected by many factors, such as daily worries, caffeine intake or working patterns, our immediate environment is vital in helping us to get a good night's rest. Despite this fact, many people around the world are trying to sleep in sub-optimum environments. For example, the World Health Organization (WHO) guidelines for community noise recommend levels of less than 30dB(A) at night. Yet, according to a recent EU publication, more than 30% of the population of Europe is exposed to noise levels exceeding 55dB(A) while trying to sleep,[27] which we can even check ourselves using apps on our phones.[28]

This means that every day a huge proportion of the population is functioning at below optimal levels, which consequently has an impact not only on how well they can perform on any given day (which is particularly scary when we think about, for example, air traffic controllers, surgeons or crane operators), but also on their relationships, mood and health.

Given the importance of sleep and how much time in our lives we spend doing it, it is surprising that so much of the focus for design work by residential architects is on the activities we undertake while awake. Issues like the amount of space around a bed and minimum daylight levels are often prescribed, but other important points, such as how dark a space should be at night, are often overlooked.

According to sleep experts, the ideal sleeping environment varies with the individual, but generally it should be cool, quiet and very dark.[29] It must also be a place in which we feel comfortable both physically and psychologically – meaning that we feel safe from threat as well as from disturbances or interruptions. The good news is, there are a wide range of factors we can do as designers to help ensure these conditions are met.

In order to keep a space cool, there are a number of options. As always, the starting point should be natural ventilation, ideally through a dual aspect or stack ventilation approach. However, in certain climates or noisy areas this may not be appropriate and additional mechanical cooling may be required. While it does often get criticised for its impact on the environment, insufficient ventilation or cooling can have significant health impacts, and with modern heat recovery systems and other innovations, these systems are becoming greener year on year. Allowing residents to cool spaces without opening windows is also one way to address the issue of noise, along with a well-insulated building envelope.

The provision of a truly dark space for sleeping is one that is often overlooked, however, and with outdoor lighting in the UK growing at around 3% a year, it is a major problem.[30] Many homes are sold without curtains or blinds to allow residents to style their own homes, but as designers we should be recommending blackout blinds or curtains to bedrooms in our schemes, particularly in urban areas.

We can also enhance a sense of safety in bedrooms through design. Ideally, bedrooms should be placed at first floor or above to harness the power of 'prospect and refuge' theory – the idea that humans have evolved to feel safer at a high level with good views outward – as well as the practical benefit of making them harder for criminals or animals to access. If they have to be located on the ground floor, they should be behind a substantial defensible space, such as a 2m-deep garden with a thick hedge, rather than simply a row of planting as we see in many new homes.

Design tips

1. Be aware of the four key aspects of an ideal sleeping environment – temperature, sound, light and safety – and consider how bedrooms can optimise these elements from an early stage of design.

2. Locate bedrooms on the quieter, darker side of projects, and recommend blackout blinds or curtains to clients.

3. Place bedrooms on upper floors where possible. If unavoidable, then ground floor bedrooms should feel protected from the world outside in other ways.

4. Artificial ventilation is not the enemy and is often necessary. Instead of boycotting it, consider ways to reduce its environmental impact.

Acoustic buffers

> 'He is the happiest, be he king or peasant, who finds peace in his home.'
> – JOHANN WOLFGANG VON GOETHE, WRITER AND THINKER

Figure 2.7: Roadside acoustic barrier, London, UK, by Beep Studio

Potential mental wellbeing benefits
- Physical health improvements
- Improved sleep
- Increased productivity
- Sense of safety
- Greater equity

Potential issues and considerations
- Build cost
- Loss of views
- Aesthetic challenges

We have already seen the impact that excess noise can have on sleep, but its effects on us during the daytime can be significant and often underestimated. WHO sees noise not only as a nuisance but as 'one of the most important environmental risks to health'.[31] Excess noise can not only cause damage to the human auditory system, leading to effects such as tinnitus or hearing loss, but it can have an impact on our bodies as a whole too. It is now believed that excess noise can be connected to a wide range of problems from cardiovascular disease to cognitive impairment in children.

We have also seen that for many people exposure to unhealthy levels of noise is now completely normal – an issue that only looks set to get worse as more of the world's population moves into urban environments in the coming decades. Some of the key sources of noise according to WHO are road traffic, railways, aircraft and wind turbines, of which the first three are much more likely to impact city dwellers. They also estimate that at least one million healthy years of life are lost every year from traffic-related environmental noise in western Europe alone.[32]

While WHO is lobbying policymakers to address these issues at source, there are also issues designers can do to help reduce the amount of noise that reaches people in buildings. Unfortunately, sound from external sources can be challenging to block, and there is still a large amount of misinformation about the best ways to do this. It's commonly believed that trees or planting can effectively block out noise, but these are actually 'very poor at screening any sound', as Nick Baker and Koen Steemers explain in their book *Healthy Homes*.[33]

To screen both high- and low-frequency noise effectively, a rigid, heavyweight barrier, such as an earth bank or a concrete wall is needed. Of these, an earth bank or bund would be preferable, given its reduced impact on the environment and the opportunity it offers to bring more nature into a project through planting.

Architects have even started to design bespoke noise-shielding barriers recently, such as Beep Studio's innovative roadside buffer in east London, which protects the local community from noise produced by cars on the busy A12.[34] The installation is around 30m long x 3m high, and made from 'silk metal' acoustic panels, which absorb sound through tiny perforations in aluminium sheets which form the front face of a closed box, trapping air inside and reducing sound vibrations. The University of East London is currently monitoring its success as an acoustic buffer.

Beep Studio's barrier is also a great example of how a functional installation can double as a piece of artwork with references to local culture and history, providing additional social value and wellbeing benefits. The piece was inspired by nearby waterways and is reminiscent of a flowing stream or river, using a biophilic language despite being clearly man-made in its materiality.

While we will ultimately never be able to eradicate all sources of external noise, especially in cities, we can at least do our best to protect people from them. In doing so, we might also find other opportunities to create joy or beauty, or to integrate nature, creating happier places as well as more peaceful ones.

Design tips

1. Carry out a noise survey early in a project to understand key sources of noise and how significant these are. Refer to WHO Environmental Noise Guidelines to understand whether they are likely to affect human health.

2. Porous or lightweight elements, such as timber fences, hedges or trees, may screen a source of noise from view, but they do little to screen the sound, particularly lower frequency noises.

3. Rigid structures made from dense materials will provide better protection. Design these not only to protect from sound but to provide a pleasant outlook or other wellbeing benefits.

Acoustic baffles and panels

> 'The quieter you become, the more you can hear.'
> – RAM DASS, PSYCHOLOGIST AND MINDFULNESS THOUGHT LEADER

Figure 2.8: Pernod Ricard offices, London, UK, featuring a slatted oak ceiling, by Stil Acoustics

Potential mental wellbeing benefits

- Physical health improvements
- Increased productivity
- Physical comfort
- Nature interaction
- Moments of joy / awe

Potential issues and considerations

- Fitout cost
- Specialist input useful

When thinking about noise in buildings, external sources are only half the issue. We design buildings for humans and within every building, be it a workplace, home or even a library, humans make noise. This is not to say that all noise is bad – in some scenarios ambient background noise has actually been shown to improve concentration and creativity[35]. However, many noises can be distracting or a cause of stress.

Historically, this is unlikely to have been such a big problem. While many dwellings of the past have certainly been more crowded and likely noisier than they are today, their construction was generally rougher, less precise and used more organic materials, which will have helped in a couple of ways. Firstly, the use of softer materials like furs, earth or timber would absorb a large amount of sound, in contrast with the hard surfaces we often use within buildings today like tile, exposed brick or concrete soffits. Secondly, ancient dwellings were simply not built to the tolerances and standards of today's buildings, meaning that walls, floors and ceilings would have had imperfections and curves that stopped sound from reflecting around spaces as well. What we have effectively created today with our rectilinear, hard-edged spaces is fantastic environments for sound reverberation.

This issue has been exacerbated by a move to open-plan living, which is not just a problem in the home but in the office as well. In spite of this, there are a number of strategies we can employ to reduce the impact of internal noise on occupant health. One such approach is 'acoustic zoning' or 'sound mapping', where an exercise is carried out to understand likely sources of noise and locate these social or collaborative spaces away from more sensitive uses like learning, concentrating or sleeping.[36] Another important tool in our armoury is that of barriers and separation through the use of acoustically insulated walls, floors and doors.

However, these strategies can only take us so far, and there are still likely to be situations where we have large, open-plan spaces in which high volumes of internal noise are generated. In these instances, it can be useful to introduce acoustic baffles or panels to help reduce reverberation times and to mitigate the impact of this noise. These were first introduced to improve the acoustics of concert halls and theatres, but have since been adopted in offices, gymnasiums and even some homes.

Baffles are typically hung from the ceiling, while panels are generally placed on walls, but they generally work in the same way by absorbing sound, typically into glass wool fibres or profiled foam, and converting the sound energy into heat energy. As well as reducing echo and background noise levels in spaces, when designed well they can also become a visual feature in a space and are often used to create aesthetic interest, add colour and create a sense of playfulness and joy.

Similar sound-dampening effects can be produced by creating any profiled surface, and evenly spaced or perforated timber elements are now being used more frequently for this role too, adding the benefit of calming natural materials into a space. Rather than see such strategies as something we 'need' to do to improve acoustics, perhaps we can reframe them as opportunities to create a sense of character within a space and to add further wellbeing benefits.

Design tips

1. Carry out a sound-mapping exercise early in the design process and ask clients how they envisage different spaces being used. This will allow you to separate loud and quiet spaces through the building's layout.

2. If acoustic dampening is required, rather than going for a simple off-the-shelf acoustic ceiling panel or carpet, explore opportunities to add natural materials or create an interesting visual effect and add character.

3. Investigate the materials that are being used in any sound baffles or panels you specify, as they could be a potential source of VOCs if made from artificial substances.

Sound-masking systems

> 'Noise pollution is a relative thing. In a city, it's a jet plane taking off. In a monastery, it's a pen that scratches.' – ROBERT ORBEN, AUTHOR

Figure 2.9: Aquent offices, Boston, Massachusetts, USA, which features a QTPro sound-masking system, by Huntsman Architectural Group

Potential mental wellbeing benefits

- Physical comfort
- Sense of privacy
- Increased productivity
- Social opportunities

Potential issues and considerations

- Fitout cost
- Maintenance

The workplaces of today look very different to those of 50 years ago. In the 1970s, it was common for offices to be divided up into separate rooms in a still largely hierarchical layout, with managers being offered the highly sought-after corner offices. The 1980s saw a boom in cubicles – seemingly offering the benefits of openness and privacy all at once – but these were soon accused of being soulless and uninspiring. In contrast, today's offices are largely open plan, arguably in a reflection of the flatter, more egalitarian corporate structures many businesses now claim to have.

On the surface, open-plan offices have a huge amount to offer. They look fantastic on the cover of architecture magazines or on a company's website, appearing open, airy and inspiring. Images of open-plan workspaces make us think of collaboration and ideas sparking in serendipitous encounters at the watercooler. However, we should be cautious about the powers of open-plan offices. One of the common arguments in their favour is increased social interaction, and while in some ways this may be true, a 2018 Harvard study showed that they increase communication by email and messaging by around 50%. The same study also found that open-plan offices decrease face-to-face interaction by around 70%, as many staff feel uncomfortable discussing things in a large, open space with little privacy.[37]

Despite this, they do offer advantages in some situations. For example, when paired with staff's ability to work anywhere in a space, they provide a great deal of autonomy over the sort of space in which one can choose to work. Staff can select a bright space, a busy space or a quiet space, or perhaps one on the warmer side of the office if they get cold easily. Open-plan spaces are, however, very noisy.

Sources of noise in offices are numerous, from business calls to mechanical equipment or personal conversations, and with video conferencing becoming even more commonplace post-COVID, these noise levels look set to rise even further. To return to Savills' 'What Workers Want' survey, the lack of a quiet place to work was the issue that surveyed staff were most dissatisfied about (37% of participants), with noise levels close behind at 34%. This can significantly harm productivity and occupant comfort, leading to frustration and ultimately a lack of job satisfaction.[38]

One approach to addressing this problem is the use of sound-masking systems. These work by introducing ambient sounds that are specifically engineered to match the frequency of human speech, which makes it harder to overhear the conversations that people around you are having.[39] While it might seem counterintuitive, introducing sound in this way can actually make a space seem quieter, as we notice fewer distracting noises.

Sound-masking systems generally consist of speakers in the ceiling or walls, which will be connected to a dedicated sound-masking generator. This can be adjusted to ensure the sound cover is adequate and can also be pre-programmed so that the volume increases gradually (and importantly, inconspicuously) as spaces get busier, and then decreases as they begin to empty.

The impact of such systems can be significant, resulting in less distracted, more productive and less frustrated occupants. While they are, of course, an initial investment that may seem costly to clients at first, there is a strong financial case for the use of such systems, given that staff are generally the biggest cost to most office-based businesses.

Design tips

1. Work with a specialist acoustician and sound-masking system provider to ensure that the system you propose will be adequate for the space you are servicing.

2. Sound-masking systems can be set up in a number of ways, but ideally speakers should be located away from building structures and evenly spaced throughout an office.

3. Sound-masking noises should vary based on background noise and occupancy levels. Explore ways in which this can be automated, such as through a timed or adaptive system.

Window shading devices

> 'Hot weather opens the skull of a city, exposing its white brain and its heart of nerves, which sizzle like the wires inside a lightbulb. And there exudes a sour extra-human smell that makes the very stone seem flesh-alive, webbed, and pulsing.'
> – TRUMAN CAPOTE, *SUMMER CROSSING*

Figure 2.10: Ladera Hotel, Santiago, Chile, by Estudio Larrain

Potential mental wellbeing benefits

- Physical comfort
- Physical health improvements
- Improved liveability
- Increased autonomy
- Environmental benefits

Potential issues and considerations

- Loss of views
- Loss of light
- Aesthetic challenges (external)

The balance between creating environmentally friendly buildings and those that provide comfortable, year-round environments presents a significant challenge. Buildings need natural light: not only is it more sustainable than electric lighting, but it is also essential for our health. However, buildings must also be airtight and well insulated to avoid heat loss and reduce their energy requirements in colder months. As a result, in summer months overheating has now become a serious problem in many modern buildings, as large windows generate substantial solar gains which can be very challenging to mitigate.

The UK's Committee on Climate Change warned about the magnitude of this problem in 2017, arguing that levels of glazing and rising u-values in current building design is 'locking in problems for future generations'.[40] A look at the history of building regulations confirms this trend. In 1965 the minimum u-value (insulation level) for walls was 1.7.[41] This rose to 1.0 (the lower figures represent more insulation) in 1976, 0.6 in 1985, and 0.3 in 2015. As a result of these factors, around 90% of UK hospital wards, for example, are now prone to overheating.[42]

While being warm in winter is very good for our physical comfort, the impact of being too hot can also be substantial, with around 2,000 heat-related deaths in the UK each year. Overheating can seriously impact our mental processes too, with several studies showing that heat-exposure impairs cognitive function, affects our behavioural responses and decreases the capacity of both our working and short-term memories.[43]

The good news, however, is that there are strategies to deal with overheating. The simplest approach is to reduce window sizes; one that the UK government suggested in early 2021 to a fair deal of criticism from the architectural profession.[44] We can also change the 'g-value' of glazing, which affects how much heat it allows through, but with current technology this also reduces the amount of daylight substantially.

The problem of how to significantly reduce the impact of overheating without reducing light levels is not an easy one to solve. The major issue is that in winter we need more heat and light from the sun, whereas in summer we can do without as much of either. For this reason, shading devices that allow us to alter how much light (and heat) our buildings receive are very powerful tools. These can ultimately be extremely simple, like the classic European split-centre wooden shutter which occupants can close to keep the sun out. As they are placed on the outside of a building they prevent the sun's heat from hitting the glazing at all, meaning they are highly effective and have benefits in terms of acoustics and privacy too. They also offer the aesthetic benefit of giving us the impression we are in a small town in the south of France; but they strangely seem to have fallen out of fashion with architects in recent years.

Even simple brise-soleil style shading seems unfashionable in current contemporary architecture, which is particularly strange given the substantial reduction in solar heat gain they can offer, especially on southern facades. When designed with angled louvres they can also allow the low winter sun through while blocking higher summer rays.

If designing from a purely human-centric perspective, designing for a pleasant indoor space in which people feel comfortable and therefore happier, such shading devices seem like an obvious response.

Design tips

1. Form follows function: design buildings that will create the best internal environment for occupants. The current architectural fashion may not celebrate shading devices, but they will result in better buildings for the people who use them.

2. Give occupants control over their environment, so that they can choose when to shade a window or opt for more daylight and heat. Shutters or adjustable louvres are perfect for this.

3. Do not compromise year-round daylight if possible; a better approach is to find ways to reduce heat gain in summer while maximising the light gains in darker months.

Awnings and shaded spaces

❝ Oh for a book and a shady nook/ Either indoors or out/ with the green leaves whispering overhead/ or the street cries all about.' – JOHN WILSON, POET

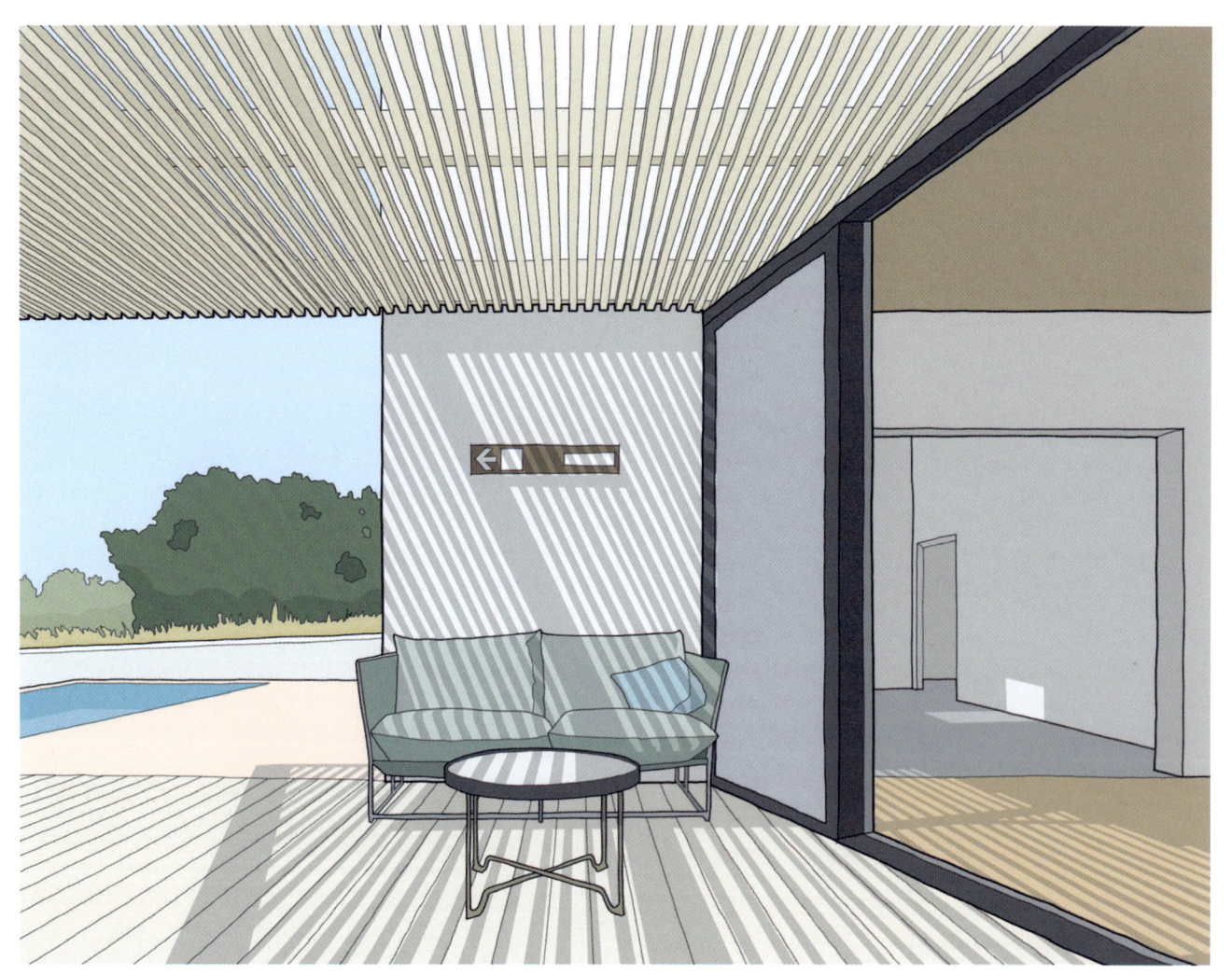

Figure 2.11: House in Comporta, Portugal, by Almeida Fernandes

Potential mental wellbeing benefits

- Improved sleep
- Increased activity
- Social opportunities
- Nature interaction
- Moments of joy / awe

Potential issues and considerations

- Build cost
- Space requirements
- Protection from elements
- Maintenance

While the data might show that generally we now spend less time outside than inside, outdoor comfort is still important, particularly if we are trying to encourage people to get out more. We know that people will spend more time in well-designed spaces that make them feel good, and the benefits of nudging people to spend more time outside can be significant, with research demonstrating that people who do so lead more fulfilling lives.[45]

When people spend time outdoors, they are exposed to much greater levels of daylight, which as we know benefits our health in a range of ways. On a clear day, the light level outside can be around 10,000 lux, compared to CIBSE's recommended indoor light levels of just 500 lux for a typical office space. Encouraging people to go outside creates an opportunity to put them in contact with more natural elements and gain biophilic benefits for their mental health, and can also result in people being more active, whether this is simply through a slight increase in standing or movement, or through encouraging them to walk or play. Finally, it can create great opportunities for increased social interactions, bolstering a sense of community and being a powerful tool for placemaking when used in the right locations.

While there are many reasons that we now spend more time indoors than in any previous age,[46] we must address deterrents to being outside, and one of the key factors in this is weather. Wherever we are in the world, people are likely to be put off going outdoors by either excessive rain or overbearing sunshine. Fortunately, it is fairly straightforward to protect people from these elements, and while there are even points available for doing just this in the WELL Building Standard, this protection is often overlooked or omitted.

A simple and cost-effective way to shade people from the sun and protect them from precipitation is through the introduction of awnings outside buildings at ground floor level. It is no coincidence that when we picture the stereotypical European café on a summer's day, we imagine tables laid out in the street with people sipping drinks, protected by a generous, retractable awning overhead. There is evidence that such devices were used as far back as ancient Egypt and Syria, in the form of woven mats that were used to shade market stalls and the spaces in front of homes.[47]

With the technological advancements that came in the late nineteenth century, retractable awnings became commercially available, meaning that these are now an excellent example of an adaptable building element. Being able to deploy or withdraw these as required gives occupants greater control over their outdoor environment, which in itself generates a psychological benefit, while also increasing usability of outdoor spaces in a range of conditions.

Finally, awnings and canopies can be a powerful way to add visual interest to a streetscape – provided they are well designed and well maintained. They offer opportunities to provide increased colour, variety and detail to the public realm, facilitating better placemaking, activating more building frontages and contributing to more aesthetically pleasing streets, which as we will discover in Chapter 6 adds its own benefits to our sense of happiness and wellbeing. While they may seem like a minor or even frivolous addition to a building, all these factors mean that awnings offer a high level of wellbeing value in relation to their relatively low cost.

Design tips

1. Review which outdoor spaces around a building's perimeter will add the most value when activated, and shelter these through some form or sun, rain or wind protection, depending on local climate.

2. In drier climates, rain protection will be less important, but some sun exposure may still be desirable. In these instances, semi-shading devices may be more appropriate, such as alternating timber battens or overhead foliage.

3. With full awnings, occupants may not always want to sit in a shaded space, so provide the option to retract the canopy, if possible, to maximise user autonomy.

A protective winter garden

> 'Who loves a garden loves a greenhouse too.'
> – WILLIAM COWPER, POET

Figure 2.12: Risuviita apartments, Seinäjoki, Finland, by OOPEAA

Potential mental wellbeing benefits

- Physical comfort
- Improved sleep
- Sense of privacy
- Nature interaction
- Improved air quality

Potential issues and considerations

- Loss of views
- Loss of light
- Possible social impacts
- Possible loss of nature interaction
- Impact on layouts

To anybody outside the world of residential design, the term 'winter garden' might be unfamiliar. Traditionally, these were conservatories or greenhouses that housed tropical plants and might also serve as additional living space. They are believed to have existed as early as the seventeenth century, but as so often, they were popularised by the Victorians, particularly in the wake of Sir Joseph Paxton's Crystal Palace. These traditional winter gardens would provide a warm, protective environment for the plants, which also made them pleasant places for their owners to spend time, even in cooler parts of the year.

Today the meaning of the term is somewhat different, instead generally being referred to a recessed balcony that is fully enclosed, often with floor-to-ceiling glazing. They are often provided in residential apartment buildings as an alternative form of private amenity space, but they can also be used to great effect in workplaces or public buildings. When comparing balconies to modern winter gardens, we cannot simply say that one is better than the other. Both have advantages and drawbacks, but in some situations and climates winter gardens do offer a number of benefits in terms of both physical and mental wellbeing.

In colder locations there are clear comfort benefits, with a winter garden offering protection from the rain, snow or biting wind while still giving the sensation of being in an outdoor or semi-outdoor space. This allows people to sit on their balcony in complete comfort, regardless of weather conditions. The same can apply in hotter climates, as the temperature of the internal winter garden can be regulated through comfort cooling – even if it is 40°C (104°F) outside.

Winter gardens can offer benefits to air quality in a similar way if a building is located in a highly polluted area, as air within the winter garden can be filtered, allowing occupants to use the space with less fear of breathing in harmful air. With studies now linking air pollution to mental health issues in children, this approach could make a significant difference to the wellbeing of inhabitants in such areas, when compared with traditional outdoor balconies.[48]

Unlike true balconies, winter gardens can also offer significant acoustic benefits to the spaces behind them, as they can provide a second buffer to any noise. This produces a more comfortable internal acoustic environment, both in the connected space and in the winter garden itself, and is a further reason they are particularly well suited to busy roads. Finally, they offer a greater level of privacy than traditional balconies, which can often feel exposed if they are positioned on the front of buildings. We know that privacy plays an important role in how free people feel to use spaces for many activities, and that it is also a key component in our sense of safety.

There are disadvantages to winter gardens that we should be aware of, however. They can reduce the amount of daylight internal spaces receive, as any light has to pass through two layers of glazing, and interior windows will likely be in shade for most of the day. There is also the potential that they can offer a reduced connection to the outside world and the natural elements it often contains, as well as reducing the level of social interaction with neighbours. However, both can be addressed by allowing some of the glazed elements to be openable, provided there is protection from falling, of course!

Design tips

1. Carry out a comparison exercise to understand the benefits that winter gardens, recessed balconies or projecting balconies might offer.

2. The suitability of winter gardens or traditional balconies may vary within the same building depending on the surrounding context. Ideally choose the best type of private amenity space for each facade rather than attempting a 'one size fits all' approach.

3. Provide openable glazing to winter gardens where possible, although on tower buildings or in areas with significant acoustic or air quality issues this may not be appropriate.

Dual aspect spaces

> *'By dint of building well, you get to be a good architect.'*
> — ARISTOTLE, PHILOSOPHER

Figure 2.13: Am Chatzebach housing development, Muri, Switzerland, by Baumberger & Stegmeier + Stücheli Pestalozzi Schiratzki Architekten

Potential mental wellbeing benefits
- Physical comfort
- Improved air quality
- Improved sleep
- Increased autonomy
- Greater adaptability

Potential issues and considerations
- Build cost
- Space requirements
- Impact on layouts

The traditional 'house' is, by its very nature, dual aspect, meaning it has windows on two or more (usually opposing) facades. There are some notable examples, such as the traditional cave houses of Tunisia or northern China, but generally most vernacular housing has at least two different 'aspects'.

Simply having openings on two sides of a dwelling – or for that matter any building – offers a raft of benefits to the quality of the indoor environments and, in turn, our wellbeing. An obvious advantage is the ability to place rooms on both facades, and in turn maximise daylight. It also gives designers and occupants greater choice over where to locate different rooms, for example by putting a living space on a facade with the best view, an eating space on the elevation where diners will be able to enjoy the sunsets, or bedrooms on the quieter facade. Single-aspect apartments, in contrast, have none of these luxuries.

Dual-aspect spaces also offer significant benefits in terms of natural ventilation, as we can harness the power of cross-ventilation, where windows are open on both sides of the building, allowing for the free flow of air through its various spaces. This does, of course, rely on internal doors between rooms being open, and ideally needs outdoor air temperature to be 2°C cooler outside than inside, but generally these conditions are achievable and give occupants an effective way to improve thermal comfort relatively quickly.[49]

This begs a simple question: if dual-aspect spaces offer so many advantages, why aren't all new buildings dual aspect? Single-aspect apartments, for example, are now highly prevalent, and despite some efforts by authorities to address them (in particular, the infamous 'north facing' variety which receive the very lowest levels of daylight), many new apartment schemes still include what one journalist referred to as homes of 'the brutal long corridor, single aspect variety'.[50]

The issue of accessing apartments does indeed play a large role in this problem. The standard model is currently a central corridor flanked by apartments on either side – which of course means all apartments bar those on the corners become single aspect. Fundamentally, this is a model that can easily be improved: by moving access to decks outside or arranging flats in a cluster of six or even eight around a central core, it is possible to create layouts in which all homes are dual aspect.

The arguments against these approaches are rolled out time and again: 'another core will be too expensive', 'we can't afford the increase in external floor area', or even 'there's a housing crisis, we must build as densely as possible'. While we absolutely do need more homes, these must not come at a cost to quality of life. If the problem were simply about providing more dwellings, we could make every home a 20m^2 studio apartment with minimal glazing and be done with it.

Ultimately, dual- or triple-aspect spaces improve physical and mental health, making them better quality and increasing their value. This can help to offset the extra spend on another core or increased external wall area and will likely improve the image and brand of a developer, too, as one who builds high-quality, health-driven environments. Again, this comes back to the question of how we define 'value': is it simply calculated in a spreadsheet or can value also be about creating excellent places where people will truly want to live for generations to come?

Design tips

1. Challenge any brief demanding single-aspect buildings: make the case for the added value created by dual-aspect spaces both in terms of their inherent value and the value added to the developer's brand.

2. Explore strategies to eliminate single-aspect spaces from schemes. This could be deck access, spaces clustered around a core or duplex apartments which only feature corridors at every other level.

3. Consider developing a company policy on single-aspect spaces. Some architectural practices outlaw single-aspect north-facing dwellings entirely, for example, or only allow them on other facades in special situations.

High-performance ventilation (when natural is not suitable)

> 'Some old-fashioned things like fresh air and sunshine are hard to beat.'
> – LAURA INGALLS WILDER, AUTHOR

Figure 2.14: Bloomberg HQ, London, UK, featuring an advanced ventilation system via its large 'fins', by Foster + Partners

Potential mental wellbeing benefits
- Physical health improvements
- Improved sleep
- Improved air quality
- Increased productivity

Potential issues and considerations
- Operational cost
- Fitout cost
- Environmental impacts
- Specialist input useful

Despite our best efforts, there may be situations in which it simply isn't possible to ventilate a space naturally. Perhaps a site is located in a highly polluted or extremely noisy area, or we are trying to ventilate a space at the very top of a tower building where operable windows aren't possible. Whatever the reasons, thankfully we now have the ability to ventilate such spaces artificially.

Artificial ventilation has existed in some form since the nineteenth century, when heat- and wind-induced low-pressure systems were introduced in a number of public buildings and dwellings.[51] Today it generally takes the form of systems which bring in cool, fresh air from outside, replacing the warm, stale air indoors.

In the last few decades artificial ventilation and comfort cooling has developed a bad name as a result of its high energy loadings, and with good reason. There are roughly two billion air-conditioning units in operation around the globe, and space cooling is now the number one driver of electricity demand in buildings globally.[52] Natural ventilation should always be our first choice if possible.

In spite of these issues, the image of mechanical ventilation received a serious boost during the COVID-19 pandemic, as the world became aware that higher rates of air change in a space reduces the risk of the virus spreading, and certain filtration systems –particularly HEPA filters[53] – could potentially offer some protection from airborne viruses.[54]

Artificial ventilation systems can offer further benefits to our health too, not least in terms of addressing indoor air pollutants. Our buildings are often home to a wide range of pollutants that can lead to a range of poor health outcomes from headaches, dry throats or runny noses to more serious respiratory problems, cardiovascular diseases or cancers.[55]

Achieving adequate air circulation, particularly in combination with high-quality filters, can have significant impacts on indoor air quality and the health of people using those spaces. In one study, when ventilation rates in an office were doubled, there was a reduction in short-term absenteeism of 35%: enough to make any employer think about improving ventilation.[56] As buildings have become more airtight and with levels of CO_2 or VOCs able to build up very quickly, it is easy to understand why good ventilation is important for human health.

High-performance ventilation has other advantages for our comfort, physical health and contentedness. It gives occupants better control over the temperature and indoor environment, resulting in greater comfort and autonomy. Systems can also address the problem of humid spaces, which can be a significant factor in unhappiness and poor mood, with numerous studies demonstrating that high humidity has an impact on concentration, increases sleepiness and is a predictor for 'lack of vigour, elation and affection'.[57]

Unfortunately, artificial ventilation seems to be an area where there is a conflict between sustainability and wellbeing. Despite them often getting lumped into one category, this example demonstrates that there can be differences between the two, and that the healthiest solution is not always the most sustainable. The good news is that in many countries the energy grid is becoming cleaner every year, with the UK achieving a 66% decarbonisation between 2013 and 2020.[58] We should also seek to use sustainable systems, such as those that recover heat to minimise energy loss and integrate green energy sources to mitigate the environmental impact of artificial ventilation in our buildings.

Design tips

1. Bring a mechanical engineer on to the project team early in the design process and carry out an initial ventilation strategy review to ascertain whether a natural or artificial approach is more suitable for the project.

2. Refer to CIBSE (Chartered Institute of Building Service Engineers), ASHRAE (American Society of Heating, Refrigeration and Air-Conditioning Engineers) or similar standards to ensure that ventilation systems are designed to provide adequate ventilation rates, and make sure system are tested and balanced after project occupancy.

3. Avoid construction pollution and dust getting into ventilation systems by sealing ducts during construction or cleaning them thoroughly prior to final installation of components.

4. Consider the use of HEPA, media or UV filters within your system, each of which achieves different things depending on project requirements.

CHAPTER 3
Control and autonomy

> 'The world is so unpredictable. Things happen suddenly, unexpectedly. We want to feel we are in control of our own existence. In some ways we are, in some ways we're not. We are ruled by the forces of chance and coincidence.' – PAUL AUSTER, AUTHOR

Figure 3.0: Arnhem primary school, the Netherlands, by Architectuurstudio HH

The World Happiness Report ranks 157 countries by their happiness (sometimes referred to as 'subjective wellbeing'). You might not be surprised to hear that the highest ranked countries tend to be Nordic and north European, with one notable outlier of New Zealand frequently appearing in the top 10. One of the things all these countries share (as well as being relatively affluent), is a fairly liberal and highly democratic culture, with high levels of individual freedom and choice.

Indeed, one of the key measures of happiness identified by the What Works Centre for Wellbeing is 'Freedom to choose what you do in life'[1] – something that is echoed by one of the co-authors of the World Happiness Report, Richard Layard, in his excellent book *Happiness: Lessons from a New Science*.[2] In the book, Layard sets out to examine happiness and its causes, concluding that there are seven key factors, one of which is 'Personal Freedom'. Citing the example of Swiss cantons, he explains that by comparing the cantons with the highest levels of political autonomy against those with the lowest, 'the difference in happiness is as great as if they had double the income'.[3]

With experts agreeing that increased autonomy correlates with happier people, how can we ensure that the buildings and cities we design empower their occupants and give them greater control over their daily lives?

Studies have shown that in terms of home satisfaction, the ability to change the layouts of our homes is more important than the size of bedrooms, showing that control over our immediate environments significantly affects our happiness within them.[4] This translates to the workplace too, with a greater sense of control over how and where people work linked to lower levels of burnout. As Dr Whitney Austin Gray, Executive Director of Research and Innovation at global wellness pioneer Delos, explains, 'many factors may impact feelings of control over the physical work environment – ranging from lighting to privacy to psychoacoustics. The ability for employees to choose where they work and how, as well as their ability to adjust factors in the physical environment to meet their needs, is central to a sense of control within the work environment'.[5]

For many people, the importance of control is intrinsically linked to concerns over uncertainty – when we have control, we feel like uncertainty levels are diminished, which is often comforting. Psychology professor Nick Carleton argues that a 'Fear of the Unknown' is a fundamental human function that we have developed to keep us safe: 'Enough fear to approach unknowns with caution (i.e. treating unknowns as potential threats) would be adaptive, so long as the intensity did not compromise survival activities (e.g. seeking food, shelter, mates). Accordingly, evolution should have produced a selection bias for assessing unknowns as likely threatening.'[6]

Part of the challenge of living in modern society is that generally our potential threat levels have decreased: most of us no longer come face-to-face with carnivorous predators on a daily basis. However, that evolutionary system still exists, meaning the part of our brains responsible for our fight-or-flight mechanisms can fire when we are faced with uncertain situations. Giving people greater autonomy over their environments can, in some part, help people to regain some sense of control and therefore support better mental wellbeing.

Flexible separating devices

'My hope is that light, flexible architecture might bring about a new and open society.' –
FREI OTTO, ARCHITECT

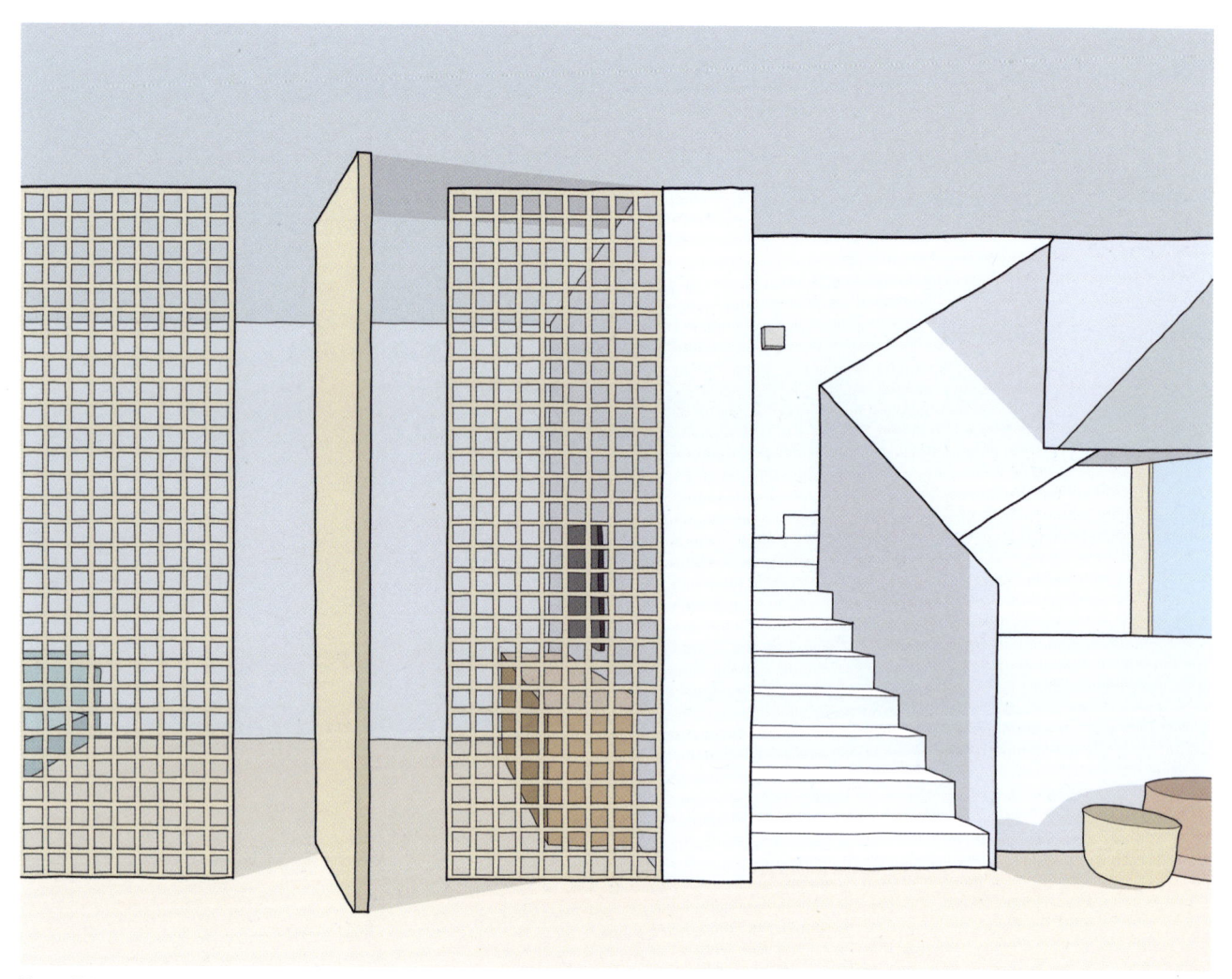

Figure 3.1: House of Tranquility, Tel Aviv, Israel, by Tal Goldsmith Fish Design Studio

Potential mental wellbeing benefits

- Greater adaptability
- Increased productivity
- Increased autonomy
- Social opportunities
- Environmental benefits

Potential issues and considerations

- Maintenance
- Use by all
- Build cost

We often think of the things that architects design as being fixed. Buildings are, generally, intended to be permanent, and materials are often selected precisely for their permanence and stability: brick, stone, steel and concrete.

However, what if there was an alternative approach that could empower the people who live and work in our buildings, giving them greater control over not just how they use spaces, but over the configuration of the spaces themselves? Research shows a strong correlation between how well our homes meet our needs and how happy we are, so the ability to adapt our homes to support how we live could play a key role in supporting good mental wellbeing.[7]

There is an alternative tradition of architecture in which walls and even windows are not heavy and fixed – quite the opposite. In traditional Japanese housing, for example, the idea of architectural permanence is less pervasive.[8] Historically many family homes (or *machiya*) were viewed as temporary and reconstructed every 20 years or so – although waste was minimised and buildings were primarily made from natural materials, including wood, paper, clay and rice straw.

These houses often featured sliding walls or doors called *fusuma*, allowing interior spaces to be dynamically reconfigured into different sized rooms for a variety of functions, such as multiple bedrooms being combined during the day into a living room. In a country where plot width was traditionally a signifier of wealth, space has always been at a premium and *fusuma* allowed Japanese families to get the most out of smaller homes.

This approach is not solely limited to Japan. Many architects around the world have integrated the use of sliding or moveable elements to create more flexible and adaptable buildings. Perhaps the most well-known of these is the Schröder House, designed by Dutch architect Gerrit Rietveld in the 1920s. The two-storey home includes an adaptable kitchen/living/dining area, along with working and sleeping space at ground floor, with a fully open first floor that could be subdivided using moving partitions.

Rietveld believed 'the reality that architecture can create is space'.[9] He understood that by giving the Schröder family greater control over the spaces they occupied, they were empowered to live life how they wanted. A century later, these issues are still just as relevant, with a 2020 report on housing design explaining that even today 'a lack of flexibility and open plan living are major issues for wellbeing'.[10] A further way to enable this flexibility is to avoid loadbearing internal partitions by moving structure to the perimeter of the building, as seen in the work of Rietveld and many of the twentieth-century modernists.

This adaptability is not just beneficial in our homes. In workplaces it can allow employees to move quickly from open-plan working to private offices or small studios, or to create ad hoc meeting rooms. In schools it can enable classrooms to transform into play spaces or be combined into an assembly hall. This not only benefits us psychologically through an increased sense of control, but makes buildings more sustainable, as they are far easier to reuse and repurpose in the future, reducing the need for demolition or likelihood of renovation.

Design tips

1. Early in a project's design, undertake an 'activities and zoning' exercise, analysing the likely activities that might take place within different parts of a building, and how spaces might ideally respond to those different uses.

2. Design any moveable systems to be low-maintenance, robust and simple enough that occupants can repair them – otherwise malfunctions could reduce the sense of user control over their environment.

3. As with all elements of a building, design systems that people with a range of physical abilities can also use – lighter elements may be better suited for this reason.

4. Modular or gridded systems naturally lend themselves well to more adaptable spaces, so start with a structural grid, then subdivide this into smaller modules for partitions.

Smart control systems

'All technology does is give us back to ourselves. So to be anti-technology in a sense is to be anti-human.' – JOSHUA COHEN, AUTHOR

Figure 3.2: Google Home Assistant

Potential mental wellbeing benefits
- Increased autonomy
- Personalisation opportunities
- Improved liveability
- Physical comfort
- Greater equity

Potential issues and considerations
- Fitout cost
- Consultation required
- Use by all
- Futureproofing

In the twenty-first century, it is tempting to think we have more control over our lives and surroundings than ever before. However, when we look a little closer at the places where many of us spend most of our time, we find this isn't always the case.

Many people do not have the luxury of being able to change their thermal environment at work, for example, despite a recent piece of research which showed that 85% of workers consider temperature to be one of the most important factors in their workplace.[11] Meanwhile, many student halls don't even trust their occupants with light switches, instead using sensors in kitchen and living areas. This gives residents no opportunity to dim the lights – instead, they are faced with the same harsh, intense fluorescent lighting at all times of day and night, whether they are trying to watch a movie or get a glass of water at 3am.

Given the technologies we have at our disposal today, it is surprising that many buildings still offer people such poor control over their environments. Over the last 80 years, computers have shrunk from the size of a house to fit in our pockets, and our phones now have more than 100,000 times the processing power of the computer that helped NASA land Apollo 11 on the moon in 1969.[12] Advancements like these mean that we now have an enormous range of smart building systems available to us, offering us control over almost any aspect of our environment.

For perhaps the first time ever, we can truly adapt our environment to suit our needs at the push of a button. Such systems have the potential to empower people and allow buildings to work for them, rather than being something they tolerate. Lighting is now available in almost any colour or temperature, and we can change the brightness with our devices or voices. We can adjust the temperature of our homes remotely and control a huge range of electrical appliances from kettles to ovens and even our showers using mobile technology. Smart tech can remove the stress of turning things on and off every day and address common worries, such as whether we left the oven on or locked the front door. It can even help cut our utility bills through use-analysis, saving us money and addressing eco-anxiety concerns over our carbon footprint while improving internal comfort.

There are, of course, challenges associated with smart building technologies. If not designed properly they can make buildings harder to use, and when they go wrong they can be far more challenging to put right. For this reason, it is important to consider such technologies early in the design process so that they are part of a fully integrated system and are futureproofed as far as possible, although we can never truly guarantee such systems will not fall victim to obsolescence, when providers go out of business or lines are discontinued.

We also need to be aware of privacy issues associated with smart control systems. While this is a subject that has been centre stage in the press recently, there are ways around many of these problems via either design or in the technical settings, and by working closely with occupants, tech teams can help to address these fears.

Perhaps more than any other tool in this book, this is one which relies on good communication with end users and a clear brief on the desired systems at an early stage.

Design tips

1. Design-in smart tech from an early stage so that the tech can complement the building's use and operations, allowing benefits to be fully realised.

2. Work with the client early to understand their priorities for the project and how smart tech might benefit them most – this can inform the products and system selected.

3. Consider possible ways to futureproof smart tech – ideally focus on one unified system manufactured and managed by a large, reliable company.

4. Provide 'How-to' guides to building occupants in a simple-to-access way, such as QR codes leading to an easy-to-use website.

Adaptable work spaces

> 'A Not So Big House feels more spacious than many of its oversized neighbours because it is space with substance, all of it in use every day.'
> – SARAH SUSANKA, ARCHITECT AND AUTHOR

Figure 3.3: Argentona Street House, Barcelona, Spain, by YLAB Arquitectos

Potential mental wellbeing benefits

- Greater adaptability
- Increased productivity
- Improved liveability
- Spatial benefits
- Increased autonomy

Potential issues and considerations

- Detailing
- Build cost
- Maintenance

We now live in a world where space is at a premium. Many cities are becoming denser year on year, with our current urban population of around 4 billion expected to grow to around 6.34 billion by 2050.[13] Though space standards in many places set minimum sizes for homes, these are often far from generous. In the UK, for example, living areas have shrunk by around 32% since the 1970s.[14] While small homes can play an important role in the housing market, they can also be restrictive if poorly designed, and as an industry we certainly should be promoting larger dwellings.

Not only are our homes often getting smaller, we are now adapting them for more uses. Between 2005 and 2017 there was a 159% increase in homeworking, which only grew further during the 2020 COVID-19 pandemic, when many people had no option but to work from home.[15] During this time many of us discovered that working from home was more challenging than we had perhaps imagined, and we also found that many of our homes were ill-equipped for homeworking.

While not promoting smaller homes, one way to maximise the space available to us is through the integration of adaptable work spaces. These are spaces which can, with minimal effort, be transformed into a desk or home office, and with similar ease return to another function. This can be achieved in several ways: through kinetic furniture, by folding down units or cupboard space, or through the use of under-used spaces, like lofts or nooks below staircases.

As well as offering benefits in terms of autonomy, this adaptability also allows us to psychologically 'remove' the workspace when our tasks have been completed. This allows users to more fully disconnect from their work at the end of the day. Research has shown that people who do not switch off properly from work are more likely to experience high stress or mental exhaustion,[16] while working a 60-hour week has been claimed to double the risk of heart attacks.[17] Despite this, according to a recent survey nearly half of Americans consider themselves 'workaholics'. Working from home only seems likely to exacerbate this problem, making it all the more important for designs to nudge people to disconnect wherever possible.

As with any home office, other mental wellbeing issues should still be considered when designing an adaptable work space. Ideally it should be in a location where it can receive generous amounts of natural light and in close proximity to plants or other natural elements, as these are shown to reduce stress and improve productivity. Natural materials are preferable and factors such as comfort and ergonomics should not be sacrificed at the expense of adaptability.

If all of these issues are considered, the ability to transform a part of the home into a high-quality workspace can be extremely empowering and can add psychological value as well as financial value to a house or apartment.

Design tips

1. A pop-up work space still needs to be comfortable and supportive. Ensure that ergonomics have been factored into the design to avoid injuries or chronic pain.
2. Locate pop-up work spaces in quieter parts of a building. If this isn't possible, review other acoustic strategies, such as extra partitions or sound-masking devices.
3. Ensure the space is easy to transform from one use to another. If this is challenging, then it is less likely to get put away at the end of each day.
4. Even though it might only be a temporary work space, remember to bring elements of joy into the design, whether it be through colour, biophilia, artwork or texture.

Personal space bubbles

> 'All space must be attached to a value, to a public dimension. There is no private space. The only private space that you can imagine is the human mind.'
> – PAULO MENDES DA ROCHA, ARCHITECT

Figure 3.4: Slack's Toronto offices, Canada, by Dubbeldam Architecture + Design

Potential mental wellbeing benefits

- Spatial benefits
- Increased productivity
- Sense of privacy
- Improved liveability
- Increased autonomy

Potential issues and considerations

- Possible social impacts
- Space requirements
- Impact on layouts

In *The Spaces Between Us*, a book dedicated almost entirely to the subject of personal space, Michael S.A. Graziano explains that we all have a personal space zone, which can grow or shrink depending on our circumstances.[18] A good demonstration of this is to imagine somebody standing less than a metre from you at an empty train platform: it would be very disconcerting, due to the emptiness of the setting and the lack of intimacy with this person. Yet, if it was a very busy platform, or a person you knew well, your personal space zone would shrink accordingly.

Graziano explains that the idea of personal space was first studied in the 1950s, when it was discovered that many animals have a 'flight zone' around them, which will trigger a flight response if anything unfamiliar enters.[19] Despite such threats being less relevant to us as a species now, we have not lost this sense of personal space.

We have already seen that cities are becoming denser and with it houses smaller, and as property values rose in the early 2000s many business owners looked to densify their office spaces as well.[20] This has effectively reduced people's personal space bubbles in both the home and the workplace, which can have some significant consequences.

A report by Matter Architecture, titled 'Wellbeing in Prison Design', explores the concept of personal space and 'interpersonal distances'.[21] As the report explains, 'in smaller spaces, personal space bubbles expand' and as a result overcrowded spaces lead to increased aggression and reduced pro-social behaviours. Height played a role as well, as overall room size with lower ceilings also resulting in expanded personal space bubbles.

While it is rare for most architects to work on prison design, we can bring these lessons into other typologies, and perhaps see them as a warning for what happens when we shrink (or overpopulate) spaces beyond comfortable levels. Jacobs, a company that has collected benchmarking data on office space use for over 20 years, has tried to understand 'how dense is too dense', and believes that between 11.5m^2 and 12.5m^2 per office employee should be seen as an absolute minimum.[22]

This is one area in which COVID-19 actually had some positive impacts around the world. People were forced to spread out, with office layouts, classrooms and even fitness classes needing a redesign. This resulting extra personal space may not be permanent, but it certainly demonstrated that through intelligent design we can all be afforded a little more breathing room. It is also important to remember that spaces must also meet our needs for connection and stimulation, so too large a space can be isolating. Jacobs argues that well-designed workspaces should provide a mix of spatial settings and activity zones; what is key is to consider how people's personal space bubbles will change as they move from one to another.[23]

Design tips

1. When considering the design and layout of any space, explore what the likely personal space bubbles might be for the uses expected in that space.
2. Be aware of what sort of relationships are likely to exist between occupants: personal space bubbles can shrink for friends, but for strangers or colleagues larger areas will be required.
3. The concept of designing with personal space bubbles can be used in landscape and urban design too – from the location of seating in gardens to the width of pavements and footpaths.

Smart storage

> 'I can't focus when there's too many things around. Whenever I used to go to the office, I used to always say, "Tidy up".' – ZAHA HADID, ARCHITECT

Figure 3.5: Apartment in Taiwan, by A Little Design

Potential mental wellbeing benefits

- Improved liveability
- Spatial benefits
- Physical comfort
- Increased autonomy
- Greater adaptability

Potential issues and considerations

- Space requirements
- Impact on layouts

We have all experienced first-hand the impact a messy space can have on us. From a kitchen full of unwashed dishes to an office strewn with paperwork, when we walk into an untidy space it tends to feel unpleasant. Research supports this too, with studies suggesting that people who live in messier homes had cortisol profiles more closely associated with adverse health outcomes and stress, and are more likely to suffer with 'depressed mood' scores over the course of the day.[24]

With the average size of homes shrinking in many parts of the world, this is perhaps some cause for concern. This is exacerbated by just how much 'stuff' we now own in industrialised countries, with the average American home containing around 300,000 items.[25] The average British 10 year old in 2010 owned over 200 toys,[26] while the average American woman owned roughly 30 different outfits in 2015, up from just nine in 1930.

The upshot of these circumstances is that well-designed storage is now more important than ever. With people demanding even more of their homes during COVID-19 lockdowns, storage became more essential to allow people to turn parts of their houses and apartments into gyms, offices or classrooms. It is no surprise, therefore, that the self-storage industry continued to grow while many others have declined.[27]

Despite this clear under-provision of storage in housing, standards for new homes demand a remarkably low amount. The UK's 'Nationally Described Space Standards', for example, require just 1.5m^2 of built-in storage for a two-person home (slightly smaller than a pub pool table), while an eight-person family is deemed to need just 4m^2 to house all its possessions. The Home Quality Mark – which was established to help house builders demonstrate high quality homes – does slightly better, asking for 0.5m^2 over these National Standards, although this still works out as just 3% of the total floor area in a three-storey four-bedroom house.[28]

In modern apartments, many developers now prioritise 'saleable' floor area in habitable rooms over storage, and without lofts, eaves or garages to use for storage, designers must think creatively about how to maximise storage. The internet is full of ingenious solutions, from drawers integrated into stairs, cupboards hidden within dropped ceilings above bathrooms or kitchens, and seemingly inconspicuous walls that open to reveal floor-to-ceiling shelving built into them. Furniture can also be a highly efficient way to add storage, such as within a sofa or divan bed.

Storage lockers can be especially helpful in keeping workplaces tidier across all industries, as well as making it easier for people to cycle or run to work. These can be situated in areas that are harder to use as 'work' space, so can be a good use of 'leftover' space.

Fundamentally, storage is an essential, yet often overlooked, part of any building. By understanding its importance and maximising how we provide it, we can not only make buildings easier to use and more liveable, but visually more appealing and better for our moods every day.

Design tips

1. Carry out an occupant and use analysis early in any design process to gain an understanding of the likely storage requirements for a given space. These will vary based on use, so there is no 'one size fits all' rule, and instead should be designed bespoke on each project.

2. Be aware that storage requirements only look set to increase, so err on the side of over provision.

3. The design of storage spaces can be as important as the overall volume – ensure it is laid out to maximise useful space and to be accessible by all.

4. Remember that minimum space standards are 'minimums'; don't treat them are targets, as they are almost certainly too small.

A sense of choice – but not too much!

> 'Everything can be taken from a man but one thing: the last of the human freedoms – to choose one's attitude in any given set of circumstances, to choose one's own way.'
> – VIKTOR FRANKL, HOLOCAUST SURVIVOR AND PSYCHIATRIST

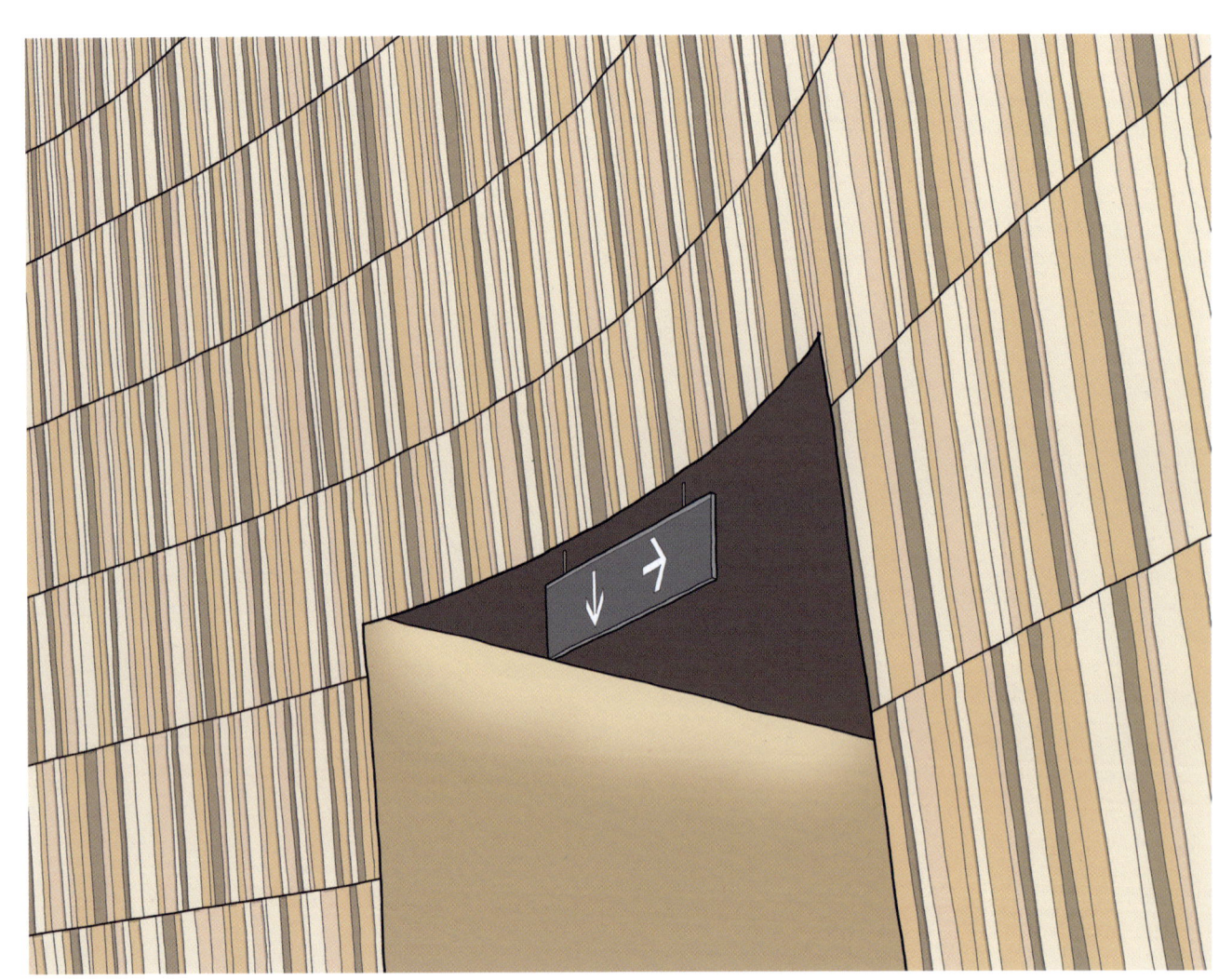

Figure 3.6: Oslo Opera House, Norway, by Snøhetta

Potential mental wellbeing benefits
- Increased autonomy
- Greater adaptability
- Improved liveability

Potential issues and considerations
- Impact on layouts

In a marketing campaign from 2017, Microsoft claimed that each day every human makes around 35,000 decisions. Our choices can be conscious or unconscious, from what colour t-shirt we wear to which hand we use to open a door. American psychiatrist William Glasser believed that in fact our 'behaviours' and our 'choices' were one and the same, and that all were driven by a combination of survival needs (such as food and safety) and psychological needs (such as belonging or power).

As humans, we certainly seem to like a sense of choice. Feeling confined to behaving in a certain way can be frustrating and leave us with a sense that we have no control. It is perhaps no surprise, therefore, that countries with higher levels of 'freedom' are shown to have higher levels of happiness, albeit patterns of correlation do seem to differ between cultures and different aspects of freedom.[29]

However, too much choice can be a bad thing, as Professor Sheena Iyengar explores in her book *The Art of Choosing*.[30] In one of Iyengar's studies, a grocery store offered customers two different 'jam sampling' stations: one with 24 flavours and one with just six. The first station, despite drawing more onlookers, sold jam to just 3% of consumers, while the second had a hit rate of 30%.

This concept of 'choice overload' is also explored by psychologist Barry Schwartz in *The Paradox of Choice*, in which he argues that our present-day abundance of choice has made us more dissatisfied and less happy.

Knowing that people like choice, but not too much, is important for designers. If we consider, say, the design of an art gallery, our instinct may be to lead people on a predetermined path so that we retain control of the visitor experience. However, this could be perceived as restrictive by patrons, making them feel 'forced' to view artworks in a specific order. On the other hand, if we offer visitors too many routes, they may feel lost or worried that they have missed parts of the gallery.

We could also integrate this knowledge into our design approach for a new urban masterplan. As humans we want our towns to provide us with some sense of choice, to encourage curiosity and to spark the joy of exploring new streets. However, if we offer up too much choice and randomness, a place might become illegible and difficult to navigate.

Finally, we can consider this understanding of choice into how we design a home or a workplace. This could be as simple as giving somebody a choice of where to eat or giving them the option to work in a variety of spatial environments with a range of privacy levels.

Design tips

1. Design spaces that people can use in a variety of ways but avoid spaces that have no clear use at all.

2. Provide a range of environment types, whether in a workplace or home, giving people more choice over privacy levels, acoustic setting, brightness, etc.

3. Offer a range of routes around buildings or masterplans, allowing people some element of exploration.

The humble corkboard

> 'A house is not a home unless it contains food and fire for the mind as well as the body.'
> – BENJAMIN FRANKLIN, POLITICIAN AND ONE OF THE FOUNDING FATHERS OF THE UNITED STATES OF AMERICA

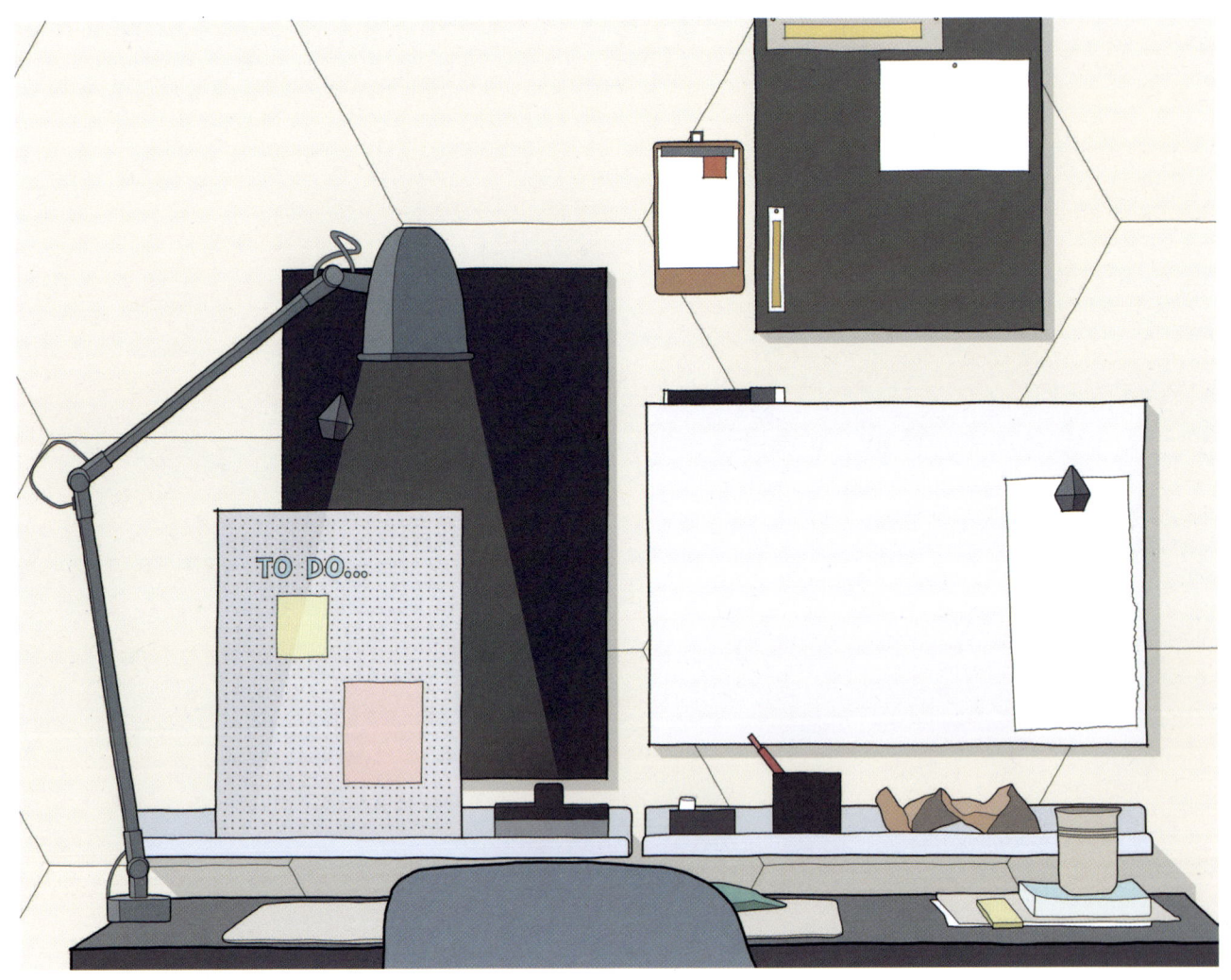

Figure 3.7: A desk space can easily be personalised with memo boards

Potential mental wellbeing benefits

- Personalisation opportunities
- Increased autonomy
- Identity / self-worth
- Nature interaction

Potential issues and considerations

- Maintenance

In 1909, Henry Ford famously stated that 'any customer can have a car painted any color that he wants, so long as it is black'.[31] Today, in contrast, we can personalise almost everything, from 'create your own' pizzas to customised watches and cars. Even our user experiences are now personalised, with products such as Netflix and Spotify using complex algorithms to suggest what might interest us. While this might seem disconcerting to some, studies show that generally people prefer these personalised experiences, as they (perhaps counterintuitively) make them feel more in control and they reduce the sense of 'information overload' that some technology can create.[32]

Research shows that giving people the chance to personalise the spaces they use can actually make them happier, healthier and more productive. This research, based on surveys of over 2,000 office workers, suggests that staff satisfaction and output can be increased if employees are allowed to take greater ownership of their workplace and are fully consulted on changes.

Despite evidence like this, many building users are often denied the ability to personalise the spaces that form the backdrop to their everyday lives. In many rented homes and in student accommodation, it is common not to be allowed to paint walls or hang pictures. Meanwhile, many workplaces operate 'clean desk' policies, preventing staff from bringing in photos or ornamentation to personalise their workspaces.

In Ingrid Fetell Lee's book, *Joyful: The Power of Ordinary Things to Create Extraordinary Happiness*, she explores how simple objects and 'sensory rich' environments can improve our moods.[33] Lee believes this concept of 'abundance' is important, explaining 'minimalist homes promise a Zen-like serenity, but to live permanently in that kind of environment seems to go against the grain of our human nature'. While the crisp lines of a blank, empty home or workplace might look beautiful on the cover of an architecture magazine, they also lack any visual stimulation or individual touches that spark joy.

How can people personalise their homes or work spaces even when faced with various restrictions? One simple solution is the humble corkboard. A corkboard can allow the user of any space to pin up things that are personal to them and can take years of punishment from the most aggressive of pinners without requiring any real maintenance. While perhaps maligned at times as unfashionable or un-architectural, there are now some very attractive designs available. As an added bonus they will bring the benefits of warming natural wood into a space, but if this isn't your preferred aesthetic, they can be found in a range of different coloured canvas finishes too.

Design tips

1. Design-in elements that people can personalise, whether it is a corkboard, chalkboard or magnetic fridge door.
2. Ensure these complement the overall aesthetic, perhaps through the use of natural materials or a harmonious colour palette.
3. Locate these in places where people will regularly see and use them, rather than hiding them away in subsidiary spaces.

Self-sufficiency features

'Self-sufficiency is the greatest of all riches.'
— EPICURUS, ANCIENT GREEK PHILOSOPHER

Figure 3.8: RHS Rosemoor, Torridge, North Devon, UK, by Gale & Snowden Architects

Potential mental wellbeing benefits
- Environmental benefits
- Increased autonomy
- Sense of safety
- Altruism benefits
- Nature interaction

Potential issues and considerations
- Build cost
- Maintenance
- Space requirements
- Impact on layouts
- Aesthetic challenges (external)

Historically, as a species, we humans have been very self-sufficient creatures. However, this is a skill that appears to be waning with every passing generation. A recent poll suggested that most young people now lack even the most basic survival skills, with only a third knowing how to naturally start a fire, 40% having never swum in open water and nearly half having never been camping.[34]

This might be expected, given that in the industrialised world our food now arrives wrapped in plastic and generally we are luckily enough to get our drinking water straight out of a tap. However, the cost of these conveniences is that we are more reliant on technologies, utilities companies and supermarkets. Many of us had never given this a second thought until genuine concerns emerged over supplies of basic groceries in spring 2020 as the COVID-19 pandemic spread around the world and panic buying led to empty stores. Amidst this, many realised that we have far less control over our own subsistence than we had previously believed. How well would many of us cope if food supplies, petrol supplies, utilities and the internet disappeared, even just for a few weeks?

There are people who prepare themselves for such eventualities – 'preppers' – who make plans for disasters or worst-case scenarios, and they appear to be growing in number. Dr Bradley Garrett, a social geographer at University College Dublin and author of *Bunker: Building for End Times*, believes that recent events have played a role, having witnessed an 'insatiable desire for self-sufficiency and safety in this age of uncertainty'.[35] These events include not only the COVID-19 pandemic, but the rising number of natural disasters around the world due to climate change.

In response to some of these issues, 'off-grid' living is increasing in popularity, with an estimated 75,000 people living in this way in the UK, as of 2018. Ironically, it is often advances in technology that allow people to return to this simpler way of life, such as photovoltaic panels with back-up batteries, rainwater harvesting systems or micro water turbines.

This approach not only lets people live a more sustainable lifestyle, tackling their eco-anxiety concerns, but it can create a sense of 'doing good' as well. This altruism has been shown to offer a number of psychological benefits, such as decreasing stress, hypertension and cortisol, releasing endorphins and even reducing a risk of early death.[36]

Whether we go fully off-grid or simply use some of the features above as back-ups – as seen in RHS Rosemoor's Peter Buckley Learning Centre on the facing page, which includes rainwater harvesting and a solar-powered thermal storage tank – as an architectural approach it can offer us a greater sense of independence, resilience and control, all of which can contribute to better mental wellbeing. As *The Ideal City* explains: 'resilience to climate change, extreme weather events and flooding is imperative for a safe city – it promotes a feeling of safety by providing protection for all'.[37]

Design tips

1. Begin by considering the different ways in which a project is reliant upon large suppliers, from utilities to food.
2. Investigate innovative solutions such as water harvesting systems, composting toilets or even low-tech fridges such as root cellars.
3. Ensure energy usage is minimised, perhaps through an improved envelope or increased thermal mass.
4. Remember the importance of a back-up system such as a battery or generator.

Openable windows

'A day spent with dreaming and sunsets and refreshing breezes cannot be bettered.'
— NICHOLAS SPARKS, AUTHOR

Figure 3.9: Kings Crescent Estate, London, UK, by Karakusevic Carson Architects

Potential mental wellbeing benefits

- Increased autonomy
- Physical comfort
- Environmental benefits
- Nature interaction
- Moments of joy / awe

Potential issues and considerations

- Air quality risks
- Use by all
- Safety
- Acoustics

We all know the physical sensations of being in a space that feels oppressively warm or too stuffy. When this happens, our immediate urge is to open a window. It is an instant and simple way to not only cool the space and allow for movement of air, but for us to take control of our internal environment.

Not only is this sensation of control beneficial for us psychologically, but opening windows can also have positive physical health impacts in terms of both respiratory and cardiovascular health. Interestingly, research has shown that naturally ventilated buildings generally have fewer people reporting sick building syndrome symptoms than mechanically conditioned ones,[38] while other studies show a productivity benefit of around 8% associated with naturally ventilated spaces.[39]

Despite this research, many modern buildings don't offer the simple benefit of openable windows to occupants. The reasons for this are numerous, but a significant factor is operator desire to maintain control over the internal environment. By introducing air-conditioning systems, it is possible to enforce a set temperature and even humidity. However, this obsession with creating 'perfect', unchanging internal conditions removes control from occupants while also eliminating any interaction with nature, such as the sensation of a 'real' breeze or the sound of birdsong we might hear if we opened a window.

A second reason for avoiding openable windows is a focus on energy efficiency and avoiding heat loss. Of course, sustainability is just as important as human health in the design of buildings, but ironically a naturally ventilated approach is often kinder to the environment, removing the substantial energy load of a mechanical system. Perhaps a better approach would be to educate people properly on how their buildings work, and when to use mechanical or natural ventilation, treating our building users with respect and trust rather than removing their control and choice.

Pollution is a further problem, with some schools and homes in the UK now banned from having openable windows due to outdoor air quality.[40] While ultimately a longer-term responsibility lies with the government to cut traffic numbers and reduce particulate matter and nitrogen dioxide levels, in the meantime there are some ways we can manage this issue. The WELL Building Standard, for example, suggests monitoring outdoor air quality and informing building users when it is unsafe to open windows via a small indicator light or an app, for example, as often this only occurs at specific times of day such as rush hour.

In many situations a hybrid solution – with a mix of mechanical ventilation and manually openable windows – may be the best approach, but removing the autonomy of building users to open windows entirely can have a significant impact on how they feel within a space and so should be avoided where possible.

Design tips

1. Consider all building users and ensure windows are openable from a seated or standing position with one hand.
2. The IWBI recommends handles that require less than 22N of force to open. Alternatives such as cranks or electric systems can make windows easier for people of all abilities to open.
3. In areas with poor air quality, provide systems to alert building users to dangerous external air quality before they open windows.
4. Aim for openable window area to be at least 4% of occupied floor area.

Safe streets and safe buildings

> 'This is something everyone knows: A well-used city street is apt to be a safe street. A deserted city street is apt to be unsafe.'
> – JANE JACOBS, ARCHITECTURAL AUTHOR AND JOURNALIST

Figure 3.10: Kensington Street, Sydney, Australia, by Jeppe Aagaard Andersen and Turf Design Studio

Potential mental wellbeing benefits
- Greater equity
- Sense of safety
- Increased autonomy
- Increased activity
- Social opportunities

Potential issues and considerations
- Impact on layouts
- Possible social impacts

Staying safe is one of our most primal instincts. Our brains are hard-wired to look for threats at all times, even when we may not be aware that they are doing this. Our amygdala is largely responsible for this, and when it thinks we might be in danger it can 'hijack' our brains bypassing our prefrontal cortex, and with it any sense of reason.[41]

This is an evolved response, which increases our chances of safely identifying threats and surviving long enough to pass on our genes. As part of this process, we generally dislike the feeling of being unsafe (putting aside the phenomenon of thrill-seeking and the associated risk-taking), which is why Maslow's Hierarchy of Needs lists safety as a 'basic need', essential to our wellbeing and happiness.

You would hope that all places would look to provide a freedom of fear from being attacked, harassed, bullied or mugged. However, unfortunately, in many cases the design or layout of streets and buildings has made them inherently more dangerous. The modern world is only just coming to terms with the fact that cities have, for the most part, been designed by men. As sociologist and expert on urban theory Saskia Sassen explains, 'we are a bit stuck with a certain type of city that was made for men to take trains to work and women to stay at home'.[42] The result is an unequal urban environment. In New York City, for example, there are three times as many male bike commuters as their female counterparts[43] – and the impact of a world designed by men extends far beyond cyclists.

Data shows that 32% of women in the UK feel unsafe when walking alone at night, while only 13% of men express the same concerns.[44] It is therefore fundamental that the design community not only becomes more diverse but also shifts its collective mindset to create places aimed at making everybody feel safe.

There are many tools and strategies that we can integrate to help design safer streets and buildings, and a number of helpful guides too.[45] One of the simplest ways to tackle this issue is getting layouts right in the first place, in particular avoiding dark corners or places that aren't properly overlooked. We can supplement this through additional, well-placed surveillance from homes and the inclusion of features like bay windows, which help people look out across a wider area. Good street lighting is key, too, with studies showing that it is generally more cost-effective than CCTV in reducing street crime.[46]

It is also helpful to have a clear definition of public and private spaces, and which sides are the 'fronts' or 'backs' of buildings. Legibility can affect how we feel in any space, so by making the use and purpose of routes clearer and avoiding vague spaces, we can reduce the risk of people being lost or confused. We often find that spaces like rear parking courts are some of the most dangerous in any given development, as they are often poorly lit, poorly overlooked and have little sense of ownership.

Design tips

1. Create diverse design teams which will have a broader understanding of how different people experience space.
2. Strive for high-quality design, as it can increase sense of ownership, respect and responsibility, which are linked to reduced crime levels.
3. Be aware of conflicts between safety and community; sometime security concerns can increase division and create more separation between spaces.

Private outdoor space

❝ A garden is a private world or it is nothing.'
— ELEANOR PERENYI, GARDENER AND AUTHOR

Figure 3.11: Wardian, Canary Wharf, London, UK, by Glenn Howells Architects

Potential mental wellbeing benefits

- Nature interaction
- Increased activity
- Social opportunities
- Increased autonomy
- Improved sleep (daylight access)

Potential issues and considerations

- Space requirements
- Build cost

For many people, their garden is an integral part of their home. It's not surprising therefore to find that often people find homes with gardens more appealing, with 72% of people in the UK saying they would pay more for a property with an outdoor space.[47] Yet, according to the Office for National Statistics, a staggering one in eight households in Britain had no access to a private or shared garden during the COVID-19 pandemic, with this figure rising to one in five in London.[48] Sadly, but perhaps not unsurprisingly, black people are nearly four times as likely as white people to have no access to an outdoor space in their building, with renters generally hit harder than homeowners as well.

On the surface, a lack of access to outdoor space might not seem like an enormous problem, but the role that our private outdoor spaces play is substantial. They can provide the opportunity to take on private projects (anything from building a treehouse to simply servicing a bike), as well as acting as highly social spaces, where we might share food or drinks with friends on a sunny afternoon, strengthening our relationships with our all-important support network and helping to combat loneliness. On top of this, when spending time in our own gardens we also benefit from direct contact with nature and opportunities for taking exercise.

These spaces don't necessarily need to be huge or ornate. A balcony or terrace can offer many of these benefits, such as the freedom to take our meals outside, to grow vegetables or flowers, or just to sit and enjoy exposure to natural daylight.

A modest balcony can become an intermediary between the public and the private, or the inside and the outside, which can play a particularly important role for people who find it challenging to get out of their homes regularly. As Vancouver city planning consultant Brent Toderian put it: 'there are a lot of benefits to balconies from the perspective of liveability, lovability, mental health, and the enjoyment of living in urban settings [...] They connect homes in higher-density cities to the streets and to the outdoors.'[49]

Juliet balconies, however, do not offer these same benefits. While they may allow us to get more fresh air and daylight into a space than even a full-height window might, they offer no true private outdoor space, and so should be avoided wherever provision for a full balcony is possible.

Ultimately, a private outdoor space's true power is in giving occupants choice over how and where they spend their time at home.

Design tips

1 Always start from the position that every home should have its own private amenity space.

2 Ensure resident privacy is provided in the design of balconies and terraces. If this is not considered, then residents may improvise with screening of their own, which is not always attractive.

3 Design balconies and terraces of sufficient depth to allow for a range of activities, furniture and all users regardless of accessibility needs.

A good entranceway

> 'Decent hall space is needed as a kind of decompression chamber between the outside and inside worlds.' – FLORA SAMUEL, ARCHITECT, AUTHOR AND RESEARCHER

Figure 3.12: Family House, the Netherlands, by Tessa Hop

Potential mental wellbeing benefits
- Sense of privacy
- Sense of safety
- Physical comfort
- Spatial benefits
- Improved liveability

Potential issues and considerations
- Space requirements
- Impact on layouts

In many parts of the world, open-plan homes are now highly desirable. They grace the pages of architecture and interior design magazines, offering functionality, social interaction and a greater sense of space. However, this has also encouraged a trend for bringing residents and visitors immediately into the heart of the home. Whether entering off the street, from a garden or perhaps a communal corridor, many houses and apartments are now designed with the primary entrance opening directly into living rooms or kitchens (or perhaps an open-plan combination of the two).

Yet this has not always been the case. When we look at many Georgian or Victorian homes (or their American neo-counterparts), they generally have a small entrance area, often labelled as 'vestibule' or 'antechamber' on the plans. Even as far back as the traditional Roman house, it appears that an entrance hall or passageway was commonplace, acting as a transition space between the public street and the central atrium.[50]

This approach was not simply confined to western architecture. Many Japanese houses and apartments include a *genkan*, which is an entryway area for removing outdoor shoes and putting on *uwabaki*, or indoor slippers.

We now know that this intention of 'leaving dirt at the door' can play a role in healthier indoor environments, particularly in reducing the transmission of air pollutants from outdoors to indoors – so much so that this is one of the features included in the Air Concept of the WELL Building Standard. For this reason, a lobby can be beneficial in residential and workplace environments.[51]

As Flora Samuel's quote, at the beginning of this section, explains, our entrance spaces act as a place for us to decompress and adjust when moving from the chaotic, exposed environment of the street to the (hopefully) calm, quiet and private world of the interior.[52] They offer an opportunity for us to pause and mentally transition from one mindset to another, encouraging us to take a mindful moment as we do so. To encourage this, we should design such spaces to be relaxing, calming and visually quiet, ideally including natural materials which soothe the parasympathetic nervous system, and perhaps images or objects that are personal to us.

As part of this ritual, proper entrance spaces can help to keep the interior more private too, in both a symbolic sense and visually. We should consider lines of sight from public to private in setting out these parts of a building. As well as thinking about privacy and lines of sight, it is also important to consider who will use the entrance space each day, and what their storage (or other) requirements might be within this space.

Design tips

1. A good entranceway should be robust and easy to maintain. It may require different detailing and finishes to the rest of the building.
2. Use changes of material, style or ceiling height to emphasise transitions between public and private spaces.
3. Be aware of direct lines of sight from public areas to private areas and mitigate these where possible.
4. A lobby space can offer acoustic and thermal attenuation too – consider these benefits in design and detailing.

Well-designed laundry spaces

‛Look after your laundry, and your soul will look after itself.'
– W. SOMERSET MAUGHAM, PLAYWRIGHT AND AUTHOR

Figure 3.13: Celsious laundromat and coffee shop, Brooklyn, New York City, USA, by Corinna and Theresa Williams

Potential mental wellbeing benefits

- Improved liveability
- Social opportunities
- Increased autonomy
- Identity / self-worth

Potential issues and considerations

- Maintenance
- Detailing
- Hygiene

If our ultimate goal is to give people using our buildings more autonomy, one of the simplest ways to achieve this is to give them more control over how they live their daily lives.

While these are not the most glamorous parts of architecture – and are unlikely to end up on the front cover of design journals – utility spaces can often be the elements that have the biggest impact on the people who use them every day. If homes and workplaces aren't designed to support the humdrum chores of life, these can eventually become far more difficult and even overwhelming.

One important part of our lives that most of us have to do, is laundry. As any parent will attest, this becomes an even bigger task as our families grow and can easily take over whole rooms of the house. The average American family now does between eight and ten loads of laundry a week, which each take an average of one hour and 27 minutes to complete, totalling around 12 hours of laundry time every week.

It is surprising, therefore, that many design standards do not require the provision of specific space for many of these tasks, such as drying, sorting or ironing clothes. The UK's Nationally Described Space Standards, for example, make no reference to these activities. Fortunately, some standards such as the Home Quality Mark do require areas for these activities, setting out minimum lengths for external drying, for example, but generally these sorts of areas are not mandatory. Without dedicated areas to activities like this, however, homes can very quickly become cluttered and messy, which as we now know can increase stress levels.

Interestingly, despite not seeming like the most exciting parts of projects, a dedicated laundry room can often become one of the most social areas in an apartment building. While the temptation might be to place them in the basement or deep within a floor plan where no daylight is available, these are spaces that people will use most weeks and therefore should be designed with care. They present opportunities for people to meet their neighbours, sit and have a conversation, or just spend a few minutes unwinding. Make sure that these rooms have good seating, a welcoming atmosphere, relaxing lighting and, most importantly, some level of joy! Many build-to-rent or student housing projects, for example, have laundry rooms with bright feature walls, spaces to read or play games, or adjoining coffee areas.

While the space in which we do our chores – be they laundry rooms, refuse stores or post-sorting areas – may not be the most high-profile parts of the buildings we design, fundamentally they are some of the elements that make the biggest difference to the people that use them. The homes that we design should empower people and make their daily routines easier rather than constraining how they live, and by not just providing these spaces but filling them with delight, we can have a significant impact on the quality of people's lives.

Design tips

1. Don't ignore people's daily chores. Instead, consider how designs can make them easier, faster or even more enjoyable!
2. Utilise these spaces as an opportunity to encourage social interaction, perhaps through well-designed seating or gamification.
3. Integrate elements that can elevate these spaces from their simple function, be it light, colour, natural materials, art or sound.
4. These spaces often become some of the most used and must therefore be robustly detailed with consideration of impacts and potential water damage.

Spaces for napping

> 'O sleep! O gentle sleep! Nature's soft nurse.'
> – WILLIAM SHAKESPEARE, PLAYWRIGHT

Figure 3.14: Sleep pods at Google's Sydney offices, Australia

Potential mental wellbeing benefits

- Improved sleep
- Increased productivity
- Increased autonomy
- Mindfulness opportunity

Potential issues and considerations

- Hygiene
- Maintenance
- Space requirements

Sleep can be one of the biggest factors in how we feel on any given day, with sustained poor sleep having a substantial impact on both our physical and mental health. A lack of sleep can also impair our performance and productivity at work, increase the chance of errors and have negative impacts on relationships.[53]

While a healthy sleeping pattern generally involves getting the majority of our sleep in one long night-time spell, research has shown that napping during the day can also have significant benefits, whether we're sleep-deprived or not.[54] Numerous studies have investigated the power of napping and found positive results associated with short (sub-30-minute) bursts of sleep, ranging from improved vigilance, reasoning, alertness, memory, creativity, vigour and mood, while lowering stress and blood pressure.[55] Even resting without sleeping – known as 'quiet wakefulness' – has been shown to be highly beneficial, reducing stress and improving mood and motivation.

Despite the huge array of advantages associated with short sleep breaks, culturally the concept of napping or even taking breaks to reset our minds within the working day has still not been embraced across much of the world. In the UK, workers are currently entitled by law to just a single 20-minute rest break in a standard working day, while if they are working less than a six-hour shift, they are not entitled to any break at all. In fact, many European and American employers still operate a 'stay at your desk' policy – whether formal or unspoken – not even allowing a 15 minute 'reset' break outside the standard lunch break, let alone a nap. Even if management allows short periods away from your desk, in many workplace cultures employees who embrace this opportunity are often labelled as slackers by their colleagues, so instead remain at their desk despite feeling like they need to step away.

This 'anti-break' culture is, in fact, highly counterintuitive, as short breaks from work have been shown to increase output, meaning staff who take breaks will produce more work than their colleagues who don't. One study, for example, found that the 'ideal' work rhythm took the form of around 50 minutes of work followed by a 17 minute break.[56] This is believed to be because the brain naturally operates best in bursts of intense energy and focus, followed by a short spell of low energy during which it can recharge. Ironically, too, the biggest productivity benefits from napping seem to take place during our afternoon 'circadian dip' – between 3pm and 5pm – when we are generally in the workplace and therefore not permitted to do so.

Some parts of the world have more of a historic connection with napping, such as Mediterranean siesta cultures. In Japan, too, sleep or relaxation pods are commonplace, even taking the form of entire capsule or pod hotels. Thankfully, this approach does seem to gradually be filtering through to British and American workplaces, with companies such as Google now providing sleep pods for their staff.

These can be bought off the shelf, with numerous proprietary sleep pod products now available, as well as bespoke systems. Sleep and relaxation pods should consider all the same points explored in the 'High-Quality Sleeping Environments' section in Chapter 2, from thermal and ergonomic comfort to strategies for reducing phone use within the pod, such as a designated phone locker. It is also important to make sure they are located within a specified quiet zone to avoid disturbance whether users are sleeping or just resting. Background music, nature sounds or sound-masking systems can also be helpful in achieving a peaceful environment.

Design tips

1. Locate sleep or resting spaces in quiet, undisturbed parts of buildings.

2. Consider ergonomic and thermal comfort.

3. Give users the option of background sounds such as white noise, soothing music or nature sounds if desired.

4. It is also important to consider hygiene, so they should be ventilated, easily cleaned and made from non-toxic hypoallergenic materials.

Meditation or rejuvenation spaces

' Meditation is not a way of making your mind quiet. It is a way of entering into the quiet that is already there – buried under the 50,000 thoughts the average person thinks every day' – DEEPAK CHOPRA, AUTHOR

Figure 3.15: Springhill House, Melbourne, Australia, by Lovell Burton

Potential mental wellbeing benefits

- Mindfulness opportunity
- Increased autonomy
- Increased productivity
- Physical health improvements

Potential issues and considerations

- Space requirements
- Fitout cost

While sleep and rest pods can offer many benefits, sometimes larger, more adaptable spaces are required. These can allow people to undertake a wider range of activities from yoga to group meditation, or simply be a quiet place to sit and read a book or listen to music. They can be located outdoors, too, giving people the benefits of sunlight, natural sounds and interaction with plants or animals. Spaces like this are recommended within the Mind Concept of the WELL Building Standard, due to the many mental wellbeing benefits such forms of rejuvenation can offer us.[57]

Despite being practised for millennia, largely for spiritual and religious reasons, we can now demonstrate the scientific benefits of meditation for our minds too. Quantitative research on meditation started in the 1930s and has become increasingly sophisticated, now using a range of modern scientific techniques such as fMRI and EEG machines, allowing researchers to observe neural activity and brain physiology of people before, during and after meditation. A detailed and thorough review of over 17,000 citations and 47 trials in 2014 concluded that mindfulness meditation can improve anxiety and depression, and also found some evidence that it can improve stress levels and mental health-related quality of life.[58]

It therefore seems not just beneficial but logical to provide spaces for such activities in our buildings, much in the same way we might provide a gym to support occupants' physical health.

The good news is that a space for meditation can be very simple and inexpensive. The WELL Standard suggests the inclusion of some natural elements, along with calming colours, textures or forms.[59] Beyond that, even seating is not essential, as it could just as easily be provided in the form of cushions or mats.

Visual and acoustic privacy, however, are important design considerations. Thermal comfort should also be considered so the space is pleasant to spend time in, and protection from the elements if a relaxation space is located outside. If the space is indoors, consider how it will be lit. Ideally, users will be able to control the brightness and temperature of the lighting to create a range of visual environments. Such spaces generally benefit from being tech-free, however, so avoid app-controlled systems if possible – although with many people now using phone-based mindfulness apps, it can be difficult to enforce a total tech-ban in shared spaces.

While such spaces might feel like a luxury, they can play a key role in helping us to stay calm and happy in what can otherwise feel like stressful environments. In the home this adds its own indefinable value, but in the workplace we know from research by academics such as Shawn Achor that happier and more relaxed staff can actually be more productive, thus adding value in a perhaps unexpected way for businesses as well.[60]

Design tips

1. Simple is often better. Stick to natural materials, gentle colours and soft, pleasant background noise.

2. Ensure lighting is adjustable to create low-light environments when required.

3. Design-in good visual and acoustic privacy for users of the space.

4. Make it clear the space is to be used for relaxation only and is not a work or social area.

CHAPTER 4
Nature and biophilia

' It is not so much for its beauty that the forest makes a claim upon men's hearts, as for that subtle something, that quality of the air, that emanation from the old trees, that so wonderfully changes and renews a weary spirit.' – ROBERT LOUIS STEVENSON, *ESSAYS OF TRAVEL*

Figure 4.0: Bosco Verticale, Milan, Italy, by Boeri Studio

Of all the subjects in this book, nature and biophilia are perhaps the most well researched and written about. We are all familiar with nature, but perhaps less so with the concept of biophilia, a term coined by the Harvard entomologist Edward O. Wilson in his 1984 book *Biophilia: The Human Bond with Other Species*.[1] In Greek, the term literally means 'love of life' and refers to Wilson's belief that human beings have an innate love of nature and a need to connect with other life forms.

Since the publication of Wilson's book, many studies by neuroscientists and environmental psychologists have explored the ways in which nature affects us. In recent years, landscape and architectural designers such as Oliver Heath have championed biophilia through their work, helping to raise awareness of this important phenomenon.

Research shows that nature can be a powerful force in supporting both our physical and mental health. The psychological benefits of, for example, adding plants to our environment, include improved mood, reduced stress levels, increased productivity, better reaction times, longer attention spans and increased tolerance to pain.[2] In a recent experiment, 38 households in Greater Manchester were given two planted containers and a tree to place in their front garden. Before the experiment just 24% of residents had healthy cortisol patterns. After three months with the new plants, this had increased to 53%, with over half the residents also saying their garden now made them happier.[3]

It is perhaps not surprising that nature is so good for us, since human beings evolved from single-celled organisms as a part of nature for at least three and a half billion years.[4] Living in the homes and cities that many of us do today, it is often easy to forget the relationship our ancestors once had with nature. As a species we are gradually losing our connection to nature, and the evidence suggests this may be to the detriment of our mental health. This was brought sharply into focus during the Coronavirus lockdowns of 2020 and 2021, when the UK media began to talk of a 'flight to the country' as many people realised the value of daily interaction with the natural world.

On a positive note, many architectural projects are now embracing what Wilson and others have taught us about biophilia: from Stefano Boeri's Bosco Verticale (Vertical Forest) apartment building in Milan to Piet Oudolf's re-greening of New York's High Line. The boundaries between landscape and interior design are blurring again as we see more green elements move inside, and on top of, buildings.

However, the integration of natural elements in our cities, homes and offices is not without its challenges. As much as we try to control nature, ultimately it doesn't like to be tamed. Roots will burrow, water will seek a path ever downwards causing leaks or damp and plants will grow in directions we didn't anticipate, blocking daylight or gutters. Ironically, this is part of what makes us love the natural world: nature's randomness and organic forms are integral to its beauty. As designers we need to embrace this uncontrollability rather than try to bend it to our will, and we will create places that are healthier for both people and planet.

Green walls and facades

> 'Nature's beauty is a gift that cultivates appreciation and gratitude.'
> – LOUIE SCHWARTZBERG, DIRECTOR AND CINEMATOGRAPHER

Figure 4.1: Pixel facade concept, by Oliver Thomas and Keyan Rahimzadeh

Potential mental wellbeing benefits
- Nature interaction
- Improved air quality
- Moments of joy / awe
- Mindfulness opportunity
- Increased productivity

Potential issues and considerations
- Environmental impacts
- Maintenance
- Operational cost
- Build cost

Without walls there would be no buildings. They are the fabric that create our cities. We may not give them a great deal of thought, but without walls it has been argued there would be no civilisation.[5] As anyone living in Berlin in the 1980s or the USA in the 2010s can tell you, walls can even be political – in fact, ever since the first city walls of Jericho 12,000 years ago, walls have been used to keep people out (or in some cases to keep them in).

However, thankfully most walls are simply, well, walls. They hold up roofs and floors, and they protect us from the elements. And they are ubiquitous. When we consider that New York City had an estimated 860,000 buildings in 2011 (and has grown substantially since then), that is an awful lot of wall.

Perhaps then, these walls are one of the greatest opportunities to bring nature into areas that need them most. Inner cities are typically dominated by brick, concrete, glass and metal – hard, man-made materials, which constantly remind us how far we are from nature. By challenging the assumed use of these typical cladding materials, we find there may be an opportunity to 'soften' our modern cities.

However, green walls are not cheap and they're certainly not simple. Designers need to consider a wide range of issues from the structural load of the wall, how it will be supported, lighting, irrigation, waterproofing and of course the plant health and nutrition itself. These issues come with substantial costs, although as technologies advance, green walls are gradually becoming more affordable.

When we compare green walls to other cladding materials, it's actually very difficult to find anything that comes close to the benefits a green wall can offer. Few other materials could remove air pollutants, reduce urban temperatures, improve biodiversity, attenuate rainwater, as well as offer enormous benefits to our mental wellbeing as effectively as a green wall.[6] What's more, by including a green wall either on the facade or the interior of a building, we are providing constant views of nature, which can have a range of positive impacts on us both physically and psychologically.[7]

Not only do green walls create visual interest and break up monotony, but they also create a tactile surface, offering direct opportunities for people to interact with nature, through touch and even smell. Beyond these obvious health benefits, there are other advantages to green walls, which may help designers convince their clients the extra cost is worth it. They provide a vertical garden in dense urban environments where ground space is limited, and also have the potential to become shading devices, as they change with the seasons.

A green wall can also be used in a symbolic way to represent a building or company that wants to improve its immediate environment, can help a scheme comply with a range of standards such as BREEAM or WELL certification and can be valuable in achieving planning permission. However, as with all wellbeing and sustainability features, care must be taken to ensure that the principles are grounded throughout the project and that it is not simply an example of 'greenwashing', where a building is made to look more healthy or sustainable than it truly is.

Design tips

1. There are a range of different green wall systems, including modular, tray and freestanding products. Explore the different approaches to understand which is right for your project.

2. Irrigation is a vital element of any green wall and should be considered from an early stage.

3. Plant species specification will depend on a number of factors, including project location, wall orientation and aesthetic intention. Consult a specialist horticulturist or landscape architect to ensure you get the specification right.

Trees for wellbeing

> 'A man has made at least a start on discovering the meaning of human life when he plants shade trees under which he knows full well he will never sit.'
> – D. ELTON TRUEBLOOD, AUTHOR AND THEOLOGIAN

Figure 4.2: House in Kyoto, Japan, by 07BEACH

Potential mental wellbeing benefits

- Nature interaction
- Improved air quality
- Moments of joy / awe
- Mindfulness opportunity
- Physical comfort

Potential issues and considerations

- Maintenance
- Build cost
- Space requirements
- Loss of light

Whichever way we look at it, trees are quite simply amazing. Some species have been alive for nearly five millennia, some can consume over 2,000 litres of water a day, and there are currently over 3 trillion of them on the planet – nearly 400 for every living person. Historically, trees have had an incredible cultural significance. In old English folklore, for example, Aspen wood was used to make shields, in part because it was believed to have magical properties of protection.[8] In West African culture, trees and forests have traditionally had a different symbolic importance, being viewed as a link between ground and sky, and being connected to ancestors, religion and healing.[9]

While they may not have the same cultural meaning in today's western society, trees, woodlands and forests undoubtedly still play a significant role in both our physical and mental wellbeing. The physical health benefits of trees are, of course, relatively well known, particularly their air cleaning qualities. Studies also link spending time in forests – known as *shinrin-yoku* or 'forest bathing' – to both improved immune function and heart health.[10]

However, there are also many ways in which trees can be beneficial to our mental health. Spending time in woodlands has been shown to make us calmer, kinder, more creative and ruminate less.[11]

Perhaps more than any other plant, trees can connect us to the passage of time through the changing of seasons and their variation in colour. Biophilic designer Oliver Heath argues that a connection to these natural systems is one of the '14 patterns of biophilic design' that can support mental wellbeing.[12] We have all experienced the real visual joy that occurs as leaves turn a beautiful range of colours in autumn, and the uplifting sense of hope as we see new shoots develop in spring. Seeing a tree that has been there for decades or even centuries can also create a real sense of awe, which has been shown to have psychological benefits, allowing us to place what might seem like big worries into context.

While we may not be able to recreate dense woodland in urban environments, a greater quantity of trees in towns and cities still has an impact, having even been shown to reduce crime in some studies. One such study demonstrated that areas of Chicago with a 10% greater tree canopy were associated with 11.3% lower assault, robbery and narcotics rates – results that were mirrored in Baltimore, New Haven and Vancouver.[13] There may, of course, be a connection between increased tree canopies and more affluent communities, but it seems clear that for one reason or another, people are prepared to pay more to live in an area with more trees, which suggests some perceived improvement in quality of life either way.

Trees can also be brought into buildings, providing even more direct contact with nature to their users. In such situations, it is important to consider issues such as root spread, access to water and exposure to daylight, as a dying tree is certainly not all that uplifting!

Design tips

1. Not all trees are right for all environments, and in fact the wrong species of tree can sometimes do more harm than good. Use an arborist or horticulturist to help you select the right species for your site.

2. From a mental wellbeing perspective, there are arguments in favour of both deciduous and evergreens: deciduous trees allow us to experience the changing of the seasons, giving a good reference to time, whereas evergreens offer a more permanent green element within a landscape.

3. Ultimately, it should come down to what works best in the context, unless the goal is 'making a statement', encouraging people to stop and engage with it deliberately or to provoke a specific moment or joy.

4. Be aware of which tree species might be prolific pollinators, and the potential impact this could have on allergies – especially if being used in enclosed spaces.

Internal water features

> 'They both listened silently to the water, which to them was not just water, but the voice of life, the voice of Being, the voice of perpetual Becoming.'
> – HERMANN HESSE, AUTHOR AND POET

Figure 4.3: Đàm lộc House, Vietnam, by V+studio

Potential mental wellbeing benefits

- Nature interaction
- Improved air quality
- Moments of joy / awe
- Mindfulness opportunity
- Physical comfort

Potential issues and considerations

- Acoustics
- Maintenance
- Hygiene
- Air quality risks

To humans, water is one of the most important substances on earth, being crucial for our survival. While this importance is recognised by its inclusion as one of the ten core Concepts of the WELL Building Standard, sadly an enormous 80% of all illness in poorer countries is still water-related.

Water has a deeper cultural importance for us too. Early humans settled near water for other reasons: to allow them to trade and travel more easily, irrigate their crops and wash themselves and their belongings. It has even been argued that our early ancestors' migratory behaviours may have been driven by changes in rain and weather patterns.[14] Water can also create powerful emotions, whether it is the crashing of an ocean, the calmness of a great lake or the awe we feel standing at the foot of an enormous waterfall.

With all these factors considered, it is perhaps no surprise that researchers tend to find that water benefits us psychologically. A 2019 study showed that people who live in close proximity to the coast are less likely to report issues such as depression and anxiety.[15] While it could be argued that this is because houses near the sea are generally more expensive, actually the study revealed that water was especially important to low-income households, who were around 40% less likely to exhibit symptoms of mental illness if they lived near the coast.

Experts such as marine biologist Wallace J. Nichols are now talking about the concept of 'blue health' or 'the blue mind phenomenon', as a way of describing the various wellbeing benefits of blue spaces like oceans, lakes and rivers.[16] Many argue that we enter a mildly meditative state when spending time on or near water, which can lower stress and heart rate, make us more creative and conversational, and even improve our sleep.

However, given that we can't always give people views of oceans or lakes, can we instead bring water into buildings to offer direct 'blue health' benefits? Despite studies showing that interior water features are perceived as calming by the vast majority of people, they are often dismissed as too costly or challenging by clients or contractors.[17]

Indoor water features can also offer physical comfort benefits to the environment, as a way to moderate temperature, combat dry air and promote air movement, all of which can be particularly helpful in hot, arid climates. Furthermore, they can be fantastic natural noise attenuators, creating a gentle background 'white noise' effect, thus improving the acoustic comfort of busy spaces.

Design tips

1. Locate water features in places where they will be visible to larger numbers of occupants, maximising the visual nature benefit.

2. Consider the potential positive (or negative) impacts of sound – a gentle background gurgle can be calming, but excessive noise can be distracting.

3. When including internal water features, be aware of maintenance and monitoring requirements due to issues like calcium deposits, oxidation and algae growth, and create a healthy maintenance strategy, avoiding harsh chemicals like bleach.

4. Be aware of other possible impacts, such as a potential increase in internal humidity. While this may be desirable in some locations, in others strategies may be needed to mitigate this.

External growing areas and allotments

❝ Gardening simply does not allow one to be mentally old, because too many hopes and dreams are yet to be realized.' – ALLAN ARMITAGE, HORTICULTURALIST

Figure 4.4: Hackney School of Food, London, UK, by Surman Weston

Potential mental wellbeing benefits

- Nature interaction
- Identity / self-worth
- Increased autonomy
- Environmental benefits
- Mindfulness opportunity

Potential issues and considerations

- Space requirements
- Maintenance
- Structural issues

Early humans existed in 'hunter-gatherer' societies – that is, they were largely nomadic people, and almost all their food was obtained by foraging for wild plants or catching and killing wild animals. This began to change around 12,000 years ago, during the Neolithic Revolution, when most cultures adapted farming in lieu of foraging, leading to more settled agricultural populations across the globe.[18]

The importance of this global change is difficult to overstate. It laid the groundwork for what we know as modern society, allowing populations to rapidly expand and to create fixed homes. In fact, without farming it is fair to say that cities as we know them would not exist, as Carolyn Steel explains in her book *Hungry City*.[19]

A fairly major downside of this is our modern-day dependence on agriculture and the global food chain. Today we are largely ignorant of where our food comes from and the processes involved in creating it, which has made us underestimate the importance of it, while simultaneously becoming overconfident of our ability to access cheap, plentiful sustenance at the tap of a contactless debit card.

A survey in 2017 showed that under a fifth of all adults in the UK now grow their own fruit or vegetables.[20] This figure is perhaps surprising when we consider how many wellbeing benefits there are to growing our own food. For a start, when we do so, we know everything that has gone into it, instantly allaying any concerns about modern supply chains. We also know that it has almost the smallest carbon footprint food is possible to have.

The mental health benefits of growing our own food extend far beyond reducing these anxieties and have been widely researched and documented in recent years.[21] This is perhaps unsurprising when we consider the multifarious benefits of gardening: it puts us in close proximity to nature; makes us more active; gives us better control over our diet and lifestyle; and creates opportunities for social interaction. Perhaps, most importantly, it can provide a genuine sense of achievement and something to look forward to next week, next season or next year. As a result, many mental health charities are now offering horticultural therapy, such as 'Thrive', who claim that 80% of people taking part report better mental health, with 93% reporting better confidence and motivation.[22]

An external growing area doesn't need to be large or costly. It could be as simple as some growing bags or fabric pots on a balcony. It needn't be restricted to residential buildings either. The WELL Building Standard awards points for growing areas in office buildings due to the benefits they can offer staff. Rooftop areas can work well due to generally warmer temperatures, although issues such as wind and structural loading will need to be considered. Finally, it's just as important to design-in space for tools and gardening supplies; without these even the most green-fingered gardeners will struggle!

It would be remiss not to say that we can't address all our food needs by turning our gardens or terraces into mini farms. One study showed that if every homeowner in Seattle turned their lawn into edible plants, it would only produce enough food for around 1% of the city's residents.[23] However, while the crop yields may be minimal, the impact on our mental health of growing our own food can be significant.

Design tips

1. Location is key. Roofs can often work well, as they have good exposure to daylight and temperature is generally higher, allowing for growth of more tropical vegetable plants such as aubergines, peppers and tomatoes.

2. A courtyard, garden space or even a small balcony can also work, although be aware that many plants need to be sheltered from the wind, so some form of windbreak may be required.

3. Growing bags or pots can be one possible approach for growing areas on roofs or terraces; they give the ability to reduce loading and can be moved around if needed.

4. In terms of sizing, WELL recommends around 1ft^2 per employee or 15ft^2 per home.

5. Supplies, tools and space to store them are vital and often overlooked – remember to factor them into your projects.

Internal growing areas

> 'To nurture a garden is to feed not just the body, but the soul.'
> – ALFRED AUSTIN, POET

Figure 4.5: Growing Underground urban farm, London, UK

Potential mental wellbeing benefits

- Nature interaction
- Identity / self-worth
- Increased autonomy
- Environmental benefits
- Mindfulness opportunity

Potential issues and considerations

- Space requirements
- Maintenance
- Structural issues
- Specialist input useful

It is all well and good promoting the benefits of gardening for our mental health, but what should we as designers do when outdoor spaces are not available to us?

Throughout the 1900s there was a global boom in residential tower blocks, so much so that they have now become synonymous with urban living. While tower blocks offer some advantages over traditional housing, there are also many issues associated with high-rise living, particularly when no private amenity space such as balconies or terraces are provided. As we have already read in Chapter 3, one in eight people in the United Kingdom have no access to outdoor space, whether private or shared, so this is clearly a very real problem, even in the twenty-first century.

However, if you do find yourself faced with this challenge as either a designer or an occupant, there are still many ways to design-in opportunities for gardening indoors. In fact, partly in response to the climate emergency and partly due to the enjoyment people get from it, over the last half a century there has been an explosion of 'urban farming movements', seeking to bring agriculture and nature directly into buildings and cities.

To some extent we all understand the mood-boosting benefits of bringing plants into our homes or workplaces – we are aware of it every time we buy someone a bunch of flowers or water one of our succulents. In a now much-quoted study, enriching an office with greenery was even shown to boost human productivity by as much as 15%.[24]

These internal growing areas don't have to be large to make a difference either. They could take the form of a simple window box or hanging external planter on windows or balconies – something which we rarely see included in modern planning applications despite their potential to have a significant emotional impact. Even small potted plants can have an effect, with no planning permission required for these, although this does make a good argument for windows with raised sills.

For the more committed indoor gardener, systems such as hydroponics or aeroponics can be incorporated into designs. These address issues of space, as growing shelves can be stacked vertically and can even be placed in 'leftover' spaces of a building, such as unused plant rooms or basements using technologies such as LED grow lights. Of course, there are sustainability issues to consider, with such methods around use of both energy and water. However, urban farms such as Growing Underground are showing that these concerns can be addressed, having utilised the natural insulation of underground tunnels, 100% renewable energy and a recycling hydroponics system to grow up to 60 harvests a year of some vegetables.[25]

If done correctly, many believe that Internal Urban Farming solutions like these could play a significant role in food production moving forward, addressing a number of ecological issues and supporting a healthier planet.[26] And as an added bonus, it can be done almost anywhere, giving people the satisfaction and mental health benefits of growing food within their own home.

> **Design tips**
>
> 1. Undertake a review of opportunities for internal planting locations at various project stages and across scales – whether this is a whole growing room or the addition of simple window boxes.
>
> 2. Ideally, internal growing areas should utilise natural light, but if this is not possible a renewable energy source should be considered for any artificial lighting. In this scenario, they can offer a good use for 'leftover' or 'darker space' in designs, for which it is hard to find other uses.
>
> 3. There are a wide range of containers and systems available on the market. Review these thoroughly, as each have their own benefits and drawbacks.
>
> 4. It is also important to consider that some foods require specific temperatures and humidity to grow, which may mean they're not suitable to be grown in the home.

Air cleansing plants

> 'Ultimately, the only wealth that can sustain any community, economy or nation is derived from the photosynthetic process – green plants growing on regenerating soil.'
> – ALLAN SAVORY, ECOLOGIST

Figure 4.6: Dracaena, or dragon plant

Potential mental wellbeing benefits

- Nature interaction
- Improved air quality
- Moments of joy / awe
- Mindfulness opportunity
- Increased productivity

Potential issues and considerations

- Fitout cost
- Maintenance
- Loss of light
- Allergies

As discussed in Chapter 2, when we looked at the impact of VOCs, the quality of the air around us can have an impact on our brain function, physical health and ultimately our mental wellbeing. Indeed, the World Health Organization estimates that around 4 million people die prematurely every year from illnesses attributable to household air pollution.[27]

However, VOCs are only a part of the issue. There are many other sources of air pollution in our homes and workplaces, including combustion appliances, such as ovens or wood stoves, mould and fungi, tobacco products, cleaning and maintenance products, and electronic equipment such as printers.[28] And even our bodies are machines for producing fairly impressive quantities of carbon dioxide; in an airtight room of around 30m^3 (3m x 4m x 2.5m), it has been claimed that a group of 10 healthy adults would turn oxygen into CO_2 fast enough to run out of breathable air in less than a day![29]

In our quest for carbon-neutrality, we are creating buildings that are increasingly airtight, which can make it challenging for pollutants to leave buildings without effective ventilation systems in place. Luckily, plants (among their other benefits) can help to address some of these issues, although it's important first to discuss their limitations.

While some studies seem to show that many plants can remove VOCs, even a small office space (3m x 3m x 2.4m) would need nearly 1,000 'typical' plants to match the performance of a standard ventilation system, explains engineering professor Michael Waring. He does, however, note that if you used the most effective type of VOC-filtering plant, this figure comes down by a factor of around 10.[30]

So, while houseplants certainly aren't going to fix indoor air quality on their own, they can play a role within a wider strategy of ventilation and healthy material selection.

So which plants are most effective at cleaning air? Unfortunately, research in this area is still limited, although some experiments appear to shed light on this question. A 2014 study, for example, investigated 28 plant species from 15 families to explore how effectively they could remove benzene, toluene, octane, trichloroethylene and α-pinene. They discovered that members of the Araliaceae (ginseng) family were particularly efficient at removing these chemicals, while ferns and herbs exhibited the highest removal rates of formaldehyde.[31]

The Royal Horticultural Society recommends a variety of species for the removal of VOCs, all of which can be obtained fairly easily.[32] These include the spider, dragon, rubber, and jade plants, common ivy, Boston fern, mother-in-law's tongue, Zanzibar gem, bamboo palm, peace lily, and dumb cane.

With regards to plants removing CO_2, there are also a limited number of studies currently available. However, a 2017 report suggested that the prayer plant was the most efficient of the seven common houseplants studied, reducing CO_2 in a 1m^3 chamber by around 14% over eight hours, closely followed by a Kadaka fern at 12.5% and a dumb cane plant at 11.1%. Spider plants performed surprisingly poorly, with a CO_2 reduction rate of around 0.1% in comparison![33]

Design tips

1. Studies show some plants absorb up to five times as much carbon dioxide at 700 Lux than at 300 Lux, so to maximise the air cleaning properties of plants, ensure they receive plenty of natural daylight.

2. Plants will not clean the air on their own, so should be used as part of a wider ventilation and filtration strategy.

3. Review CIBSE (or equivalent) guidance for further information on recommended air changes per hour, and the WELL Building Standard (Concept 1: Air) for best practice on filtration systems.

Chances for special views

> 'A good photograph is knowing where to stand.'
> – ANSEL ADAMS, LANDSCAPE PHOTOGRAPHER

Figure 4.7: Path of Perspectives, Innsbruck, Austria, by Snøhetta

Potential mental wellbeing benefits

- Nature interaction
- Moments of joy / awe
- Mindfulness opportunity
- Physical health improvements

Potential issues and considerations

- Impact on layouts
- Aesthetic challenges (external)

We may not always realise it, but a view is a powerful thing. We have already touched upon the positive impact that views of nature can have on our mental wellbeing, and we now know that even photographs of nature can make people feel less anxious and reduce pain levels.[34]

'Prospect and refuge theory' argues that we have evolved to feel innately safer in spaces which allow us to see without being seen. Giving people outward views can not only allow us to connect with nature, it can enhance our sense of safety, calming our overactive 'fight or flight' systems. We also know that experiencing a sense of awe can have a positive impact on wellbeing, with research showing it can lift us out of our day-to-day concerns and make us feel connected to something larger and more significant.[35]

However, not all views are equal. A 1995 study by Clare Cooper Marcus, emeritus professor in landscape architecture at the University of California, and Marni Barnes, a landscape architect specialising in therapeutic design, analysed a series of hospital gardens and interviewed their frequent users. They discovered that the most appealing views were 'tree-bordered vistas of fountains or other water features, with lush, multilayered greenery'.[36] Cooper Marcus explains that we should try to promote greenery over hard surfaces generally, stating that 'a ratio of at least 7:3 seems to work best'.

Of course, we don't always have control over the landscape elements of our surroundings, but it is possible to use windows or other openings in a building to enhance or draw attention to certain views. While many architects from Le Corbusier to Mies van der Rohe loved the use of a large, glazed wall which could almost disappear, this is not a universally accepted approach.

Christopher Alexander, author of *A Pattern Language*, disputed this philosophy, arguing that a view should be carefully framed so as not to lose its significance. Alexander explained that 'gradually [the view] will become part of the building, like the wallpaper; and the intensity of its beauty will no longer be accessible to the people who live there'.[37]

Alexander's approach is standard practice in Japanese architecture, where windows are not seen as simply a source of lighting or ventilation, but are celebrated as a 'picture' in their own right; a way of 'cutting out' a piece of the scenery and enjoying nature in a unique way.[38] As architectural historian and critic Igarashi Tarō explains, 'we regard windows not only as a part of architecture, but as being related intimately to people's lives and physical actions'.[39] The Japanese even have a special name for a 'window for seeing snow', *Yukimi Shoji*, the idea behind which is to hide the sky, focusing the viewer's attention on snow-covered surfaces, drawing them into mindfully observing the snow falling quietly.

Perhaps then, we should choose our views from certain windows carefully, celebrating them as the special things that they are, and using window frames as the 'crop' for a beautiful landscape composition. With modern software we have no excuses not to simulate the view from any point of any building, and we should be using this technology to create views that are informed by the research of Roger S. Ulrich, Jay Appleton, Cooper Marcus, Barnes and the many other environmental psychologists to make us feel better.

Design tips

1. Consider views of nature from the earliest design stages, as this can have an impact on the orientation, position and layout of your building.

2. While all views of nature offer benefits, identify any 'special' views from initial site visits and consider how the benefits of these can be maximised for residents.

3. Identify which parts of your building would benefit most from special views of nature – ideally spaces in which people spend the greatest amounts of time, or perhaps in which more stress-inducing activities – such as work – take place in order to support people where they need it most.

4. Where real views of nature are truly not possible, images or paintings can offer some of their benefits.

Natural forms and language

> 'There are no straight lines or sharp corners in nature. Therefore, buildings must have no straight lines or sharp corners.' – ANTONI GAUDÍ, ARCHITECT

Figure 4.8: Maggie's Leeds, UK, by Heatherwick Studio

Potential mental wellbeing benefits

- Psychological response
- Nature interaction
- Moments of joy / awe
- Spatial benefits

Potential issues and considerations

- Build cost
- Impact on layouts
- Useability challenges

Architectural language, or 'style', is a contentious issue. There will no doubt be many architects reading this book who would never dream of using a curve, for example. I still remember my first week of architecture school, where in my first tutorial I was told unequivocally 'never use a curve unless you have a very good reason'.

We might look back at architectural history and think there is a good reason for this philosophy. From the pyramids to the acropolis, Vitruvius to Palladio, through to modern architectural greats such as Frank Lloyd Wright and Le Corbusier, there is a rich history of rectilinear, orthogonal forms. When we look at vernacular architecture from around the world, however, we find that this is not always the case. Traditional typologies such as igloos or yurts have been used for millennia and utilise round forms, which offer structural and thermal benefits.

There are many modern day architects and designers who have broken the orthogonal mould too, such as Alvar Aalto, Eero Saarinen, Oscar Niemeyer, and more recently Frank Gehry, Zaha Hadid and Thomas Heatherwick. Perhaps one of the most famous and recognisable proponents of this approach was Antoni Gaudí, who, as the quote at the beginning of this section reflects, did not believe in straight lines or sharp corners in architecture.

In her book *The Shaping of Us*, environmental psychology consultant Lily Bernheimer explains that curved forms make us calmer than angular ones, while a 2011 eye-tracking study found that at just five months of age, infants show a clear visual preference for contoured lines over straight lines.[40] Other studies have shown that sharp-cornered objects activate our amygdala (the part of the brain associated with fear and our fight or flight mechanisms) more strongly than rounded objects and that 'the degree of amygdala activation was proportional to the degree of angularity or sharpness of the object presented'.[41]

The theories behind these findings are numerous. It is perhaps connected to the idea that curved things are safer, whereas sharp things like a rock or knife can hurt us more easily. It may also be that up until very recent history (in an evolutionary sense), we would have encountered very few straight lines and even fewer truly flat surfaces – with the exception of water, which ceases to be flat the moment we interact with it. Plants, animals and hills are generally inherently 'curvy' to some extent.

How then can we integrate this into projects while staying within budget? One approach is to pick and choose your 'organic' moments; it doesn't have to be applied across the whole building. Certain elements and details may be better suited to curves, such as arches above openings or circular elements within entrance lobbies or central atria such as in Louis Kahn's Phillips Exeter Academy Library. In contrast, a circular bedroom or kitchen may present real functional problems, so should be avoided. We can also learn from vernacular architecture and nature, where curves are often utilised because they are most, not least, efficient.

We need to weigh up the benefits of organic elements against the downsides and appreciate that in many circumstances they won't be the most appropriate choice. However, they are certainly a way to create joy and visual interest and are not an architectural approach that we should simply write out of our toolkit due to cost.

Design tips

1. Identify opportunities for curved or organic elements within projects. While they won't be right everywhere, find special moments or objects which could allow for the integration of more natural forms.

2. When working with certain materials such as timber, stone or even brick, curves or arches can actually complement a material's inherent properties. Consider how organic forms can celebrate these, rather than trying to force linear materials into curves which may be jarring.

3. Organic forms do not necessarily need to be dramatic: a gently curving sofa or parapet can have a significant impact without being overstated.

Parks, large and small

❝ I go to nature every day for inspiration in the day's work.'
— FRANK LLOYD WRIGHT, ARCHITECT

Figure 4.9: Stevenage Town Centre Gardens, UK, by HTA Landscape

Potential mental wellbeing benefits
- Nature interaction
- Increased activity
- Greater equity
- Social opportunities
- Physical health improvements

Potential issues and considerations
- Use by all
- Space requirements
- Consultation recommended
- Maintenance

Parks and green spaces, particularly in cities, play an important role in helping to maintain good physical and mental health. We know, for example, that people who live over a kilometre away from a green space have nearly 50% higher odds of experiencing stress than those who live within 300m.[42]

Similarly, the more often people visit green spaces, the less stress they tend to experience, which is supported by evidence from the Netherlands showing that in residential areas with the lowest levels of green spaces, people were 44% more likely to be diagnosed with anxiety disorders.[43] These effects were sadly seen most strongly among those with children and lower levels of education and income.

Many homes in the UK and beyond do not have access to private gardens or balconies, particularly in disadvantaged areas, making the importance of access to open green spaces even more important. In these instances, parks provide a vital escape from the indoors. They offer an opportunity for direct contact with nature – something that can be rare in dense urban environments. In fact, this is the origin of the city park, which evolved from pasture lands within the safe confines of towns into a means of preserving a sense of nature and greenery in cities during the Industrial Revolution.

Parks help keep people active too, with one study showing that people who live nearer parks are more likely to use them, having an average of 38% more exercise sessions per week than those who lived over a mile away.[44] They give us a safe place to walk, jog, cycle or take part in team sports, as well as offering places for children to play safely and for people to meet, and as such often become the centre of a community. Given all these benefits, it is perhaps no surprise that houses and flats within 100m of public green space in England and Wales are on average £2,500 more valuable than they would be if they were over 500m away.[45]

Fundamentally, green spaces, from pocket parks to Central Park, offer fantastic value when it comes to our wellbeing. A Public Health England report from 2020 argued that £2.1 billion per year could be saved in health costs if everyone in England had good access to green space, due to increased physical activity in those spaces. It also explained that for every £1 spent on maintaining parks in Sheffield, a benefit of £34 in health costs had been saved.[46] They can also offer benefits in terms of air cleaning and urban cooling, whether through green spaces or the inclusion of water.

When proposing such amenities, it is common to meet some resistance on the grounds of cost and viability. However, the figures above illustrate that the provision of a park benefits everybody, both financially and in terms of quality of life. Property developers can increase the values of the homes or offices they build, local authorities and health services reduce their costs and other burdens, and finally the public benefits from access to a fantastic new communal space to enjoy.

Design tips

1. Engage with local communities and local authorities from an early stage in projects to understand what sort of green spaces would be most beneficial to the area.
2. Prioritise access to green space in areas of deprivation. While it benefits everyone, research tends to show this is where it can have the greatest impact.
3. Use robust evidence, such as the sources referenced in this book, to offer a broad evidence base for the importance of green spaces in your schemes.
4. Design parks which facilitate a wide range of activities and cater for a diverse range of people.

Nature walks and emotive learning trails

> 'If you lose touch with nature you lose touch with humanity.'
> – JIDDU KRISHNAMURTI, PHILOSOPHER AND WRITER

Figure 4.10: Brownsea Island Nature Reserve, Dorset, UK, with Tracker Packs for children to explore the themed trails

Potential mental wellbeing benefits
- Nature interaction
- Learning opportunities
- Increased activity
- Identity / self-worth
- Engagement with emotions

Potential issues and considerations
- Space requirements
- Build cost
- Maintenance

Whichever way we look at it, we are losing our connection with nature. Worldwide, 55% of us live in urban areas – a figure that is set to rise to 68% by 2050.[47] This is not necessarily a bad thing. Density and urban life have many benefits, from increasingly sustainable modes of transport to greater access to culture and larger, more diverse communities. However, in this move away from rural life, we are reducing our exposure to the natural world and becoming disconnected from it, which may have a negative impact on our wellbeing.

From studies showing that one in three British people can no longer identify an oak tree[48] to others revealing that even our modern songs have a third of the references to nature than they did in the 1950s, wherever you look the picture is fairly clear.[49]

As psychology professor Miles Richardson explains, 'a connection to nature predicts wellbeing to a similar extent as established factors such as income and education', so it is not a huge leap to assume that losing our connection to it might have a long-term detrimental effect on the wellbeing of society as a whole.[50]

Richardson's focus is on finding the best ways to connect people with nature. His studies suggest that direct contact with nature alone, for example on a traditional outdoor nature trail, actually has very little increase in nature connectivity in children, even when actively learning about the wildlife they are seeing. What does seem to make a big difference is engagement with these elements through the arts, by either writing about or producing artworks of their experiences with nature. This suggests that a connection to nature isn't necessarily related to knowledge of it, but rather an emotional connection or finding meaning in it.

This somewhat changes the way we as designers need to think about creating nature trails – less about teaching and more about experiencing. Rather than information points, we should consider activity stations, promoting sketching, bark rubbings or asking children to write about their experiences with nature that day. As Richardson puts it, 'rather than conveying knowledge and hunting clues, make the perception of nature central – signpost joy and wonder; emotion and beauty; and experiencing nature with the senses'.

An excellent example of this can be seen at Brownsea Island Nature Reserve, where a Creative Nature Trail has been established. This features crayon rubbing tiles for children to find and make art with, and 'mini beast safaris' for children to form emotional connections with creepy crawlies.

Another positive side of Richardson's research is that it means the most effective way to strengthen nature connections isn't necessarily the most expensive. Many of these features could easily be contained within a modest urban garden or linear park. It also means that clients don't need to spend vast quantities of money on rare or even scientifically interesting species of flora. Our focus should instead be shifted to designing a high-quality 'experience', where children and adults alike get the opportunity to strengthen their emotional bond with nature.

Design tips

1 To best strengthen children's relationship with nature, design projects that create an emotional bond.

2 Consider innovative ways in which this can take place, be it through:
- writing stories or poems
- drawing pictures
- making natural collages or exploring curiosity and wonder

and seek to provide design interventions that encourage these.

3 Don't always design projects that keep people clean and out of the dirt: we get a number of benefits from getting mucky, including better immune systems.

Planter furniture

> 'In an age of constant movement, nothing is more urgent than sitting still.'
> – PICO IYER, ESSAYIST

Figure 4.11: Kerb Garden, London, UK, by The Edible Bus Stop

Potential mental wellbeing benefits

- Nature interaction
- Social opportunities
- Increased activity
- Moments of joy / awe
- Improved air quality

Potential issues and considerations

- Build cost
- Maintenance
- Detailing

As designers, we have a powerful ability to nudge and influence behaviours through the places we create. So, if one of our goals is to encourage people to spend more time in close proximity to nature, how can we achieve this – especially in urban areas?

One element of landscaping that all of us will use from time to time is public seating. Good public seating is much more than a place to stop – it is a way to meet new people, create positive social interaction, and it also makes cities easier for people of all abilities to use.

Given that everybody will inevitably use seating at some stage, it therefore presents a great opportunity to promote nature adjacency. By integrating plants into seating, we can put people in much closer contact with nature than they usually would. It can also make seating more pleasant to use, encouraging a greater number of people to stop more regularly and take a break from the rush of modern life, and perhaps even to use them as places for social interaction. A study from the University of Illinois suggested that having more nature around us can create stronger feelings of unity with our neighbours and improve a sense of community.[51]

The addition of plants to street furniture can also be utilised as a way to bring colour and visual interest into city centres. Another advantage of this approach is that by embedding planters within street furniture, it becomes harder for these green elements to be removed, due to cost-planning exercises.

When it comes to designing or specifying planter furniture to support better mental wellbeing, there are lessons we can take from various parts of this book. The use of natural materials such as timber or stone is a way to create further nature interaction. This can also have a further benefit in an environmental sense and help to address some people's concerns over the use of materials that are harmful to the planet.

In order to create a sense of pride in place, any furniture should also be well detailed, durable and resilient. Urban neuroscientist Robin Mazumder argues that urban design and a city's built 'hardware' can have a significant impact on civic pride, and we should bear this in mind when value engineering the furniture people use every day.[52] We also know that people won't dwell on furniture that's unpleasant to use, however pretty, so seating should be ergonomically suitable for its function, and ideally tested by those specifying it.

Finally, we need to get the plant choice right. Flowerbeds that look unappealing for half the year might actually have a detrimental effect on the quality of space, so consider plants for all seasons. Planter furniture also offers an opportunity to engage other senses, such as smell and touch, so specify species which are not just visually engaging, but that offer pleasant scents and are tactile and non-toxic.

Design tips

1. When designing planter furniture, remember to consider all the practical issues you would with any other planter, like water and drainage requirements.

2. Fill these elements with joy! Consider the use of colour, materials, shapes and plant species to encourage interaction and use.

3. Explore and test different orientations of any street furniture to encourage social interaction and serendipitous interactions.

4. Use evidence and data to support and justify the provision of such elements, to promote client buy-in and help ensure they don't get value engineered out.

Homes for animals as well as people

> 'An understanding of the natural world and what's in it is a source of not only a great curiosity but great fulfilment.'
> – SIR DAVID ATTENBOROUGH, NATURAL HISTORIAN, BROADCASTER AND AUTHOR

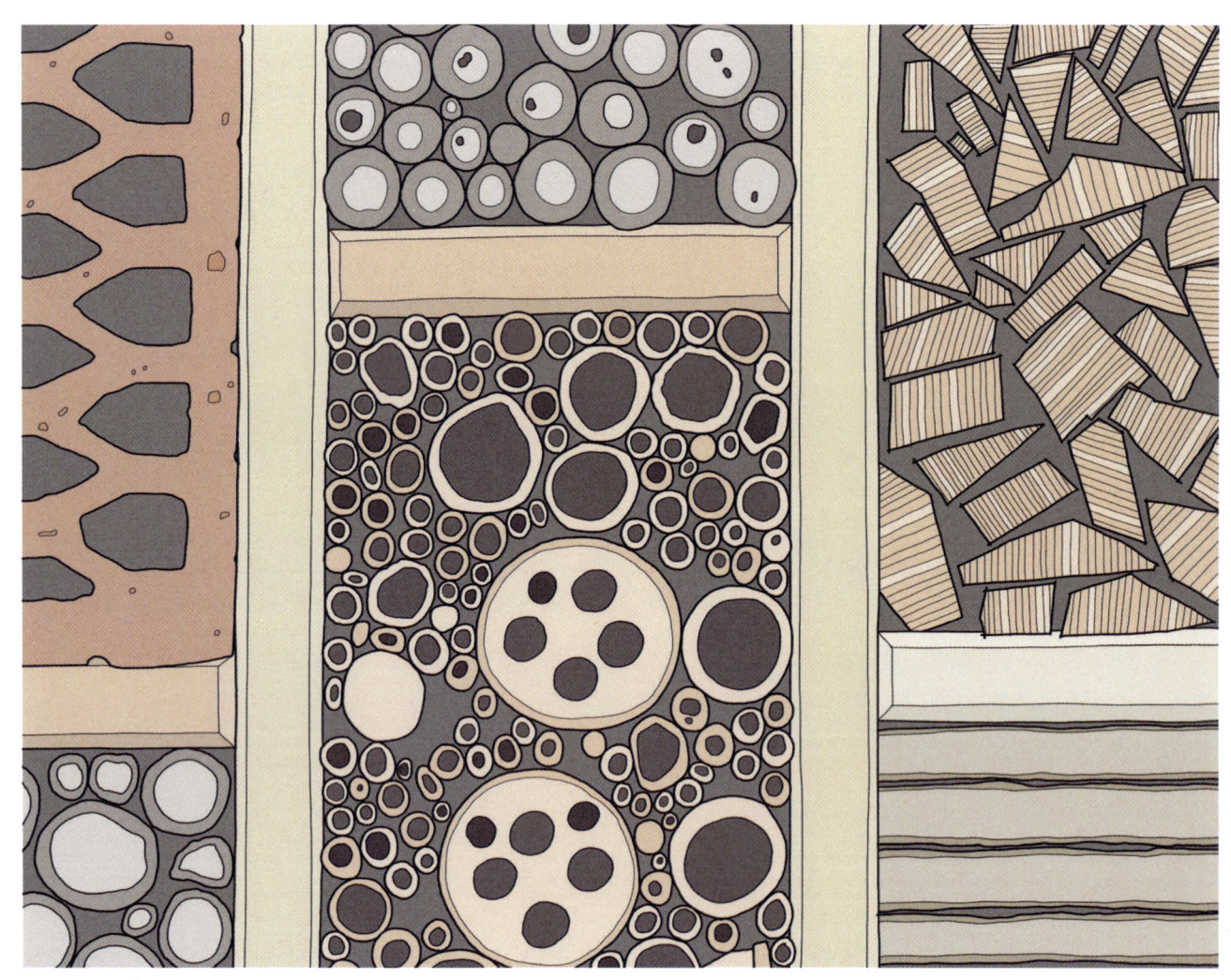

Figure 4.12: A DIY insect hotel

Potential mental wellbeing benefits

- Nature interaction
- Moments of joy / awe
- Environmental benefits
- Mindfulness opportunity
- Altruism benefits

Potential issues and considerations

- Build cost
- Maintenance
- Specialist input useful

When talking about biophilia, it is tempting to get caught up in the idea that it's all about plants. However, as we've already seen, biophilia is about our connection to all aspects of nature, including the sea, the sky and of course the animal kingdom too.

There is now a growing body of evidence that animals make us happier. Owning a pet has been shown to be good for our mental health,[53] and animal therapy is increasingly being used as a way to help people cope with, and recover from, a range of physical and mental health conditions.[54] There are now studies showing that interaction with animals can decrease anxiety, stress, fear and worry, reduce depression and even be helpful for people with schizophrenia.[55]

Therapy animals include dogs, cats, horses and birds, as well as smaller creatures like fish; even crickets have been shown to improve people's symptoms of common mental health problems.[56] This presents an opportunity for architects and designers, as while we might not be able to 'design' dogs into a scheme, we can certainly create opportunities for many types of wildlife from bats to honeybees. This can not only promote animal interaction in people, it can also address issues around eco-anxiety by reassuring people that their home, workplace or school is making positive steps to support biodiversity and animal populations.

There are now a huge number of ways to encourage fauna through our designs. Perhaps one of the most simple and well-known 'tools' to bring nature to a site is the humble bird box. These can take many forms; what is important is that they provide a good nesting environment. To achieve this they must be secure, weatherproof and safe from predators. They can be 'standalone', affixed to trees or facades, or even integrated into the building fabric itself.

Bat boxes are similarly straightforward to integrate into projects and are particularly important at present, as at the time of writing many roosting spots are being damaged or destroyed. Prefabricated 'bat bricks' are available to buy off the shelf and can form part of a standard brick facade. Bat boxes can just as easily be built from timber, but make sure the wood is untreated, as bats are particularly sensitive to smells and chemicals may harm them.

Another easy-to-build feature to attract wildlife is the wonderfully named 'insect hotel'. These can be made from an enormous variety of found, recycled or upcycled materials, and can provide vital places for all kinds of bugs to shelter year-round. The best examples have a variety of twigs, wood chips, leaves, hollow reeds, cardboard tubing and blocks of wood with holes drilled into them to provide a safe refuge for bees of different sizes.

Finally, without creating any special structures it is possible to design a garden that is friendly for bees. With bee populations in decline as a result of habitation loss, climate change, toxic pesticides and disease, this is an area where we can potentially make a big collective difference to the environment. Bees love traditional garden flowers and wildflowers, as well as herbs, which can be grown in small pots at minimal cost and maximum design impact.

Design tips

1. Bird boxes, bat boxes and insect hotels can be bought 'off the shelf' or built bespoke to suit a project – while they can take a variety of forms, there are some key rules to follow, so check out the endnotes in this book for advice and guidance.

2. It is possible to design a bee-friendly garden without creating any special structures. Bees love traditional garden flowers and wildflowers, such as primrose, buddleia and marigolds, as well as certain herbs like marjoram, thyme, chives, sage or creeping rosemary.

3. Plan a garden so that it will have a range of flowers throughout the seasons, to ensure a variety of wildlife is attracted year-round.

Ponds and lakes

> 'If I'm ever feeling tense or stressed or like I'm about to have a meltdown, I'll put on my iPod and head to the gym or out on a bike ride along Lake Michigan.'
> – MICHELLE OBAMA, ATTORNEY AND FORMER FIRST LADY OF THE UNITED STATES OF AMERICA

Figure 4.13: Lower Factory Pond, Ziegelbrücke, Switzerland, by Beglinger + Bryan Landschaftsarchitektur

Potential mental wellbeing benefits
- Nature interaction
- Increased activity
- Mindfulness opportunity
- Moments of joy / awe
- Environmental benefits

Potential issues and considerations
- Specialist input useful
- Safety
- Maintenance
- Use by all

Some of the positive impacts that water can have on our mental health were confirmed in the World Happiness Report 2020, which cites evidence that proximity to rivers and canals improves our moods.[57] As well as bringing water into buildings, we can also integrate it into the broader landscapes of projects in the form of ponds, swales or lakes, depending on the site area and the available budget.

Perhaps the most obvious wellbeing benefits are the direct views of nature from in and around buildings that a pond or lake can offer. As we now know, these can have significant mood benefits for residents and can also add values to properties, perhaps going some way to offsetting the cost of a water feature.

Integrating water into a scheme can also be a way to make us more mindful, which again can support better mental wellbeing and reduced rumination and worrying. A wonderful example of this is Holland Park Playground by Erect Architecture, which the architects saw as a 'celebration of rain', demonstrating that water can provide an opportunity for users to engage with the elements and the physical sensations offered by water, and be more mindful of weather and environment.

Lakes, in particular, are excellent ways to encourage people to leave buildings and become more active, whether that's by walking around them, swimming in them or engaging in water sports on them. As we will see in Chapter 6, the mental health benefits of exercise are substantial and demonstrable, so opportunities to 'nudge' people into being active should be harnessed wherever possible. This is highlighted within the WELL Building Standard, where it is recognised that 'blue spaces' can have a positive impact on human health due to the opportunities for exercise they offer.

Safety is of course a key consideration here, as swimming in open water is inherently more dangerous than swimming in a pool. It is harder, people tire faster and the murkiness can make it difficult to find a struggling swimmer or child who has fallen in. These increased risks are not always obvious and therefore it is very important to make people aware of them, which can be achieved through simple signage at regular locations around a body of water.[58]

Bodies of water can have significant benefits to biodiversity, acting as another helpful tool to provide human/animal interaction. They can also act as landmarks or places for people to meet, encouraging greater social interaction.

A further benefit of lakes, ponds and swales is that they can be used as a way to store excess water, and potentially reduce flood risks when designed properly. In my design career this has been a helpful way to justify the provision of such features – and, of course, giving residents reassurance that their homes are well protected from flooding removes a significant element of worry, particularly in certain parts of the world.

As with many of the features in this book, not all ponds and lakes are equal in regard to the wellbeing benefits they offer. There is a substantial difference between a simple water-filled hole in the ground and a well-designed aquatic feature rich with wildlife, visual amenity, exercise facilities and high-quality furniture. We know how to make these spaces exceptional, but unfortunately this is still not always achieved.

Design tips

1. Designing a small pond can be a relatively simple undertaking, which can be achieved with little more than a pond liner, some builders' sand and gravel, as well as a spade and some elbow grease!

2. Designing a lake is a much bigger undertaking, so it is advisable to consult with an experienced landscape designer to ensure the design is achievable and safe.

3. Whether designing a small pond or a lake, consider flood risk. Think about where the excess water will go if it overflows and how this might be managed or mitigated.

4. The ultimate aim should ideally be to create a place that has both visual and physical amenities, from seating to exercise equipment, and which maximises biodiversity.

Water channels

> 'The sound of water is worth more than all the poets' words.'
> – OCTAVIO PAZ, POET AND DIPLOMAT

Figure 4.14: The Rill at More London, UK, by Townshend Landscape Architects

Potential mental wellbeing benefits

- Nature interaction
- Legibility benefits
- Moments of joy / awe
- Historic / cultural references

Potential issues and considerations

- Specialist input useful
- Maintenance
- Hygiene
- Safety

Despite the many benefits of ponds and lakes, it is not always possible to bring them to urban environments. They generally require a fairly large area, and towns and cities often present depth constraints too. However, there are many other ways to bring water into built-up areas, one of which is the simple water channel.

Historically, streams would often run through towns, and later on leats and aqueducts were often introduced – artificial watercourses that were dug into the ground to supply a watermill, its associated millpond or perhaps a reservoir for drinking water. In time these sometimes became used as aesthetic features known as 'rills', such as at Shute House in Wiltshire or the Palacio de Generalife in Granada, which boasts impressive fountains above the rill itself.

Nowadays the practical uses of such waterways may largely have disappeared but water features like this, whether natural or artificial, can offer a visual connection to water-dense urban environments, particularly in places where rivers have now been moved underground. As an example, dozens of 'lost rivers' run below London and it is often possible to bring these back to the surface in selected places, or to use an artificial water feature to reference those lost below the ground, providing references to a place's history and making it culturally richer, with the aim of increasing the sense of local pride and community.[59] Such features can also bring other benefits of water as previously discussed, including the calming sounds of a flowing stream and bringing a simple moment of joy into what could otherwise be a dull urban environment.

As well as providing references to history and stimuli for the senses, water channels can be used as a linear wayfinding element to guide people along a specific route, making towns or cities more legible and less stressful to navigate. In this way they present a distinct advantage over a traditional fountain, which exists in a single point and therefore provides fewer wayfinding benefits.

An urban waterway can be as simple as a sunken channel no wider than a handspan, or something much more complex, like a wider, tiered element which can include plants, water jets or sculptural features. However, they present little room for error and can require careful design and engineering, so it is definitely worth investing in a water garden specialist or landscape architect if considering the inclusion of even a basic water channel.

There are also safety considerations of which to be aware, as with the sad case of the rill at More London, near Tower Bridge.[60] This landscape reference to a historic tributary of the Thames was bricked up in 2018, with the media blaming mobile phone use for repeated cases of twisted ankles as people didn't notice the small water feature.

It is also worth raising the issue of water cleanliness, which can be an issue, as any water system can become infected with bacteria like legionella, as well as viruses, yeasts, moulds or algae. These issues can be prevented through disinfection methods such as a UV treatment system, which are worth factoring in from an early stage.

Design tips

1. Identify how water channels could be used to achieve various mental wellbeing benefits, such as improved legibility, references to history or simply the joy of interaction with water.
2. Be aware of potential public safety concerns (tripping, falling in, etc.) and workshop ways to mitigate or avoid these – width, depth, location and visual cues can all play a role.
3. Simple is often better – there will be less to go wrong, and your design will be more likely to stand the test of time. Collaboration with specialists will help avoid potential problems.
4. Ensure water hygiene has also been considered and discussed with the final site operations team, ideally avoiding harsh chemicals where possible.

Roof gardens

> 'I've always felt that having a garden is like having a good and loyal friend.'
> – C.Z. GUEST, ACTRESS AND AUTHOR

Figure 4.15: Capitol Hill Urban Cohousing, Seattle, Washington, USA, by Schemata Workshop

Potential mental wellbeing benefits
- Spatial benefits
- Nature interaction
- Social opportunities
- Sense of privacy
- Increased activity

Potential issues and considerations
- Detailing
- Structural issues
- Use by all
- Protection from elements

So far in this book we have examined the importance of views, the benefits of peace and quiet, and the impact of spending time in nature. Surely if there was a way to combine all three, every home and workplace would have one?

Fortunately, roof gardens can do exactly that. As urban spaces become denser as ever more of us move to cities, utilising flat roof spaces for private or shared gardens seems like an obvious choice. Recent research by Marsh & Parson's estate agents has shown that a roof garden can add between 10% and 25% to the value of a property in certain parts of the UK, so it is peculiar that they are not more commonplace.[61]

The good news is that they do seem to be growing in popularity. According to the UK Green Roof Market Report, this industry is increasing by 17% a year across the UK. Groups such Living Roofs, set up by Dusty Gedge in 2002, have long been promoting green and biodiverse roofs, citing their many benefits from reducing climate impact to cutting building management costs.

In many respects, when it comes to wellbeing, putting a garden up in the air makes a lot of sense. We have already discussed prospect and refuge theory and the sense of safety that we obtain from being up high, with good views out over surrounding areas. A further benefit of this is that it can take us up and away from the noise and air pollution more commonly found at ground level. Like any garden, they can also encourage socialising in shared apartment buildings or workplaces.

There are, of course, many design considerations when moving a garden on to a roof. As the DIY Green Roof Guide from Living Roofs notes: 'The roof must not leak', 'The roof must not collapse' and 'The roof must allow excess rainfall to escape'. It is also important that the roof build-up is considered to allow for a level threshold for equality of access, something that can often cause problems, as habitable roofs can require deeper floors.

Once these detailing and structural issues are resolved, we can consider elements that will have a further impact on our mental wellbeing. Privacy is key – both from neighbours and within if a shared garden, so consider how areas can be screened and potentially subdivided, particularly within larger communal spaces. It is also important to consider user comfort, by providing both shaded and sunny spaces, as well as protection from wind and rain.

Ideally (in the northern hemisphere at least), roof gardens should be south facing, but of course this could vary depending on how space is likely to be used. If it is intended for use as a brunch spot, it may be better facing east to soak up the morning sunlight and warmth, while a cocktail bar may want a west-facing roof garden, allowing visitors to enjoy the best sunset views. You may also want to consider other natural elements from this chapter, such as growing areas, elements promoting biodiversity or water features to create a truly exceptional space for mental wellbeing and restoration.

Design tips

1. Whether working on the design of a new building or a refurbishment, consider each available roof space and analyse its potential merits as a roof garden.

2. Key issues to consider in the selection of possible roof gardens include privacy, acoustics, views, orientation and accessibility.

3. Be aware of the various technical challenges presented by a roof garden, such as structural, drainage and safety requirements, and engage with specialists where required

4. As roofs are often very exposed, consider potential exposure to wind, rain and sun, and provide protection if appropriate.

Garden streets and *woonerfs*

> 'Children must play, and children, if they live in the cities, must play in the streets.'
> – THE NEW YORK TIMES, 1914

Figure 4.16: *Woonerf*, Groningen, the Netherlands

Potential mental wellbeing benefits

- Increased activity
- Nature interaction
- Social opportunities
- Improved air quality
- Acoustic comfort

Potential issues and considerations

- Consultation required
- Servicing
- Local opposition

Despite all the suffering and tragedy that resulted from the COVID-19 pandemic, there were some small positives to emerge, especially in the way we as a society began to reconsider how we use our cities. One example of this can be seen in the closure of many residential side roads in towns and cities to cars, to create Low Traffic Neighbourhoods (or LTNs).

Instead of being packed with nose-to-tail cars during rush hour, roads became available for use by pedestrians, cyclists and children playing, and in many cases became filled with flowerbeds and were even used for street markets or café spill-out spaces. This was all achieved very cheaply too, using simple street furniture like bollards or planters.

It was clear that this strategy would work well to reduce car use and make streets safer, as similar experiments in Hackney in 2000 and Waltham Forest in 2013 both cut traffic use on residential streets by around half, with pollution plummeting and bike use soaring in both areas. Many cities around the world did the same, with Barcelona announcing it would turn a third of city centre streets into permanently car-free green spaces.[62]

The Dutch have embraced this idea more wholeheartedly with what they call the *woonerf*. The *woonerf* was invented in Delft in the 1960s by a community who decided there were too many cars using their neighbourhoods as rat runs. By introducing planting and trees into the road itself, they forced cars to slow down and as a result reduced the number of people using it as a shortcut. Many of these principles have since been adopted in other countries, for example in the UK's many 'Home Zones' or 'Play Streets'.

Such initiatives reduce noise and air pollution, and promote active travel as streets become safer, allowing people to cycle to work and children to walk to school. LTNs allow children to play more too, creating stronger social connections while they exercise. They also offer the opportunity for streets to be taken over by more positive uses than cars – be this planting and more greenery, or events and amenities such as markets or street parties, improving and strengthening community bonds and subsequently people's support networks.

This approach is supported by WELL Certification, which makes points available for projects located on streets with restricted vehicular traffic as they lead to more pedestrian-friendly neighbourhoods,[63] based on evidence from the *Global Street Design Guide*, which was created by experts from 72 cities across 42 countries.[64]

With most experts predicting that car use will decrease in urban environments over the next two decades, there is no reason why many of the LTNs introduced in 2020 can't become permanent. One thing we all realised during the global pandemic was that it is possible to change how we use streets in a positive way. It is up to us as designers to harness that momentum and improve the public realm that we all use every day.

Design tips

1. Prioritise pedestrians and cyclists through the use of generous shared street space.

2. Reduce or remove vehicle access if not absolutely necessary, as well as any surplus parking.

3. Planters or street furniture can be effective tools to help slow traffic, particularly when they are used to create a curving street form.

4. Many other elements from this section can contribute to a successful woonerf, such as trees for shelter and air cleaning, integrated planter furniture and even water channels or growing areas.

5. Be sure to consider practicalities like servicing and parking for people with disabilities. As an example, many Dutch neighbourhoods use centralised refuse disposal rather than individual bins.

Sensory gardens

> 'Nothing is more memorable than a smell. One scent can be unexpected, momentary and fleeting, yet conjure up a childhood summer beside a lake in the mountains.'
> – DIANE ACKERMAN, POET, ESSAYIST AND NATURALIST

Figure 4.17: Magneten Sensory Garden, Copenhagen, Denmark, by MASU Planning

Potential mental wellbeing benefits

- Nature interaction
- Moments of joy / awe
- Mindfulness opportunity
- Learning opportunities

Potential issues and considerations

- Allergies
- Maintenance
- Use by all

One of nature's key attributes in design terms is its power to address all of our senses, presenting opportunities we might not often be able to create through buildings alone. As part of our attempts to create spaces that make people more mindful, this can be harnessed as an extremely potent tool, encouraging people to engage with their surroundings in ways that many of us rarely do on a day-to-day basis.

Sensory gardens are perhaps one of the best ways to achieve this. They can take many forms and sizes, giving them the further advantage that they can be included in almost any location or project type. They are reported to be beneficial to people with autism and other sensory processing disorders, anxiety, ADHD and Alzheimer's, as well as being generally calming and encouraging mindfulness in all of us.[65]

Initially developed for specific environments such as hospitals and rehabilitation units in the 1970s, many contemporary examples focus on one sense, such as sound or scented gardens at a school for people with sight problems, for example. However, sensory gardens can be of value to all, and it is possible to use them to engage all five of our primary senses and design outdoor spaces that can be physically stimulating for all.

When it comes to the visual impact of a sensory garden, aim to provide a range of shapes and colours that will be on display year-round, including a balance of bright and more calming shades. These don't need to be provided solely by plants: butterflies and birds can be another way to bring visual stimulation into a garden.

Sounds can also be easily designed into sensory gardens in a number of ways, and the concept of non-rhythmic sensory stimuli is helpful to consider here. Features such as ornamental grasses, water fountains, wind chimes or even the rustling of leaves are all examples of this.

Smells can be slightly more problematic. As Bill Bryson explains in his book *The Body: A Guide for Occupants*, smells are closely associated with the limbic system, namely the amygdala (where emotions are processed) and hippocampus (where learning and memory formation take place), meaning that they can trigger strong and specific feelings in some people. They can also be unpleasant for people undergoing chemotherapy and other medical treatments, so in certain locations such as hospital gardens, care may need to be taken. Perhaps the best approach is to create 'smelling stations', or areas where strong smells such as lavender, lemon scented geraniums, wild marjoram or even curry plants can be experienced if desired.

To engage people's sense of touch, provide a range of tactile stimulations such as tree bark, plants like lamb's ear (woolly to touch), grasses and water. Signage letting people know that plants may be touched can also be helpful.

Finally, gardens can even allow people to explore their sense of taste by including edible herbs and fruits. This can create issues around hygiene, and care may need to be taken if it is a garden intended for use by children, so consider these issues and potential strategies to allow taste to safely play a role in your sensory garden.

Design tips

1. All gardens offer a valuable opportunity to encourage people to be more mindful. Consider each of the five senses and how you can engage them when designing any garden space.

2. Think about who will be using your garden space when thinking about which senses to address and how: strong smells may not be suitable at a cancer centre and edible foods may not be appropriate at a nursery school.

3. Use lessons from elsewhere in this book for ideas on how to engage the senses, perhaps through use of materials, increased biodiversity or use of colour.

Geveltuin, or facade gardens

> 'We don't have to engage in grand, heroic actions to participate in change. Small acts, when multiplied by millions of people, can transform the world.'
> – HOWARD ZINN, HISTORIAN AND PLAYWRIGHT

Figure 4.18: *Geveltuin*, Antwerp, Belgium

Potential mental wellbeing benefits
- Nature interaction
- Environmental benefits
- Aesthetic benefits
- Identity / self-worth
- Moments of joy / awe

Potential issues and considerations
- Maintenance
- Loss of light

If you have not heard of *geveltuin* before, do not be dismayed – before researching this book I hadn't either and there is no word in English for this design feature. To find out much about them, you will likely need to visit a Dutch or Belgian website or library, as – like the *woonerf* – this is where they originate. Unlike the *woonerf*, however, this concept seems to have remained firmly in this small part of northern Europe.

In the Netherlands a *geveltuin* is a facade garden, more commonly known as a tile garden in Belgium, and these names give us a fairly good idea of what they are and how they are created. Either during construction or once a home is occupied, a few tiles or a narrow strip of paving adjacent to the facade is removed. In this leftover space, a shallow hole is dug and soil suitable for plants is inserted.

Generally, plants are chosen that can climb the building's facade or form a small area of ground cover in the form of a bush or flowers. Dutch local municipalities are so keen to advocate these tiny patches of green that they even have advice pages on how local residents can create their own,[66] as they appreciate the ways that green streets can contribute to the quality of life in cities, particularly in cities like The Hague and Rotterdam, where front gardens aren't always common. They argue that *geveltuin* improve the streetscape, keep houses cooler, make the city more resistant to climate change and flooding, and promote biodiversity.

It is also interesting to note that despite their location on a public street and the fact that the land remains the property of the municipality, residents are responsible for the maintenance of their own facade gardens, instilling a sense of ownership for the public realm, as well as a sense of involvement and belonging.

Given all that the *geveltuin* can offer, it is somewhat surprising that they have never really migrated to the UK or other nearby countries in the same way. However, it is very easy to integrate these into new projects and (depending on land ownership) may also be possible once a building is occupied.

For new schemes, a simple planting strip along a building's facade will suffice, whereas for buildings already in occupation you may need to remove an area of tiles or paving. In certain parts of the Netherlands you don't need permission as long as you follow a set of rules, but in much of the world you must own any area of land to which you want to make changes, so do be aware of any local laws regarding changes to the built environment before you start ripping up the pavement! If it is not possible to make such changes post-completion, you could always consider a substitute, such as a low horizontal planter at the foot of a facade.

Some Dutch authorities require *geveltuin* builders to leave at least 1.8m of pavement for people to walk. They then recommend adding fertilised soil to a depth of at least 30cm. It is also important to consider root growth and soil shrinkage, and the potential damage this could do to both structure and services, so it's recommended not to use plants that grow into large shrubs or bushes, but smaller plants such as perennials or climbers.

Design tips

1 Before creating your own *geveltuin* ensure you check local laws and regulations around land ownership and changes to property.

2 Consider the specific conditions of the plot in question, such as whether plants will be in the sun or in shade, and whether the soil will be wet or dry, as this will affect the types of plants that are suitable for your facade garden.

3 If designing *geveltuins* into a new development, consider the impact on pavement width and make sure enough space is left for pedestrians.

4 Be aware of potential damage caused by plants and roots, and select species accordingly.

CHAPTER 5
Aesthetics and legibility

> 'The life of a designer is one of fight: fight against the ugliness.'
> – MASSIMO VIGNELLI, ARCHITECT

Figure 5.0: 'Happy Street', Thessaly Road, London, UK, by Yinka Ilori

Throughout history, aesthetics has been a divisive topic, largely because it is so subjective. Our own idea of what is and isn't beautiful is strongly shaped by our personality traits and our cultural background. One person may sit longingly for hours in front of a Rothko painting, while their best friend or partner might dismiss it as nothing more than splodges on a canvas. However, in an age when so much of our lives is dominated by our sense of sight, and the way places look on a screen is sometimes prioritised over how they actually 'feel' in real life, it is important to understand the ways in which we can use aesthetic features to our advantage.

A good example of the subjectivity involved with aesthetics is the debate over the issue of beauty that has recently re-emerged in British architecture, with a trend emerging of older buildings being hailed by some politicians as 'beautiful' and contemporary architecture as ugly. Returning again to the government's 'Living with Beauty' report (see Chapter 1), a new planning and development framework was proposed which promised to 'Ask for Beauty' and 'Refuse Ugliness'.[1] Not all architects responded positively, with some suggesting that 'beauty' cannot be written into a design code, given its highly subjective nature.[2]

As with art, music or film, the truth of the matter is that buildings can be beautiful to some, regardless of their age or their architectural 'style'. To some, a brutalist building will be more aesthetically appealing than a classical church, while others may prefer an Art Nouveau facade to a contemporary one. There is no 'right' and 'wrong' here, simply a sense of personal taste. What is far more important than either taste or style is *quality*. Michelangelo's *David* is still undeniably beautiful today, whether you are into the work of the Renaissance sculptors or Damien Hirst.

This section of the book focuses on visual strategies and aesthetic approaches that can demonstrably affect how people use spaces or how they feel in them – an area in which new research is still constantly emerging.

While we may not have as strong a set of data about how aesthetics affect us psychologically in comparison to, say, exercise or biophilia, how things appear certainly has the power to create joy and change the way in which we perceive places. For an even more in-depth analysis of these issues, I would recommend Elina Grigoriou's *Wellbeing in Interiors*,[3] which explores a range of concepts including visual symbolism, colour psychology, pattern and the ratios and volumes of spaces.

In connection to the navigation and understanding of a place, legibility is also undeniably one of the most important functions of aesthetics, and it certainly plays a role in how we feel. A visually illegible place can make us feel unsafe or highly uncomfortable.[4] As one visitor to the Seattle Public Library wrote in an online review: 'I left the building as soon as I could figure out how to get out, hoping I wouldn't have an anxiety attack first.'[5] In *Happy City*, Charles Montgomery explains that this is a natural biological response: 'places that seem too sterile or too confusing can trigger the release of adrenaline and cortisol, the hormones associated with fear and anxiety'.[6] In contrast, a city or building we feel we understand can provide us with a sense of reassurance and confidence, and knowing this can affect anything from the way we design a door handle to how we organise a masterplan.

It seems we also like legibility in visual patterns and motifs, with research showing that we humans are drawn to visual interest and variation, provided there is some decipherable logic or system behind it – connecting back to theories of biophilia and nature preference. We also have underlying psychological associations with certain visual elements from checkerboard patterns to pitched roofs, and just a glimpse of them can powerfully remind us of places or emotions.

By understanding the impact of visual choices like this, we can alter our design approach in a way that is likely to create positive responses and emotions in the people using our buildings and cities. Whatever style we choose to design in, there are tools and strategies we can use to create visually better places, which are likely to improve the day-to-day lives of their occupants.

Colour for joy and colour for wayfinding

> 'Colour is life; for a world without colours appears to us as dead.'
> – JOHANNES ITTEN, PAINTER

Figure 5.1: Superkilen Urban Park, Copenhagen, Denmark, by Bjarke Ingels Group

Potential mental wellbeing benefits

- Legibility benefits
- Aesthetic benefits
- Sense of safety
- Moments of joy / awe

Potential issues and considerations

- Use by all

Colour, it seems, has been a feature of architecture for as long as there have been buildings – or perhaps even earlier if we are to consider, say, the cave paintings of Lascaux, which date back an estimated 17,000 years. While we may picture classical buildings, such as those at the Athens Acropolis, as being devoid of colour, we know that ancient Greek temples and dwellings were actually painted in vivid colours (and have known this since at least the 1850s, although it still seems to surprise many people).[7]

In spite of this, a number of contemporary architects seem fairly reluctant to use colour, a trend that seemed to emerge in the twentieth century with many seeming to perceive colour as a decorative, ornamental or unnecessary element, linked to outdated architecture or regionalism.

Putting taste and fashion to one side and looking instead at the psychological benefits of colour, it is challenging to find robust scientific evidence to support the idea that certain colours make us universally happier or sadder as a species, in part because of the role that cultural values seem to play. However, it does seem to affect behaviour in some ways, with one good example being the now famous experiment at Tokyo train stations, in which introducing blue lighting seemingly reduced suicide rates. While follow-up research has challenged the extent to which the lighting had an impact, even the revised results show it had a noticeable impact on behaviours.

Even if we can't measure or understand it fully, colour undeniably has an ability to create joy and inspiration in people, as we can see in the pleasure created by the work of painters such as Jackson Pollock or Patrick Heron. Colour in architecture can have a similar effect, as Ingrid Fettell Lee explains beautifully in her book *Joyful*. Lee describes how Tirana's mayor, Edi Rama, restored the city from a dangerous place to a vibrant, safe, joyous one through the repainting of historic buildings with bright colours.[8] Much of the city soon followed suit and the impact was enormous, winning Rama 'World Mayor of the Year' award in 2004.

As designers, we should not therefore be afraid of using colour, but instead seek to understand its power to spark joy, create pleasure, to surprise or to reference a place's history or heritage. We can find examples of colour's power in buildings around the world, from the deep reds in traditional Japanese temples to more recent examples, such as PLP Architecture's Kaleidoscope offices in Farringdon, London.

Colour can also be used as a helpful tool in terms of wayfinding and legibility, as it has been demonstrated to improve memory storage and retrieval.[9] If you were to tell someone how to find a certain house, it is very common to hear phrases like 'it's the one with the red door' or 'it's the white house at the end', as colours stick strongly in our memory.

Understanding this phenomenon can be useful when designing easily navigable places. Through the use of colours we can give otherwise very similar places, such as different parts of a hospital, floors of an apartment building or large multi-storey car parks, their own distinct identity, making them more legible and more pleasant to use. While we could do this in other ways, for example through numbers, letter or visual styles, colours are a simple strategy that are proven to be easily memorable.

While the evidence on specific colours may not yet be clear, one thing is certain: colour can be a powerful tool to create better places from Tirana to Yinka Ilori's 'Happy Street' in Nine Elms, London, which transformed a previously forbidding environment into a vibrant and engaging space. And while some designers may avoid colour, in doing so they are missing opportunities to create more inspiring and more legible places.

Design tips

1. Colour is a powerful tool that can create joy and evoke emotions – seek to harness these in your projects. However, its power can make it divisive, so engagement with local stakeholders is key.

2. Ask for evidence over claims on the effects of specific colours, e.g. 'blue will make us feel sad' or 'red makes us creative'.

3. Colour can be a powerful memory aid and can help to give a place a strong identity. Use different colours as a helpful wayfinding aid to make places easier to navigate and understand.

Artworks, murals and sculptures

> 'A mural can make a street corner into a social hotspot.'
> – EVAN MEYER, ARTIST AND FOUNDER OF *BEAUTIFY*

Figure 5.2: Bendigo Hospital, Australia, by Silver Thomas Hanley + Bates Smart

Potential mental wellbeing benefits

- Aesthetic benefits
- Historic / cultural references
- Identity / self-worth
- Social opportunities
- Moments of joy / awe

Potential issues and considerations

- Consultation required
- Fitout cost
- Specialist input useful

There is some debate about when exactly the first pieces of human 'art' were created, but we are sure now that they significantly predate the aforementioned Lascaux cave paintings. In 2017, a painting of three wild pigs was discovered in a limestone cave on the Indonesian island of Sulawesi, which is now believed to date back over 45,000 years.[10] Other archaeologists believe that red markings in a South African cave are the world's first known human drawings, dating back 73,000 years, although many experts are unsure that either were created by homo sapiens.

What does seem clear is that for tens of thousands of years, humans (and perhaps our now extinct 'sister-species') have had an inherent desire to create and look at art. The reasons for this are believed to be numerous, whether it is to create records or tell stories of what has happened; to express or communicate ideas; to celebrate religious beliefs; or simply to make the places around us more beautiful. Some experts have even suggested that the earliest 'artists' painted their cave walls in an attempt to attract mates, much like the bowerbirds that use elaborate nests as part of their courtship rituals.[11]

Whatever the reasons, art is certainly a powerful force in affecting our mood and can significantly support better wellbeing. Looking at artwork has been shown to reduce stress levels in participants, while studies demonstrate that creating art or music can help with an enormous range of physical and mental health problems, reducing pain levels, tiredness, drowsiness, breathlessness and blood pressure in patients before, during and after eye surgery, for example.[12] Researchers have also discovered that looking at art we consider to be beautiful triggers similar pleasurable physical and psychological responses as when we fall in love.[13] The reasons for these collective benefits of art are not clearly known, but in part at least it may relate to the idea of mindfully appreciating our environment, rather than being lost in our own thoughts or ruminations again.

Artwork offers an opportunity to add visual interest to what might be otherwise unengaging spaces, as well as bringing some colour into a space, with the associated benefits we have previously seen. One of the major challenges is that we all seem to like different art. In the largest study ever done on this question, 91,162 people were asked about their art preferences.[14] As you might predict, everybody has different tastes (and of course some people simply don't enjoy art as much as others) but, interestingly, these preferences tend to correspond more closely to personality traits than to demographic factors. It seems the important factor is providing art in some capacity, as it is quite simply impossible to provide pieces that will please everybody.

External artworks can be incredibly powerful too, be they murals, sculptures or temporary performance pieces. These have the ability to transform not just their immediate surroundings, but also their wider neighbourhoods. This has been demonstrated by street art around the world, but perhaps most powerfully by the work of Jeroen Koolhaas and Dre Urhahn, who create community art by painting entire neighbourhoods and involving those who live there in locations as diverse as the streets of north Philadelphia to the favelas of Rio de Janeiro.[15]

What is clear is that viewing or making art can substantially benefit our wellbeing and wherever possible we should explore opportunities to integrate it, whether it is through working with local artists and communities or simply by consulting with occupants on what art would make the building better for them.[16]

Design tips

1. Create an 'art strategy' for your project from an early stage. It may be that there is a common theme throughout all pieces, or that they are deliberately varied: the important thing is that it has been considered.

2. Involve members of the local community, grassroots artists or stakeholders to give any art in the space an extra layer of meaning, value and significance.

3. Because everybody has different tastes, it is important to consult with building occupants about the type of art you install. Consider using a company like ARTIQ, which uses 'intelligent art curation' to obtain the views of the people who really matter – the people using your building every day.

Signage and legibility for all

'One thing that is guaranteed to make people feel negative about living in a city is a constant sense of being lost or disorientated.' – MICHAEL BOND, AUTHOR OF *WAYFINDING: THE ART AND SCIENCE OF HOW WE FIND AND LOSE OUR WAY*

Figure 5.3: Underhub Language School, Kiev, Ukraine, by Emil Dervish Architects

Potential mental wellbeing benefits
- Legibility benefits
- Greater equity
- Sense of safety
- Increased autonomy

Potential issues and considerations
- Specialist input useful
- Fitout cost

If we select two people at random from the general population and show them the same image, you may be surprised to find that they are unlikely to see them in exactly the same way. A wide number of factors can affect how we see or interpret the things in front of us, including age, sight conditions, memory, disability or the language we speak. For anyone dubious about this statement, consider the viral 'white and gold', or 'blue and black' dress debate of 2016, where people looking at the same image on the same screen would often disagree about the colours of the garment.[17]

This can have a significant impact in the way we design spaces, in particular when trying to ensure we support a range of needs and neurodiversities. A good example of this is in the design of retirement homes or care centres for older people. As we age, our recognition of colours often deteriorates, with studies showing that abnormal colour vision affects over half of people in the oldest age groups.[18] Our lenses can yellow, particularly disrupting blue-yellow vision, and our ability to read contrast between light and dark deteriorates as well.[19]

In design terms, this means it is important to use high levels of contrast to draw attention to items such as signs and doors.[20] These don't need to be garish colours, but the level of brightness should differ. Adversely, it is important to avoid strong contrasts between, say, two areas of flooring, as it could appear to an older person (particularly when coupled with other issues such as dementia) like a change of level, resulting in a fall.

This example illustrates just how differently two people can visually interpret the same picture in front of them and can teach us some lessons about designing places that are easier to use and to navigate. For example, what may seem like a clear piece of signage to a young, non-disabled, English-speaking designer, may be unclear to people using it once installed. For people with additional needs, good signage can be especially important, so it is vital that we consider the needs of all when designing these parts of a building or masterplan.

We have already explored one way of improving signage to make it more easily legible: the use of colour. By colour-coding parts of a building or masterplan, we provide a way for people who struggle with text or who don't speak the same language to navigate them.[21] Shapes or pictograms can perform a similar function. Imagine arriving at an airport in a country where not only is the language different, but the alphabet is too. In this instance an image of a taxi is far more helpful than the word written in, say, Cantonese.

Such strategies can also help those with visual impairments, who can generally identify numbers and shapes far more easily than words or names. For severe visual impairments we may need to consider embossed, braille or audible signs.

Ultimately, when we design buildings that address the needs of all, everyone benefits. Unfortunately, accessibility features are often one of the first factors to be cut from designs, due to cost or perceived extra effort: how many places do you know that provide braille signage, for example? Fundamentally, though, when we improve accessibility, places become easier and more pleasant for everybody to use, supporting better wellbeing for all.

Design tips

1. Using shapes, colours or numbers instead of text can make signage more accessible to a wider range of occupants.
2. If text is required, provide it at a generous size, with clear, easily defined lettering and medium text weight and stroke width.
3. Ideally use sans serif fonts with larger inter-letter and inter-word tracking, as this improves readability for dyslexic occupants.
4. Consider the best height for your signage based on the anticipated building use – like all aspects of signage, this should be consistent throughout your scheme for clarity.

Architectural detailing and a sense of quality

> 'Details, when they are successful, are not mere decoration. They do not distract or entertain. They lead to an understanding of the whole of which they are an inherent part.'
> – PETER ZUMTHOR, ARCHITECT

Figure 5.4: Gainsford Road Housing, London, UK, by Gort Scott

Potential mental wellbeing benefits

- Identity / self-worth
- Mindfulness opportunity
- Aesthetic benefits
- Improved liveability

Potential issues and considerations

- Build cost
- Detailing
- Design programme / budget

In Edward Allen and Patrick Rand's book *Architectural Detailing*, they highlight the three key aspects of a good detail: function, constructibility and aesthetics.[22] Without well-designed details, the authors argue, a building will not function as well, it will be harder to construct and it will be both less visually appealing and less cohesive in its overall appearance.

When we look at architectural detailing through these three lenses, it is easy to make a case that all three aspects can have an impact on our psychological experience of using a building, particularly if any of these three elements is done poorly. Take function, for example. If a detail is designed to function well, it will control heat flow and air ingress, making a building more thermally comfortable, and it will keep sound out, improving acoustic comfort.

A high-quality detail which is designed with constructability in mind will be more forgiving of small inaccuracies or tolerance issues, allowing it to achieve these functions better. This means ultimately an easy-to-construct detail is more likely to keep water out and control water vapour, preventing problems such as damp and mould – which not only create maintenance headaches, but can lead to a number of physical health problems too.

Finally, the aesthetics of a detail can have a significant impact on how people read not just that part of the building, but the building as a whole. High-quality detailing suggests a level of overall design quality,[23] that a building has been put together with care and attention, and thoroughly thought through. Perhaps, most importantly, it says that this is a building in which the occupants *matter*; in which their needs were considered and adequate time and effort afforded to ensure those occupants enjoy using the space.

The value of this has been understood since certainly the ancient Greeks with their elaborate column orders, and likely even earlier. In the words of environmental psychologist Toby Israel, 'Our sense of self and sense of the environment are intimately and profoundly intertwined.'[24] The places that we design for people can have a substantial impact on their sense of self-worth or personal value. If we design buildings or cities with good quality details that are built to last, we are communicating to those who use them that we value and respect them, with potentially powerful consequences on how those spaces make them feel.

Yet, sadly, when we look at some of today's buildings, a relatively low value seems to be placed on high quality or 'generous' detailing. Where there once would have been brick or stone arches, we may instead find cheap steel lintels, and in most cities it isn't too challenging to find modern apartment buildings that are pock-marked with ventilation outlets because there wasn't the budget to conceal them.

It is important to explain that this is not a question of 'modern vs traditional' either. While a Georgian cornice can express quality and care at the junction between a wall and a ceiling, a more contemporary shadow gap can achieve the same effect. As with so many of the features in this book, it comes down to a question of cost versus value. It is our job as designers or advocates for better places to communicate the added value that well-built places add – to the appearance of a place, to the quality of people's lives and to their sense of pride in where they live or work – and to champion better detailing to improve the world around us.

Design tips

1. When considering any architectural or interior detail, consider the three cornerstones of a good detail: function, constructability and aesthetics. These could form a good framework for reviewing details as well.

2. Be aware of the psychological impacts of value engineering a detail to the point where a building feels 'low quality'; you can use this to defend the additional cost of buildings or features that are high quality in appearance.

3. Design details in three dimensions, not just plan or section. BIM and CAD allow us to see how detail will really look, so use these tools to ensure your designs will work in the real world.

4. Remember, this is not a question of taste or trends: a sense of overall quality is what matters, and this can be achieved in any architectural style.

Varying visual identities

> 'What we all dread most is a maze with no centre.'
> – G.K. CHESTERTON, *A FATHER BROWN MYSTERY: THE HEAD OF CAESAR*

Figure 5.5: Valetta House, London, UK, by Office S&M

Potential mental wellbeing benefits
- Legibility benefits
- Identity / self-worth
- Aesthetic benefits
- Historic / cultural references

Potential issues and considerations
- Design programme / budget
- Build cost

What makes a good maze challenging to navigate your way out of is visual homogeneity: the fact that each wall looks largely the same and that there are no distinguishing features by which you can identify places you have seen before. When designed poorly, a city, neighbourhood or masterplan can act in much the same way, with every facade consisting of seemingly identical glass office buildings or two-up, two-down brick terraces.

In our attempt to make places more legible, towns more inviting to explore and cities less intimidating, one powerful tool that we can have in our design armoury is that of giving different areas subtly independent identities. This is not to say that we should diverge entirely from the surrounding language or historical context – as we will come to see later, this can also play an important role in how we think about place – but we should gently make people aware when they are moving from one area to another.

While there are many psychological theories about identity and ego, we do know that having a sense of individual 'self-identity' is extremely important. 'Regional identity', or the identity created by our immediate environmental and social context, has also been claimed by the *International Encyclopedia of the Social and Behavioral Sciences* to be a 'basic need of human beings'.[25] As humans, we like to have a strong sense of identity in where we live and work, as well-known places provide us with trust and security. This also highlights the psychological importance of giving places their own distinctive characteristics, so that we do not simply feel we are living in a cookie-cutter neighbourhood that might be the same as another one on the other side of the country.

This idea of 'cut and paste' developments has become more of an issue in recent years, as we have witnessed a loss of local character within some new developments, both in the UK and beyond. Historically, communities had to build with the materials immediately available to them, resulting in a wide variety of languages even across any single country. In Britain, for example, older houses are most likely to be built using limestone in the Cotswolds, granite and slate in Cornwall and flint in Norfolk.

Today, however, materials can easily be transported around a country or even internationally, with around a quarter of the UK's building materials now coming from abroad.[26] Designing buildings in the local vernacular is no longer the most cost-effective way to work; in fact, due to economies of scale, it is cheaper for large developers to use the same language, materials and details across all schemes, regardless of location.

Ideally, however, developments should embrace local character, while having some elements that make them unique. This might mean referencing the local material palette using details such as fenestration or roof profiles in such a way that it gives an area its own sense of identity. Alternatively, it could involve matching the contextual typology (such as two-storey terraced housing or mid-rise mansion blocks) but using materials in a way that gives a project a sense of individuality.

By designing in such a way, we are not only creating places that are easier to read and recognise, making cities and towns easier to navigate, we are also designing neighbourhoods which people feel is truly 'theirs', enhancing their sense of belonging and identity, and allowing them to be proud of where they live or work.

Design tips

1. If re-using typologies and layouts from previous projects, be sure to revisit and update them to provide references to local context and give them a sense of identity and individualism.

2. Find a balance between blending in and providing useful wayfinding features such as unique details.

3. Augment traditional typologies or material palettes to create a contemporary design that is grounded in its surrounding area.

Visible, well-designed entrances and arrival points

> 'The door handle is the handshake of the building.'
> – JUHANI PALLASMAA, ARCHITECT

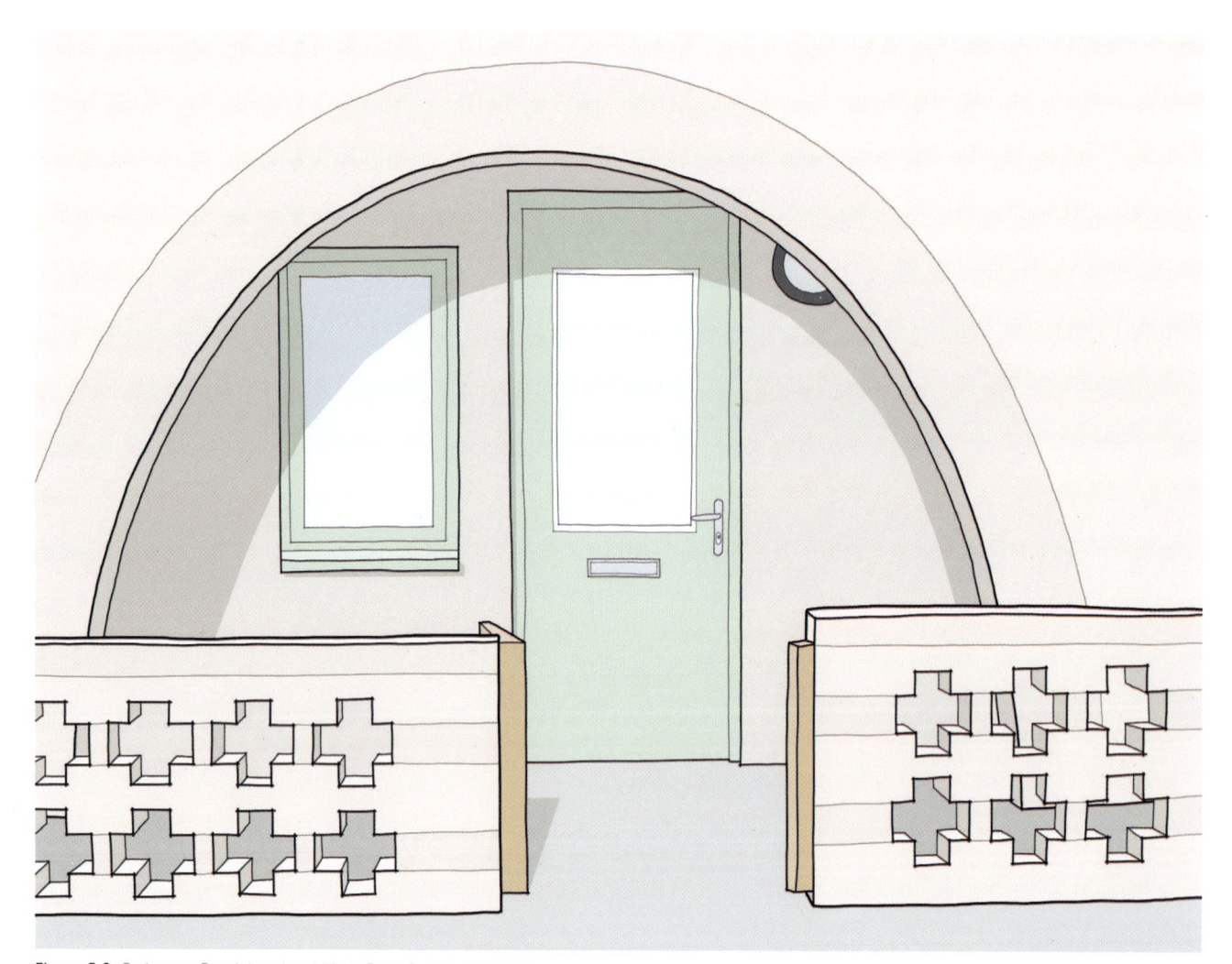

Figure 5.6: Ordnance Road, London, UK, by Peter Barber Architects

Potential mental wellbeing benefits

- Legibility benefits
- Identity / self-worth
- Aesthetic benefits
- Historic / cultural references
- Improved liveability

Potential issues and considerations

- Use by all
- Protection from elements
- Build cost

Another important aspect of making buildings legible is to clearly signpost access and arrival points. The entrance is the starting point for any building, and if we arrive somewhere confused, perhaps shuffling in through a secondary entrance, we are not only likely to be frustrated with our initial experience of that building, but further uncertainty about how to navigate internal spaces will generally follow. Illegible buildings can cause unnecessary stress, with numerous reported cases of anxiety attacks or people breaking down in tears as a result of confusing, poorly laid-out places.[27]

Historically, designers have understood the importance and weight that entrances can have, from the golden doors of the Baptistery of San Giovanni in Florence, designed by Lorenzo Ghiberti in 1452 and known as the *Porta del Paradiso* (Gates of Paradise), to the grand bronze doorway to the US Capitol building, which chronicles the life of Christopher Columbus, designed by Randolph Rogers in 1910 and weighing around 20,000 pounds.[28]

As well as making a place more legible, what both these designers understood is the symbolic significance of doors and entrances. Much as we subconsciously judge people by their body language and dress before we have even hear them speak, we make deductions about a building before we have stepped foot inside. A doorway sets the tone for our whole experience in a building, and a good one can lay the foundations for a more positive relationship with the spaces beyond, while a poor one can, like a bad opening line, set us off on the wrong foot.

Entrances should therefore seek to express and represent the same things as the rest of the building. This might be a sense of homeliness and safety, an openness to all, or perhaps a sense of intrigue and wonder. As much as we may try to represent these things through other parts of our projects, the entrance has another advantage in communicating to occupants: it is the only part of a building that people are almost guaranteed to use every time they visit.

Entrances and doorways also have a strong impact on the way the streetscape feels. They can be a way to create active frontages, which, as we will see in Chapter 6, can play an important role in people's moods and behaviours. High-quality entrances can be harnessed as a way to engender a greater sense of pride in place and support a better sense of self-worth.

Signalling entrances need not be as literal as providing signage or placards. As designers there are a whole host of tools at our disposal that allow people to understand how they enter a building, in a slightly more sensitive way. Similarly, creating special doorways need not be as elaborate as casting them in bronze or plating them in gold like Rogers or Ghiberti. It can be as simple as a splash of colour, an understated recess or a projecting element, surround or canopy – all of which can be used to draw the eye to the doorway and celebrate the entrance. The wider language of the building and landscape should also make the intended approach to the building clear, reducing legibility problems and enhancing the visitor experience.

Design tips

1. Use architectural language and landscape design to 'signpost' a building's entrance more clearly, or to nudge people to naturally head towards it.

2. Remember the importance of an entrance in our initial perception of a building and ensure that it reflects the wider design intent for the project.

3. Entrances are a justifiable place to stretch the project budget or to create one of the building's 'special' moments. Consider ways to make this experience a positive one for visitors.

4. Make entrances accessible and easy-to-use for all, and ideally provide some level of shelter from the elements too.

Engaging, complex or biophilic patterns

> 'Nature uses only the longest threads to weave her patterns, so that each small piece of her fabric reveals the organisation of the entire tapestry.' – RICHARD FEYNMAN, PHYSICIST

Figure 5.7: Nottingham Contemporary, UK, featuring lace-patterned concrete, by Caruso St John Architects

Potential mental wellbeing benefits
- Aesthetic benefits
- Historic / cultural references
- Nature interaction
- Identity / self-worth

Potential issues and considerations
- Build cost
- Fitout cost
- Specialist input useful

Wherever we look in the world we can find architectural patterns, from Angkor Wat to the concentric circles of Stonehenge. While these can sometimes be purely decorative, they often have a deeper meaning. Islamic architecture, for example, has one of the richest histories of geometric patterns, which act as both a decorative element and a reflection of the language of the universe, often intended to help the viewer reflect on life and the greatness of creation.[29]

Patterns can be useful within architecture due to their structural benefits, as can be seen in the geometric order of Inuit igloos or indigenous Kanak huts. This structural strength comes from the inherent mathematical order of patterns and the shapes they generate, which allow for compression and tension to work together in harmony – as seen in Buckminster Fuller's geodesic domes.

Partly because nature is constrained by the same physical forces, pattern is also common within the natural world, from the hexagonal symmetry of a snowflake to 'Turing Structures', which appear everywhere from sand dunes to the patterns on animal skins.[30] As wild as it may seem, most elements in nature are not random, but rather the result of highly complex mathematical systems.

Perhaps as a result of this, we as humans have an innate preference for what Lily Bernheimer calls 'ordered complexity' – patterns which include repeated elements at different scales, symmetries or rotations.[31] Bernheimer argues that over-simplicity deprives us of the sensory stimulation that we need, but that over-complexity can be confusing or disorienting. Instead, what we seem to like is patterns which are complex enough to intrigue us, but repetitive enough to be deciphered. In this way, even human-made or computer-generated ornamentation can take on a natural quality.

Modern technologies have now given us even more opportunities to integrate pattern, be it through parametric design tools, laser cutting, 3D printing or even brick-laying robots. Many newer architectural practices seem to be embracing these opportunities, from the colourful pattern work of Atelier Manferdini, or the repeated elements often featured in the work of Bjarke Ingels. Unfortunately, it seems that this is frequently reserved for 'high-end' architecture, and often doesn't trickle down to the everyday 'architecture of the people'. Either as a result of value engineering or a lack of understanding of the visual benefits of such an approach, many new housing schemes or workplaces are fairly plain, minimal buildings.

There are many ways in which we can introduce pattern into buildings in a cost-effective way, however. We have already discussed the fact that bricks offer a form of pattern which can be made more playful and engaging, and when taken to an extreme the effects can be spectacular, such as at The Interlock by Bureau de Change. Pattern can also be integrated effectively in balustrading or panelling, where perforation is needed. Another simple, yet effective, approach is through the repetition of elements such as windows or tiles, where small variations are introduced to create that sense of ordered complexity that we humans find so satisfying.

While these are just a few of the ways that pattern can be brought into architectural projects, we know that people tend to respond positively to them, and they can add something positive to the visual reading of a place and its perceived 'quality'. Once we are aware of this, it no longer seems frivolous, but in fact becomes a powerful way to improve a space and add value.

Design tips

1. Integrate pattern into your project to add visual richness, an enhanced sense of quality or a deeper meaning and connection to place or history.

2. Explore ways in which this can be done without significant impact on the budget, perhaps through tweaks to existing elements or the way things are set out within an elevation, and ascertain the parts of the building in which pattern introduction can have the biggest impact.

3. A 'fractal' approach – where patterns on a smaller scale reflect the larger language of the building – or natural patterns which are themselves often inherently fractal, can produce positive responses in humans.

Handmade furniture or detailing

❝ That's the thing with handmade items. They still have the person's mark on them, and when you hold them, you feel less alone.' – AIMEE BENDER, *THE COLOR MASTER: STORIES*

Figure 5.8: Nomad Collection handmade furniture by Nathalie Deboel, which does not use any screws or bolts

Potential mental wellbeing benefits

- Psychological response
- Aesthetic benefits
- Identity / self-worth
- Altruism benefits
- Environmental benefits

Potential issues and considerations

- Fitout cost
- Design programme

The concept of 'machine-made' furniture is a relatively new one. Until the Industrial Revolution, arguably every piece of furniture in existence was 'handmade' to some extent. The mass-manufacture of furniture, as we now know it, was reliant on two things: mass-production techniques and a big enough consumer market. When these emerged as a result of new technologies and the resultant shifts in the labour market, a reduction in handmade objects was inevitable.

While all of this is understandable, many people wonder whether we have lost something in the mechanisation of what was once a true craft. Research seems to show that people do indeed prefer handmade objects, with one study from the American Marketing Association finding that consumers are willing to pay up to 17% more for handmade items. As *Science Daily* explains: 'Consumers seemed to believe that the creator's love for the handmade product had somehow transferred to the product itself, and that the product now "contained love".'[32]

In some sense, the idiosyncrasies, flaws and tiny variations in each handmade piece are what make it special. The Japanese have a word for this, *wabi-sabi*, which refers to 'a beauty of things imperfect, impermanent or incomplete'.[33] Characteristics of *wabi-sabi* include simplicity, roughness and asymmetry, and has been described as the most characteristic feature of what we think of as traditional Japanese beauty – in direct contrast to the classical ideals of beauty or perfection in the western world. While it can be a challenging idea for many of us to get our heads around, we can perhaps look at it in this way – when you know that your bookcase is identical to 100,000 others around the world, it somehow has less of a sense of being 'yours', and it becomes less special and less beautiful.

Other studies suggest that people prefer handmade objects because they are more 'creative', higher quality, better for the environment, more personal, or because they are keen to support local and artisan communities.[34]

Almost all these factors can make us feel more positive and most are explored in this book. Improved quality goods or those with a sense of belonging personally to us have the potential to support a sense of higher personal value and a more positive self-image. Supporting the environment can address eco-anxiety concerns, and championing local traders can provide a sense of altruism, which can promote physiological changes in the brain linked with happiness.[35]

Handmade furniture generally offers greater transparency, too, in terms of both a product's ingredients and supply chain. These can give its owners a sense of reassurance: firstly that the item doesn't contain toxic or harmful materials that could release VOCs into the air, and secondly that it has been produced in an ethical way.

Of course, there are challenges when it comes to sourcing handmade furniture, primarily relating to cost. One of the great advantages of mass-produced furniture is that it can be made quickly and efficiently, making it much generally much cheaper. One way to address this is to specify handmade furniture in the places that they will make the most difference – at the reception desk or at a feature table for example. However, given the potential impact that a large order can have on a small supplier, local craftspeople may often be prepared to negotiate on price as economies of scale come into play, so don't rule out using handmade furniture without a thorough investigation of the possibilities.

Design tips

1. Look to specify locally sourced and handmade furniture to reduce impact on the environment, support local communities and give occupants the sense that these objects are special and unique to them.

2. Much as with healthy ingredients, consider ways to communicate such strategies to occupants – through strategies like 'transparent sourcing' documents or information sheets accessible through QR codes or online.

3. While handmade furniture might seem unaffordable on paper, local artisans may be prepared to negotiate, so visit local markets and workshops to get a true understanding of price.

4. If the budget will not stretch to handmade objects throughout, consider where they will have the biggest impact and communicate the social and psychological value of these pieces to the client.

Nooks and crannies

'The essence of interior design will always be about people and how they live. It is about the realities of what makes for an attractive, civilized, meaningful environment, not about fashion or what's in or what's out.' – ALBERT HADLEY, INTERIOR DESIGNER

Figure 5.9: Tivoli Building, Cartagena, Spain, by Martin Lejarraga Oficina de Arquitectura

Potential mental wellbeing benefits

- Personalisation opportunities
- Greater adaptability
- Aesthetic benefits
- Historic / cultural references

Potential issues and considerations

- Impact on layouts
- Detailing

Up until the last century or so, the places in which we lived and worked were full of 'imperfections'. Humanity's earliest structures were shaped by nature, and certainly wouldn't have consisted of perfect straight lines. As most of the world's population moved into more 'formal' buildings, fireplaces became essential, and these generally demanded a hearth with some sort of chimney breast, leaving two recesses on either side. These became an accepted feature and sometimes even a symbol of prestige, and as a result many occupants (even to this day) added 'false' chimney breasts.

Other types of niches can be found in older buildings too, for a number of reasons. They might be left over as a remnant of historic building features, such as a window that was bricked up as a result of William III's infamous window tax of 1696. Sometimes niches were deliberately designed-in, too, perhaps as a place for a piece of art or simply as a recessed cupboard.

As we moved through the twentieth century, a general trend away from such features emerged. Be it partly as a result of Mies van der Rohe's 'Less is more' philosophy, new construction methodologies that allowed for longer spans and clean lines, or the replacement of chimneys with gas boilers, many modern buildings are now characterised by flat, straight walls with few, if any, niches and nooks.

While these make great showhouses, they arguably make worse buildings to occupy. When spaces have nooks and crannies, furniture can slot into them, resulting in usable, orthogonal footprints. Without niches, furniture can often project into the room, creating strange, leftover spaces between them. Ironically, perhaps, these 'surplus spaces' are anything but surplus: they can make a room easier to inhabit or furnish.

Smaller recesses or cubbyholes can be useful too, offering opportunities for storage, which as we already know play an important role in how we psychologically perceive a space. They might be appropriated as a bookshelf or place to keep keys, offering a sense of control as occupants adapt these features to make them their own. They provide opportunities for personalisation too, as places for ornamentation, such as photographs, sculpture or vases.

On the previous page we saw some of the benefits that can be provided by giving places a sense of individualism and uniqueness, and perhaps such nooks and crannies can be a way for homes to have their own sense of *wabi-sabi*. We have also explored the negative impacts associated with the feeling you are living in a 'cookie-cutter' house identical to all those around you – and again these features could be a simple way to give homes their own distinct character.

We can use nooks and crannies to incorporate other tools from this book. For example, by designing-in a protruding window bay in place of a flat wall with a window, we can create an occupiable space that receives far more daylight, reaping many of the benefits discussed in Chapter 1. Alternatively, we could build in a window box within a small niche, adding biophilic value. Ultimately, we should rethink our position on these features, which are often seen as inconvenient leftovers from the way we used to design buildings. In actual fact they offer a number of benefits in terms of both liveability and quality of occupier experience, generally leading to a richer, more characterful space.

Design tips

1. In the design process we often focus on eliminating peculiar recesses or odd junctions: consider whether this is truly necessary and whether in fact they may offer benefits.

2. When working on historic buildings, avoid 'fixing' strange leftover features, alcoves and cubbyholes. These are often the parts of buildings that give them their character and will no doubt be useful to future occupants.

Pitched roofs and playful typologies

> 'Form follows function.'
> – LOUIS SULLIVAN, ARCHITECT

Figure 5.10: Gray Villa, Maku, Iran, by White Cube Atelier

Potential mental wellbeing benefits

- Psychological response
- Aesthetic benefits
- Moments of joy / awe
- Historic / cultural references
- Legibility benefits

Potential issues and considerations

- Design programme / budget
- Consultation important

Generally, as a species, we like things to look how we would expect them to. We see this perhaps most obviously in foods: when Heinz trialled a purple tomato ketchup, people found it disgusting and it was an enormous commercial failure. Green ketchup did alright, as tomatoes can be green but, overwhelmingly, consumers prefer red ketchup.[36]

We seem to react similarly when it comes to buildings. Ask a British child to draw a house and they will most likely sketch a square box with a pitched roof, two or four windows, a front door and a chimney. As Alison Lurie explains in her book *The Language of Houses*, we find simple buildings reassuring, because we immediately understand them.[37] Other projects tend to be better received at consultation if they are 'visually fitting', that is that they look how we expect them to look. Louis Sullivan's quote at the beginning of this section is perhaps the most frequently used in architecture, and for good reason — we really do seem to prefer buildings that meet our visual expectations.

This is particularly strong in housing, perhaps because of our highly personal connection to our homes. To quote Lily Bernheimer, 'our emotional attachment to our homes can be almost as strong as our emotional attachment to other people'.[38] Environmental psychologists often refer to this phenomenon as 'place attachment', and the design and appearance of buildings can play a large role in this. Indeed, without humans assigning meaning and value to somewhere, it is not a 'place' at all, but simply a 'space'.

Whether it is an apartment, terraced house or mansion, where we live must encapsulate that almost indefinable quality of 'homeliness' — and one of the first steps to achieving this is to make it look more like a home. In much of the world, this means having a pitched roof.

Before modern construction techniques, in wetter climates a pitched roof was essentially the only way to protect your home from the elements. Rather than pooling water or snow, pitched roofs can shed precipitation with ease, reducing risks of water infiltration and enhancing durability and lifespan. As a result, we now visually associate pitched roofs with the idea of home and protection, with some studies showing that adding one to your home can offer up to a 63% return on investment, as buyers find them more enticing.[39]

The same approach can be applied across all typologies. We might expect an office to have a flat roof, for example, but could find it strange if its facade was covered in balconies. Similarly, we would probably expect a school to be low-rise, and maybe more colourful than other building types. We can also apply the same way of thinking to local context: ideally a project should look like it belongs to a place, while of course achieving the varied visual identity we have previously explored.

By understanding such typologies, it also offers us the opportunity as designers to become more playful, and to adapt or tweak expectations to create moments of joy through architecture. One contemporary exponent of this approach is FAT (Fashion Architecture Taste), who often play with viewer expectations of both typology and context to bring genuine intrigue and delight into their projects, such as in their 2006 social housing project at Islington Square, Manchester.[40] It is important, however, to be aware of the pitfall of 'the architectural joke'. As many postmodernists discovered in the 1980s, a funny piece of design or use of materials could bring a smile to somebody's face the first time they see it, but after ten years the joke will likely feel pretty tired.

Design tips

1. Buildings that reflect their typology and context tend to be viewed more positively — design places in such a way that their use is easily identifiable.

2. This doesn't mean that flat roofs aren't appropriate for any residential buildings, just that pitched roofs are one of many techniques to bring to mind ideas of home and suggest protection and safety.

3. Play with typologies to create visual interest or moments of joy in places.

4. Aim to imbue a building with meaning, nostalgia or psychological associations, turning it from a 'space' to a 'place'.

Urban legibility features

> 'The mark of a great city isn't how it treats its special places – everybody does that right – but how it treats its ordinary ones.' – AARON M. RENN, URBAN ANALYST

Figure 5.11: The Shard and City Hall, London, UK, by various architects

Potential mental wellbeing benefits
- Legibility benefits
- Sense of safety
- Increased activity

Potential issues and considerations
- Large-scale interventions
- Consultation required

Feeling lost within a building can be an unpleasant or even anxiety-inducing experience. Given that cities can contain thousands or even millions of buildings, they are infinitely more complex than a single building. This means it is vital to provide legibility at a larger, urban scale – and there are a number of strategies that can help us achieve this.

The first approach is to support people in maintaining a clear sense of direction. A layout such as a grid can be a powerful tool in achieving this, as seen in Manhattan or the newer parts of Barcelona. Stray into the older parts of Barcelona, however, and the streets become notoriously difficult to navigate. Because these places have evolved over time like a layered palimpsest, there is often no clear pattern or discernible logic, meaning it is very easy to lose our sense of direction.

Humans generally like exploring and respond well to some level of intrigue, so it is important to break from a rigid grid on occasion, perhaps with a diagonal street or a zig-zagged path. However, there is also the argument that if we make places more legible, people will feel safer to explore them, so we should strive for a balance of clarity and mystery. It is also important to avoid rotational symmetry, of which London's Piccadilly Circus is a good example.[41] For someone unfamiliar with the area, whichever direction you approach it from, it looks quite similar, meaning it is very tricky to get a sense of north or south. Grid layouts can also result in this effect, but fortunately there are other strategies we can use to support us here – not least the introduction of landmarks.

Much as we can use colour as a feature to support better wayfinding, a similar approach can be used with landmark buildings or urban features such as statues or monuments.[42] Research has shown that within the hippocampus, animals have 'place cells', which fire up when we are in a place we recognise, as well as when we see 'landmark' objects. Studies reveal that landmarks must have a key set of properties: distinctiveness (they should be unique), stability (they must not move or change), and position (they should be visually prominent).

For this reason, historically this role was often played by cathedrals or church spires but is now more frequently taken up by office buildings or cultural landmarks. For all the criticism that tall buildings receive, when done well they can offer benefits to a city's legibility and offer high value in the right location. By providing such landmark elements we can provide a reference for the place cells in occupants' hippocampi, helping them to recognise locations more easily.

Corner buildings provide a good opportunity to create such markers, as corners generally signal places we may need to alter our trajectory, which is why we often hear architects and planners talk about the importance of a 'strong corner'. An alternative approach is to place a landmark building next to a recognisable linear element such as a river – for example, the Shard next to the Thames, or St Louis' Gateway Arch adjacent to the Mississippi.

Whichever strategy is used, the key is to create places that people can understand and of which they can build a mental map. Without this, we risk designing cities that deter movement, exploration and the formation of new communities that can follow.

Design tips

1. Review strategic locations for potential 'landmark' elements early in any large-scale project.

2. These can work well at key junctions or next to other linear elements like rivers, parks or roads.

3. To be effective, landmarks must be visually distinctive from other, similar elements: a generic residential or commercial tower is unlikely to be effective in activating the hippocampus.

4. Consider how streets and masterplans are laid out – they should seek to follow existing organisational structures or introduce other strategies to support a clear 'sense of direction' in occupants and visitors.

CHAPTER 6
Activity and exercise

'Not only does the city shape the way we move, but our movements shape the city in return.' – CHARLES MONTGOMERY, *HAPPY CITY*

Figure 6.0: Xiamen Bicycle Skyway, China, by Dissing+Weitling

As a species, humans have historically needed to be active to survive.[1] Around 1.8 million years ago, we began to develop tools for butchering animals, so we know that by this point we were reliant on hunting and running down animals for at least some of our food. As hunter-gatherers, we were almost entirely a nomadic species, walking an estimated 12,000 to 18,000 steps a day, so it is little surprise that exercise generally makes us feel better both physically and psychologically.

With all of that in mind, we also evolved to conserve energy wherever possible.[2] We need energy (often measured in 'calories') to perform our daily tasks, not to mention to keep our bodies' internal mechanisms running, from our immune systems to our hormone production.[3] As a species, our brains are so large that a quarter of all the oxygen we breathe goes to feeding our brains, and as a result they use a lot of energy. This is why, if most of us were given the choice between relaxing on the sofa or going for a jog, the majority would pick the sofa – it is an evolutionary response.

We therefore find ourselves with a dilemma that underlies a huge number of modern-day health problems: we need to be active to stay fit and healthy, but our bodies and minds are, on the whole, telling us not to be. As a result, nearly a quarter of the general population of the United States fails to achieve the recommended physical activity levels, rising to around 80% in adolescents and 53% in older populations.[4] In 2011, people globally self-reported sitting time from three to nine hours a day.

This is a pattern we see across developed countries, with substantial health impacts. Inactivity is a major contributor to premature mortality and chronic illnesses and can be linked to a host of health problems, including cardiovascular disease, strokes, type 2 diabetes, dementia and some types of cancer. As a result, physical inactivity is responsible for one in six deaths in the UK.[5] What's more, physical exercise not only affects our bodies, but is closely connected to our mental health, and inactivity can be connected to depression, anxiety, negative mood and lower cognitive function.

This is, in part, because when we exercise, we put our bodies under physical stress and pain, and our bodies react by releasing a number of 'feel good' chemicals. I imagine most people reading this book have heard of the connection between exercise and endorphins – a neurochemical which is structurally similar to morphine and is considered a natural painkiller – with some studies claiming that just 20 minutes of exercise can release endorphins that improve our mood for up to 12 hours.

However, this is only part of the story. A recent study discovered that while endorphin levels are higher post-workout, they cannot pass through the blood-brain barrier, meaning they may not have as much to do with the 'runner's high' as we had previously imagined.[6] Exercise does increase production of other chemicals though, including serotonin and norepinephrine, which may play more of a role in reducing stress and depression.

Exercise has also been found to alleviate symptoms such as low self-esteem and social withdrawal.[7] It makes us feel better about ourselves and our self-image, and it can encourage us to interact with more people, both key factors in mental health. When combined with the knowledge that regular exercise can also improve our sleep, our sex drive and our general energy levels, it is perhaps not an understatement that getting active is one of the biggest things we can do to improve our mental health.

The question this chapter poses is a simple one: what ways can we, as designers of the built environment, encourage people to become more active? We know that our design decisions can make a big difference in how people behave and the choices they make. This could range from taking the stairs instead of the lift because they are bright, colourful and inviting, to deciding to buy a bike and cycling to work rather than driving, because there is a safe, tree-lined cycle path that runs past your house. Given that our default evolutionary setting is to choose inactivity, it is vital that we as designers make it as easy as possible to choose exercise and movement instead – and this chapter will give you a number of tools to achieve exactly that.

Urban running trails or green routes

'If you don't think you were born to run you're not only denying history. You're denying who you are.' – CHRISTOPHER MCDOUGALL, AUTHOR

Figure 6.1: Running and cycle friendly routes, FDR Park, Philadelphia, Pennsylvania, USA

Potential mental wellbeing benefits

- Increased activity
- Physical health improvements
- Feel-good chemical release
- Environmental benefits
- Nature interaction

Potential issues and considerations

- Large-scale interventions
- Build cost
- Safety

If you want to live longer, there are few exercises better than running. Studies have shown that runners have, in general, a 25% to 40% reduced risk of premature mortality and tend to live roughly three years longer than non-runners.[8] Running is also shown to make us feel great, with research suggesting that when we run our brains might even produce endocannabinoids[9] – cannabis-like molecules that could be part of the reason people fall in love with running.[10] And whether it's through running, cycling or walking, outdoor activities that allow us to travel through other locations are excellent ways to experience more nature, in the form of flora and fauna or simply through exposure to the natural light of the sun.

However, in many parts of the world, running often isn't a pleasant, nature-filled experience. As anyone who has tried to run in a busy city will attest, it frequently consists of dodging pedestrians and trying to cross dangerous roads. With current figures estimating that approximately three million people around the world are moving into cities every week, less and less of the global population has access to high-quality running environments.

It is possible, however, to provide greener routes and better places to run in even the most urban of locations. From 1960 to 1980, for example, Sweden embedded an emphasis on urban forests and peri-forests within its national 'leisure planning' guidelines, and as a result now boasts a rich legacy of woodland within its towns and cities, benefitting not just runners but the wider population as well.[11]

London is another excellent example of how to integrate nature and green space into an urban environment, and in 2019 became the world's first National Park City.[12] Despite its density, Greater London's public green space makes up 16.8% of its total area, and the city is home to around eight million trees. Residents are also fortunate to benefit from the 'Walk London Network', comprising of seven key routes that connect into major parks and abut the River Thames. The importance of providing such routes and open spaces should not be underestimated. A 2007 study showed that people who live nearer to parks are not only more likely to use them, but also had an average of 38% more exercise sessions per week than those who lived over a mile away.[13]

In other cities, designers have been even more daring, moving the route for runners and pedestrians up, above the urban sprawl below. In 2009 Diller Scofidio + Renfro transformed an abandoned freight rail line in New York City into the now world-famous 'High Line', a safe and nature-filled route that spans 1.5 miles across Manhattan, drawing 8 million visitors a year.[14] Since completion, the architects themselves accept the model has 'gone viral', with perhaps one of the most notable examples being MVRDV's 'Seoullo 7017 Skygarden': a kilometre-long park in South Korea's capital that is home to a staggering 24,000 plants,

However you choose to implement them, urban running trails are an excellent way to encourage a city's residents to run or walk more, and to improve the quality of their experience. They can make running safer, bring us closer to nature, and even introduce elements of gamification to make the experience even more fun. What's more, when implemented at a city-wide level, they result in a high-quality green network of connectivity, benefitting the entire population.

Design tips

1. Identify opportunities to create routes for runners early in a project and consider using these as key drivers for a masterplan or urban design project.

2. Enhance these routes through strategies such as the introduction of nature, lighting, better running surfaces or gamification to make the experience more appealing.

3. Connect into existing walking or running networks (or other green features) where possible.

4. If an opportunity doesn't exist at ground level, consider creating a high-level route. While it may be more costly, if done well it can become the USP of a project and draw far more visitors to an area.

Walkable neighbourhoods and cycle-friendly streets

> 'Everyone has the right to walk from one end of the city to the other in secure and beautiful spaces.' – RICHARD ROGERS, ARCHITECT

Figure 6.2: Cambridge Cross City Cycling project, UK, by Greater Cambridge Partnership

Potential mental wellbeing benefits

- Increased activity
- Physical health improvements
- Social opportunities
- Improved air quality
- Greater equity

Potential issues and considerations

- Local opposition
- Build cost

Historically, towns and cities were walkable places. This all changed with the mass production of cars earlier in the twentieth century, leading to a shift in town planning from person-centric design to car-centric strategies. This is highlighted starkly in two aerial photos in the 'Living with Beauty' report, one of Siena town centre (featuring hundreds of buildings) and another of a highway interchange in Houston, Texas. Both, incredibly, are around the same size.[15]

This change in urban design approach resulted in megacities like Los Angeles, in which it is almost impossible to move around on foot once you move outside the downtown city centres. However, even in smaller towns and cities, it can often feel that non-car users' needs have been overlooked. As one UK Borough Councillor put it: 'As a driver, I know that every road has been designed with my comfort and needs in mind. As a cyclist & pedestrian, I know that my needs and often my safety, have been compromised away.'[16]

Perhaps in designing places based around the car, we have misplaced our priorities. Of course, they are convenient, and they tap into our evolutionary desire to conserve energy, but low car neighbourhoods with amenities within walking distance are demonstrably better for our physical and mental health. They have cleaner air, stronger communities, less road fatalities, less noise pollution, more active populations, and people even spend more money in their shops.[17] Allowing people to walk has benefits for our mental health as well, with studies showing that as walking is a 'bilateral activity', it engages both sides of the brain and can prevent irrational, ruminative thinking, where the right side of the brain typically takes over.

Encouraging people to walk and cycle is better for the national economy too. In the Netherlands, where cycling is far more commonplace than other countries like the UK or the US, the economic health benefits of cycling have been placed at around €19 billion (about £16.2 billion at the time of writing) a year – a substantial figure when you consider that the London Infrastructure Plan 2050 estimates the cost of building a comprehensive, high-quality cycle and pedestrian network to be around £2–4 billion.[18] What's more, children who walk or cycle to school are shown to be more attentive and achieve better results, meaning that the long-term economic impacts of encouraging active commuting could be a better educated, higher performing population.[19]

There are various strategies to create and encourage more walkable places. One approach is the '15-minute city', in which all the amenities people need are located within a short walk or cycle from their home. Mobility advocates like Robin Chase, creator of the Shared Mobility Principles for Livable Cities, argue that without having shops, schools and community facilities within walking or cycling distance, we can never realistically expect people to reduce their car use.[20]

At a more granular level, the design of streets and public space can play a key role as well. This might be as simple as creating safe, segregated cycle lanes, widening pavements, increasing numbers of pedestrian crossings, reducing road speeds, increasing natural surveillance or making streets more interesting places to walk.

There are enough strategies and approaches to create people-friendly streets to write an entire book on the subject, but fundamentally this all comes down to one simple principle set out by Chase: prioritising people over vehicles. If this can be the starting point for all projects, we will end up with richer, healthier towns and cities for all.

Design tips

1. Start designing from slowest methods of travel and move outwards: prioritise pedestrians, then bikes, then public transport and finally cars.

2. Seek to make walking and cycling safer, easier and more enjoyable. A number are listed in this book but the strategies for achieving this are wide-ranging and will vary from site to site.

3. Create masterplans with a range of uses and amenities. These will not only make a place richer and more interesting but will also reduce car reliance.

4. Connect into public transport wherever possible. If one doesn't exist, propose one – whether it's a simple bus stop or a new mass transit hub.

Good street lighting

> 'We regulate our behaviour automatically; we keep our keys in our hands, we stay on high alert, we pay extra to take a cab because we're worried about walking home.'
> – ARWA MAHDAWI, JOURNALIST[21]

Figure 6.3: Campbells Cove, Sydney, Australia, by Context Landscape Design

Potential mental wellbeing benefits

- Sense of safety
- Increased activity
- Physical health improvements
- Social opportunities
- Improved sleep

Potential issues and considerations

- Build cost
- Maintenance
- Environmental impacts

We are fortunate today to have the ability to light our streets with relative ease, with an estimated 350 million street lights globally.[22] Unfortunately, these are not always best positioned or optimally designed in terms of human health outcomes. One of the most important functions of good street lighting is its role in both actual and perceived safety. This is a subject that came to the fore in the UK in early 2021, with women taking to the streets to protest how dangerous they felt streets were after dark. As many women pointed out, they would not feel safe going out for a run after nightfall and effectively live under a curfew from mid-afternoon until dawn in winter months.

This clearly has a significant impact on people's psychological sense of safety, transforming neighbourhoods from happy places into threatening ones and undermining any sense of 'home'. It also has a major knock-on effect on night-time activity, something that has been highlighted as an important aspect of good communities within documents such as the London Plan and the WELL Community Standard. Moreover, many people feel unable to exercise outdoors before 8am or after 5pm in winter, effectively forcing them to take time out of the traditional workday if they would like to go for a run or bike ride.

Fortunately, there are strategies available to improve safety for all after dark – and one of the most effective is also the most simple: good lighting. While this has been challenged by some bodies, not least the International Dark Sky Association, literature reviews of the available evidence suggest that both violent and property crime are reduced in areas with improved street lighting, on average by 21%.[23]

Furthermore, lighting can play an important role in 'perceived safety', make a place seem less frightening. This plays a very important role in how active people are, with studies demonstrating that there is a strong link between perceived neighbourhood safety and the odds of residents being physically active, which coincidentally also increased by 21% when people felt safer.[24]

It is therefore important to consider external lighting design from an early stage in projects, ideally through an external lighting plan or narrative. It is worth bearing in mind which areas need to be best lit, and where there might be potential conflicts around light pollution. This is particularly important in residential areas, where light infiltration into homes can impact sleep quality. In these instances, strategies such as luminaire shielding to prevent light emission beyond 90° above the nadir can help to avoid such issues.[25]

Another approach that is growing in popularity is smart street lighting systems. These typically consist of LED streetlamps which can adjust in response to movement. They can form part of a wider network and can become brighter well in advance of people or traffic arriving at them. Cities such as Dublin are already looking at introducing such strategies, which not only reduce the impact of light pollution, but can also cut energy usage by up to 80%.[26] While this may be seen as too costly by some developers, alongside the added wellbeing value the estimated return on investment can be as little as three years. By 2023, 15% of global streetlights are expected to be connected in such a way, which will hopefully pave the way to cities that are both safer at night and allow us to sleep a little better.[27]

Design tips

1. Create a lighting strategy or narrative early in a project, identifying which areas of a scheme need to be brightest and which might be most sensitive to on-street lighting.
2. Pay particular attention to areas with high footfall and locations where traffic accidents are more likely to occur, such as pedestrian crossings or cycle-road intersections.
3. In specifying lighting, be aware of the potential impacts of light pollution above the horizontal plane and select products that use shielding to avoid this.
4. Use intelligent lighting systems to reduce the impact and cost of lighting when an area isn't in use.

Active commuting facilities

> 'The city needs a car like a fish needs a bicycle.'
> — DEAN KAMEN, ENGINEER AND INVENTOR

Figure 6.4: Casselden office basement cycling centre, Melbourne, Australia, by Gray Puksand Architecture & Design

Potential mental wellbeing benefits

- Increased activity
- Physical health improvements
- Increased productivity
- Improved air quality
- Feel-good chemical release

Potential issues and considerations

- Space requirements
- Maintenance
- Hygiene
- Use by all

In the last 50 years, how we get around has changed dramatically. In 1952, less than a third of all passenger kilometres travelled in the UK were made by car. In 2016, that figure was above 80% and rising.[28] While rail travel has actually increased slightly, bus use has dropped, as has travel by foot or bike. Another poll in that year found that only 9% of British people cycle to work, despite people generally acknowledging that it is beneficial for their health and can save them money.[29]

When we look into the main reasons for these low 'active commuting' figures, the top answers given are that people live too far from work, or that road safety or a lack of confidence puts them off. The good news is these are factors we can solve through design, via the 15-minute-city or the provision of better cycle infrastructure. The other main barrier preventing people from cycling to work seems to be a lack of facilities when they get there, with 17% saying their workplace offers no shower facilities and 10% having nowhere to store their bike.

Fortunately, as part of the planning requirements, all new workplaces in the UK have to provide some level of parking for staff, although this is not the case worldwide. There is also currently no mandatory requirement for showers, changing spaces or staff lockers within planning guidance, implying that the norm is for people who cycle to work to spend the rest of their working day in sweaty clothes. And, of course, most workplaces are not new-builds, leaving many older buildings with no facilities for active commuting.

Other, optional standards do suggest the provision of all of these features. The WELL Building Standard, for example, requests bike parking, bike maintenance tools, showers and lockers – albeit as non-mandatory 'optimisation' features.[30] It also only requests enough long-term cycle parking for 5% of regular building occupants, which would clearly not cater for the 9% of Brits commuting by bicycle. If the world's leading healthy building standard is setting the bar so low for the provision of cycling infrastructure, perhaps it's no wonder so few people are commuting actively.

Given the obvious benefits of active commuting, this all seems fairly surprising. Running, walking or cycling to work is one of the easiest ways for people to integrate physical activity into their daily routine. Research shows that we think better after exercise too,[31] partly because of the increased blood flow (therefore more energy and oxygen) to our brains, with active students tending to outperform less active ones in tests. It is therefore in the interest of employers to encourage their staff to commute actively, rather than driving to work, as performance levels will be better throughout the day.

Cycle parking is shown to add value to properties and neighbourhoods. Per square metre, residential property values rise 1% if motor vehicle traffic is halved.[32] It is therefore in the interest of developers to provide cycle parking – and of course this is just as important in our homes as it is at our workplaces if cycling is to become a part of our daily routine.

Design tips

1. Provide facilities for all forms of active transport, including cycling, running, walking and even riding scooters. Propose storage, showers, changing facilities and maintenance tools to enable all of these where possible.

2. Understand the potential value add of active commuting, which might be used to offset the extra floor area required for these facilities.

3. Cycle storage must be designed well to ensure it is utilised. Consider security issues, robustness, good lighting and weather protection.

4. Similarly, comfort and hygiene are key considerations if showers and changing facilities are to be widely used. Consider thermal comfort, privacy, tactility and ease of cleaning.

Active transport hubs

❝ Transportation is the center of the world! It is the glue of our daily lives. When it goes well, we don't see it. When it goes wrong, it negatively colors our day, makes us feel angry and impotent, curtails our possibilities.' – ROBIN CHASE, TRANSPORTATION ENTREPRENEUR

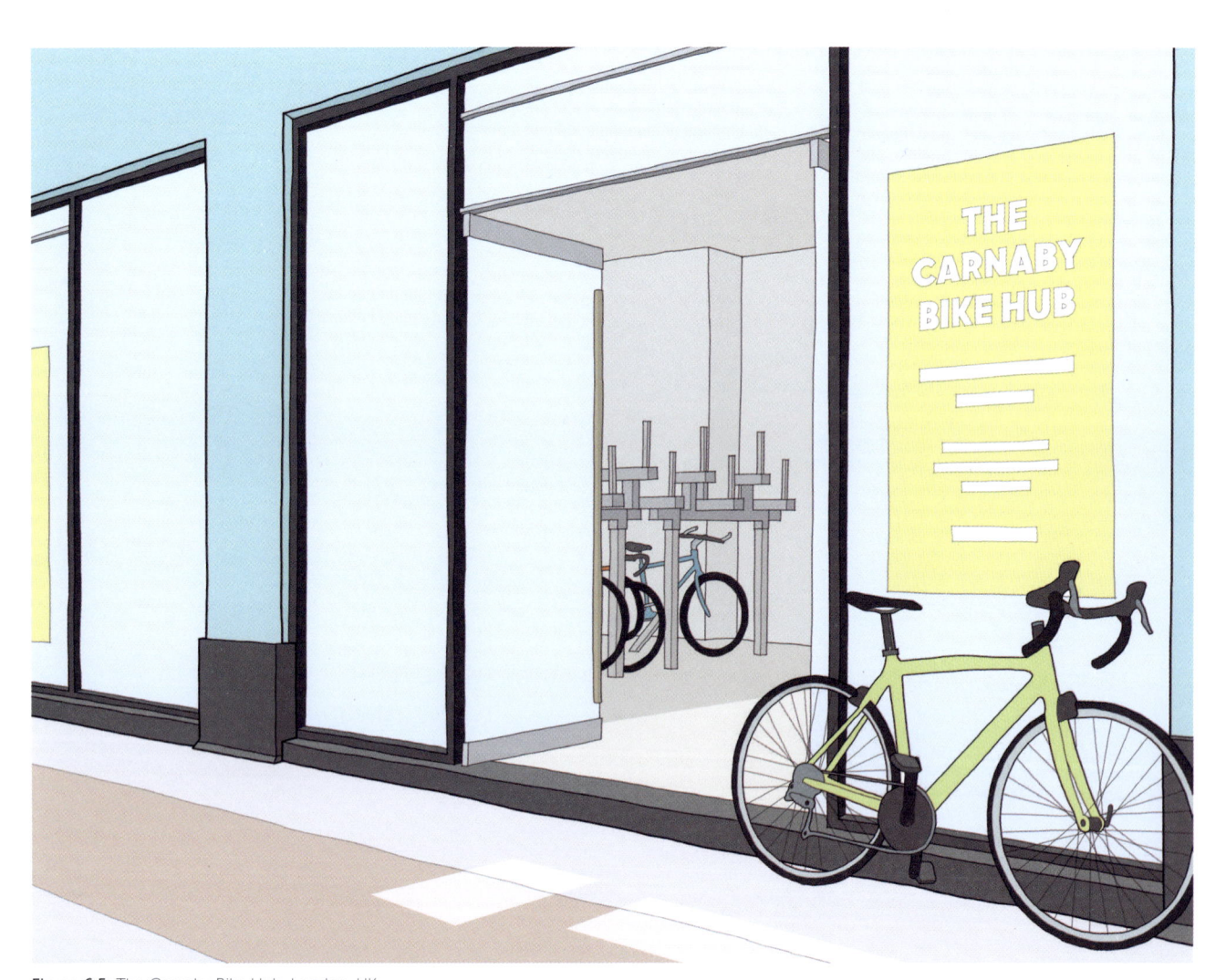

Figure 6.5: The Carnaby Bike Hub, London, UK

Potential mental wellbeing benefits

- Increased activity
- Environmental benefits
- Economic benefits
- Physical health improvements
- Greater equity

Potential issues and considerations

- Space requirements
- Local opposition

With the rise of online shopping, city centres around the world are facing a new challenge. People are increasingly choosing to shop from their sofas rather than use high streets, while out of town shopping centres provide further competition. In the UK, for example, between 2010 and 2020 the number of high street shops dropped by around 50,000.[33] One thing is clear: if town centres are going to thrive, they need to improve and innovate.

Various ideas have been floated to enhance these locations and to make use of many of the empty units that have sprung up in city centres. These include turning disused shops into office or residential uses, both of which have their supporters and critics. Another, more alternative, suggestion has been to transform them into 'active transport hubs'.

An active transport hub is a space dedicated to encouraging and supporting the use of active methods of travel. These have appeared in increasing numbers in recent years, with examples such as Stirling's Active Travel Hub which has the mission of making its city 'the best for cycling and walking in Scotland'.[34]

These can provide a number of facilities to support pedestrians or cyclists, from storage for bikes, pushchairs and scooters to cycle rental facilities, electric charging points, public toilets and even crèches. Provision of essential amenities like these not only make the city centre more appealing to cyclists, but also make it more accessible to people who may have otherwise found it challenging, from those with severe disabilities to parents of very young children.

They also offer a way to reactivate empty shop frontages, which can harm the image of a high street, and research shows that having a safe place for people to store bikes can have more than just a visual impact. High-quality cycle parking has been shown to increase the amount that people will shop in a given location, delivering five times higher retail spend than the same area of car parking.[35] As a result, many city centres are actually providing such facilities completely free of charge, having understood the wider benefits these can offer to the local economy. An example of this is the Carnaby Bike Hub on London's famous Carnaby Street, which even offers the chance to win prizes from nearby retailers when you store your bike there.

As the Stirling Active Travel Hub identifies, such facilities can be beneficial to the health of both humans and the planet, aligning with many of the UN Sustainable Development Goals, including Good Health and Well-being; Reduced Inequalities; and Sustainable Cities and Communities. By providing a secure place to store cycles, they address many people's worries about bike theft in busy cities, and if designed correctly can become a form of advertisement for healthier modes of transport. Numerous studies have found that we often decide how to behave based on how those around us are acting, so showcasing positive behaviours such as cycling can be a powerful tool in encouraging others to do the same.[36]

The hubs needn't be expensive or exclusive – at their most basic an active transport hub could be as simple as a row of bike stands with some space for prams and scooters, perhaps with a single member of staff or CCTV. Even something as modest as this can offer a powerful way to promote exercise, supporting better mental and physical health, and can help to reactivate our high streets.

Design tips

1. Location is key. An active transport hub must be in an area of relatively high amenity to offer good value.

2. Identify the key goals and target users of your hub. These might be parents, cyclists, electric scooter users or people with disabilities – although, of course, an exemplar project would support all of these groups and more!

3. Engage with local businesses and stakeholders to hear their priorities and potentially gain their support for the scheme.

Benches and outdoor stopping places

❝ The bench and, perhaps in particular, the park bench, has become the symbol of the democratic city – of free, accessible and equitable public space provided by the city for its citizens.' – EDWIN HEATHCOTE, ARCHITECTURE CRITIC

Figure 6.6: Green Circular Benches, by Streetlife

Potential mental wellbeing benefits

- Increased activity
- Physical health improvements
- Social opportunities
- Greater equity
- Nature interaction

Potential issues and considerations

- Build cost
- Use by all
- Maintenance

When encouraging people to be active, it is important to not just think about sports and high-intensity activities, but also gentler ways of being active, such as a stroll around the village. CABE's 'Value of Public Space' report sets out some of the benefits of walking, which has 'been proven to reduce the risk of a heart attack and diabetes by 50%, colon cancer by 30% and fracture of the femur by up to 40%'.[37] The report also highlights the social benefits of walking, which makes it a valuable tool in supporting our minds as well as our bodies.

For some, however, even a short walk around the local village can be an intimidating prospect. For older people or those with disabilities, walking longer distances may be significantly harder than for a young person without any accessibility needs. Research with older people in Brighton and Hove found that the availability of seating directly affected the extent to which older people felt they could participate in the city's activities, playing an integral role in its broader strategies for reducing loneliness and social isolation.[38] The Young Foundation – a think-tank that looks to tackle structural inequalities – also discovered that benches and seating play a particularly important role 'for people who may find themselves at the margins of society', as they are effectively a free amenity which can help them to meet new people and have conversations they otherwise may not have had.[39]

Seating does not simply make places more walkable and more social, however. It can also be a powerful way to celebrate a great view, encourage people to stop and appreciate a piece of art or a beautiful building, or to encourage them to interact with nature (see Chapter 4, 'Planter Furniture'). The power of seating has been embraced by many design bodies, such as the Project for Public Spaces, who listed 'being sittable' as one of their 36 key criteria for 'what makes a great place'.[40]

However, with many public parks in the UK having had their funding cut in recent years, there is a risk that benches will be lost or not maintained. Similarly, we often hear of local authorities demanding a minimum amount of play space or minimum pavement width, but it is rarer to find minimum standards around seating, although thankfully this has started to infiltrate documents such as 'The National Design Guide'.[41]

It is generally recommended that seating should be provided at regular intervals, no more than 50m apart in pedestrian areas. It should also be designed to consider the accessibility needs of all: off the main footway, with an area of at least 400mm in front of the seat and a 900mm-wide wheelchair parking area on both sides. Recommended seat levels are approximately 475–500mm from the ground, and width should be around 500mm with a good, well-angled back support provided.

Natural materials offer the biophilia benefits, and materials such as timber can also be beneficial, as they have low thermal conductivity, meaning they stay cool in summer and don't get too cold in winter. 'Bonus items' like cup holders or space for a shopping bag or walking stick have also been shown to improve the appeal of seating. Finally, the very best landscape designs will anticipate where people will want to stop – perhaps by a coffee shop, a churchyard, a playground or a great view, and ideally somewhere that will provide good opportunities for social interaction.

Design tips

1 Champion the importance of public seating, ensure it is integrated into landscape designs and challenge those who seek to value engineer it out.

2 Place seating in high-quality, high-footfall locations that will encourage its use and promote social interaction.

3 Design seating to meet the needs of all users, as per the guidance on dimensions above or by referring to other ergonomic design guidance.

Active staircases

'Stairs may be one of the most emotionally malleable physical elements that an architect has to work with.' – DAVID ROCKWELL, ARCHITECT

Figure 6.7: Panagram Office, London, UK, by Buckley Gray Yeoman

Potential mental wellbeing benefits

- Increased activity
- Physical health improvements
- Social opportunities
- Moments of joy / awe
- Aesthetic benefits

Potential issues and considerations

- Fitout cost
- Impact on layouts

It is claimed that the world's first lift (or elevator) dates back to 236 BC, with Vitruvius reporting that it was designed by Archimedes himself.[42] Throughout history there have been many attempts to use lifts as a means of vertical travel, but it was not until Elisha Otis invented the safety lift in 1852 – which ensured the cab wouldn't fall if the cable snapped – that lifts within buildings became a viable solution.

Today it is common to find a lift in any building of three storeys or more, and of course they have their value, not least as a way of making buildings more accessible to people with restricted mobility and those with a young child in a pram or pushchair. However, there is an argument that many of us have become over-reliant on these clever devices. Even though it is generally faster to walk up to even the fourth or fifth storey than take the lift,[43] studies tend to show that more people will choose lifts or escalators over stairs unless the stairs are significantly more convenient or if time is a critical factor.[44]

Perhaps this is another example of our evolutionary urge to conserve energy, but choosing to take the lift instead of the stairs every day is likely to have a fairly negative impact on both our physical and mental wellbeing. Climbing stairs is an excellent form of exercise, working almost every muscle in our lower bodies, as well as challenging our core strength. While there is often an assumption that homes without stairs are better for older people, improved lower-body strength is actually associated with better balance and a reduced number of falls, with research suggesting that training these muscles (through exercises such as stair use) could have a significant improvement on the wellbeing of people over 70.[45]

In terms of cardiovascular benefits, one Canadian study found that climbing stairs is twice as difficult on the body as walking up a steep incline or lifting weights, while another found that men (but interestingly not women) who lived on higher floors of elevator-less apartment buildings had lower BMIs than their neighbours on lower floors.

Given the clear health benefits, it is therefore important that the design of buildings encourages stair use, and there are numerous ways to do this. One of the simplest strategies is to make the stairs a more convenient choice. In one case, doubling the distance between the stairs and the nearest escalator in a shopping centre increased the likelihood that someone would take the stairs by 95%.[46] This approach does need to be considered early in the design and layout of a building, but if pursued is an inexpensive way of improving occupant fitness.

Improving the experience of taking the stairs can be another way to encourage their use, with the WELL Building Standard explaining that integrating 'aesthetic' features into staircases can do exactly that. The standard recommends strategies such as music, artwork, daylight or light levels of at least 215 lux, natural design elements such as plants, water or images of nature, or even gamification of stairways.

Another successful approach is to include 'skip-stop' lifts, where all except one lift stops at designated floors only, as recommended in the City of New York's 'Active Design Guidelines'.[47] This guide also suggests 'incorporating stairs within the main orientation lobby', and there are certainly many great examples of stairs being used as strong visual features, and even stopping or meeting places. These tools are all powerful ways of increasing stair use and should be considered from an early design stage across all use types.

Design tips

1. Place stairs physically or visually before lifts.
2. At lifts, provide clear wayfinding or signage that indicates the location of the stairs.
3. Consider ways in which staircases can be enhanced, perhaps through making the user experience more fun or engaging.
4. Make staircases a central visual feature where possible.

Intriguing routes and characterful corridors

> 'We like streets that curve out of sight around the corner, leading us on with a tantalising hint of what lies beyond. We love mystery.'
> – LILY BERNHEIMER, ENVIRONMENTAL PSYCHOLOGY CONSULTANT

Figure 6.8: Sutherland Road, London, UK, by Levitt Bernstein

Potential mental wellbeing benefits

- Psychological response
- Increased activity
- Physical health improvements
- Moments of joy / awe

Potential issues and considerations

- Safety
- Urban legibility

One approach to designing streets is to use long roads, perhaps in a gridded system – a common approach in 'younger' countries like the United States. As we have already seen, this has various benefits in terms of legibility: on a grid it is very easy to understand where in the city you are, and to maintain a sense of direction. In contrast are cities like Marrakesh, Bruges or Venice, which are characterised by narrow, winding streets and are famously easy to get lost in. In spite of this, such places draw huge numbers of tourists every year and we seem to find them strangely appealing, from which we can infer that there must be something beyond simple legibility that makes us enjoy using a city.

This phenomenon seems partly because we enjoy a sense of intrigue and mystery, which Lily Bernheimer explains in *The Shaping of Us*.[48] When we see a corner up ahead, it is natural to us to wonder what is around it, stirring our inner explorer and perhaps even making the city feel more fun. With long, wide, gridded streets, this sense of curiosity is lost, and as a result people tend to prefer winding streets. Creating a certain mystery within cities can therefore be a way to get people to walk more, meet new people and discover new places, all of which are good for our mental wellbeing.

Longer and wider streets present a range of other challenges too. Jan Gehl has argued that the optimum dimensions for a public square are between 30m and 35m, as this is the distance at which we can generally recognise other people, and with gridded streets stretching on seemingly into infinity this sense of familiar security can easily be lost.[49] We also know that on long, straight, wide streets, cars tend to drive faster, which, as Charles Montgomery explains in *Happy City*, causes our bodies to release stress hormones, makes people more easily agitated and makes streets feel less social and 'more lonely'.[50]

However, it is also important to be aware of the risk of creating dark corners or unsurveilled parts of streets, as these can have a negative impact on actual and perceived safety. Fundamentally, there is a balancing act in street design between making places safe and legible, and retaining a sense of character and intrigue.

At a micro-scale, corridors, like streets, can be either pleasant and engaging or dull and seemingly endless. In today's buildings these can unfortunately often be the latter, with circulation spaces frequently coming at the top of the list in value engineering exercises. However, these are parts of a building that we use every day, and when designed well can potentially lift the entire experience of a building and also encourage people to explore, albeit on a smaller scale.

As a result, there does thankfully seem to be a trend towards improving the quality of corridors again, particularly in the hospitality sector. Like staircases, there are a number of simple tools that can be used to enrich these spaces, such as natural or artificial light, views to the outside, art or colour, natural materials or plants – many of which can be achieved with a minimal impact on overall project budget but can have a dramatic effect on how people perceive a building.

Whatever scale we are considering, there is one key rule: encourage people to move more, to be explorers and to enjoy the experience.

Design tips

1. While grids are good for legibility, they create less intrigue and might make people less inclined to explore. Curving or zig-zag routes as part of a gentle, larger grid are a way to achieve both.

2. Long, wide straight roads also encourage faster car movement which has a negative impact on occupant mental wellbeing. Curves or narrow stretches can help to reduce speeds and improve safety.

3. It is also important to think about the internal walking environment. Use strategies such as art, colour, light or natural materials to improve spaces such as corridors to create a better experience for people moving around buildings.

Swimming pools and lidos

> 'There is still every reason for healthy people to take cold showers, or swim outside in cold water. It gives you the feeling that you are alive.'
> — WIM HOF, EXTREME ATHLETE

Figure 6.9: Jubilee Pool and geothermal baths, Penzance, Cornwall, UK

Potential mental wellbeing benefits	Potential issues and considerations
▶ Increased activity ▶ Physical health improvements ▶ Feel-good chemical release ▶ Mindfulness opportunity ▶ Social opportunities	▶ Build cost ▶ Operational cost ▶ Maintenance ▶ Space requirements

Unlike many mammals, humans are not 'natural swimmers'. Despite the myth that babies possess an innate swimming ability (they simply hold their breath as part of their 'mammalian diving reflex'), humans, like apes, cannot swim instinctively. We must learn to swim, much like we must also learn to walk.[51]

Humans learned this skill many millennia ago, although exactly when is the subject of some debate amongst anthropologists, and it appears this ability may have all but vanished at various points in history – for example, during part of the medieval period.[52] Today, swimming is an almost ubiquitous skill and a common hobby. Around a third of British adults go swimming every year, while over 10% swim twice a month or more.[53] In children the figures are even higher, with over 25% of those aged seven to 16 swimming on a weekly basis, perhaps because swimming is part of their school timetable or because children generally have more free time and enjoy going to the swimming pool.

It is no surprise that people find swimming so appealing. As exercise goes, it is perhaps one of the best for our bodies and minds. Because it provides greater resistance than air, 30 minutes of exercising in the water is worth 45 minutes of the same activity on land. Regular swimming can help to reduce long-term health conditions such as heart disease and diabetes by up to 40%, and because it is a low impact sport, it is much kinder on joints than many land-based forms of exercise.

Like other forms of exercise, swimming is excellent for the release of our bodies' post-workout feel-good chemicals and can help us to get in better physical shape, creating mood benefits in terms of self-image and a sense of pride in ourselves. When compared to other sports, though, it is perhaps the best exercise for getting in touch with our bodies and our physical sensations. Much like mindfulness, when we swim we naturally focus on our breath and on our body's feelings, and some swimmers are now combining the two to swim in a more mindful way. Unlike in the gym, there are very few distractions in the water. We can't look at our phones or watch TV while we swim, meaning we have little choice but to tune into the present moment.

As a result of these factors, regular swimming has been shown to lower stress levels, reduce anxiety and depression and improve sleep patterns. A 2018 poll discovered that 1.4 million adults in Britain significantly reduced the symptoms of anxiety or depression through swimming, and of this group 43% felt happier, 26% felt more motivated, and 15% believed life was more manageable as a result of swimming.[54]

The design of pools can encourage swimming, through strategies like gamification or a more appealing environment using tools such as light, colour or natural elements. The operation, management and maintenance of buildings can also play a key role here, whether it is through making occupants aware of the benefits and availability of swimming, putting on activities from beginners' lessons to aqua-fit sessions or water polo matches, or by maintaining a clean and inviting environment.

The construction and management of a swimming pool comes with inherent costs, which can be off-putting to developers and residents alike. It is therefore important to design pools at an appropriate scale for the scheme to make them as cost-effective as possible. Ultimately, however, swimming facilities can be a powerful tool to encourage activity, support better mental health and improve overall quality of life.

Design tips

1. Provide pools that are appropriately sized for the occupant level of a scheme: pools that are too small won't get used, while pools that are too large won't be maintained.
2. Integrate strategies to encourage more people to swim through design, such as gamification, tactile engagement or a high-quality, enticing space.
3. Explore ways that swimming areas can promote engagement with the senses, perhaps through different temperature pools or the addition of other features such as saunas or steam rooms.

Filtered water dispensers

'To be thirsty and to drink water is the perfection of sensuality rarely achieved. Sometimes you drink water; other times you are thirsty.'
— JOSÉ BERGAMÍN GUITIÉRREZ, AUTHOR, PLAYWRIGHT AND POET

Figure 6.10: Ljubljana drinking water fountains, Slovenia, which offer free drinking water around the city

Potential mental wellbeing benefits

- Physical health improvements
- Increased activity
- Improved liveability
- Environmental benefits
- Altruism benefits

Potential issues and considerations

- Hygiene
- Maintenance

When it comes to sport, water is a big deal. Losing just 2% of body weight in fluid can decrease the performance of top athletes by up to 25%, and while most of us may not be at this level, staying hydrated is still important.[55] During exercise we can easily lose a litre of water an hour through sweating and breathing, and this can increase further depending on other factors such as weather or fitness.[56]

Staying hydrated is vital to good physical health, helping us to maintain a healthy body temperature, fight off infections, deliver nutrients to our bodies' cells and keep our organs working properly. According to Harvard School of Public Health, it can also benefit our mental wellbeing, helping us to sleep better and improving our cognition and mood.[57]

In spite of this, studies have shown that inadequate hydration is a prevalent issue, even in parts of the world where safe water is available from the tap.[58] It is therefore important to provide water dispensers where possible, both indoors and outdoors, to encourage more water consumption. Water dispensers can take a range of forms from simple taps to fountains and bottle fillers or bottled water coolers. While some research does show the latter to have success in increasing water consumption, water coolers like these use plastic bottles and often plastic cups too, so could have negative connotations in terms of the environment and health with regard to microplastics.[59]

A number of successful examples around the world use simple taps or fountains to great effect, such as the Ljubljana, which boasts over 30 drinking water fountains dotted around the city, free for use by the general public, each with a unique, creative design. Paris has taken a more modern approach, with a series of fizzy water dispensers around the city, provided for free by municipal water provider Eau de Paris. The scheme was introduced as a way to reduce plastic bottle use, and by providing sparkling water the hope is that residents will find it more appealing to drink.[60]

This can also be achieved by making water taste better – something that is suggested in the WELL Building Standard.[61] Chemicals such as chloride in water can give it a saltier taste, while metals such as iron or aluminium at trace levels can also affect flavour or appearance. By using filters to reduce levels of such chemicals in water, we can improve the experience of drinking water and encourage people to drink it.

Fortunately, in most of the UK water tends to meet WELL's fundamental quality measures regarding factors such as coliforms (bacteria), turbidity (cloudiness) and more harmful chemicals like lead or arsenic, although sadly in other developed countries like the USA this is not always the case, as seen by the tragic events in Flint, Michigan, where nearly 9,000 children were supplied lead-contaminated water for 18 months.[62] Fortunately, there are now many affordable solutions to these problems, such as activated carbon filters, ion exchange resins and reverse osmosis systems. It is therefore worth testing water quality at the outset of every project and carrying out an analysis of whether any improvements to safety or taste are necessary.

Fundamentally, providing water dispensers not only helps people to stay more active, it can also improve health through cleaner water and better hydration, supporting both our physical and mental wellbeing. It can also address eco-anxiety concerns through supporting a circular economy approach of keep-cups and reusable bottles, benefitting the planet too.

Design tips

1. Design water dispensers into buildings, landscapes and masterplans, particularly in close proximity to playgrounds, sports facilities and cycle or running routes.
2. Make these visual enticing and eye-catching to maximise interaction and usage.
3. Seek to improve water quality. At a bare minimum this should be brought up to safe standards, but ideally other soluble elements will be addressed as well to improve water flavour and appearance.
4. Consider hygiene concerns and put operational guidance in place so that dispensers are regularly and properly cleaned.

Active frontages, high-quality streetscapes and colonnades

> 'A good city is like a good party – people stay longer than really necessary because they are enjoying themselves.' – JAN GEHL, ARCHITECT AND URBAN DESIGNER

Figure 6.11: Bartlett School of Architecture, London, UK, by Hawkins\Brown

Potential mental wellbeing benefits

- Aesthetic benefits
- Increased activity
- Physical health improvements
- Social opportunities
- Physical comfort

Potential issues and considerations

- Build cost
- Impact on layouts
- Design programme / budget

Another strategy that we know can make people more active and increase social interaction is the creation of amenity-rich neighbourhoods with high-quality, active facades – any area of building frontage that has been 'activated' through ground-floor occupation by retail, hospitality, workspace or residential uses.

Research shows that if an area has a higher number of amenities, residents are more likely to feel a strong sense of community, with one study showing that 45% of people in high-amenity neighbourhoods rate their community as an excellent place to live, compared to just 26% when amenities were more scarce.[63] However, providing these is only part of the solution, they must also contribute positively to their townscape and create richer, better quality streets.

Experts have discovered that the design of building facades has a strong effect on people, with visually interesting elevations affecting us far more positively than simple, monotonous ones.[64] Test subjects repeatedly spend longer in front of the active facades of restaurants or shops, while they speed up to 'escape' dead zones.[65] Readings from electronic devices and reaction surveys even show that mood and arousal states drop in these areas, giving us a clear indication that blank frontages have a negative impact on how people feel. Creating active facades has a further advantage of creating natural surveillance, as occupants look directly out on to the street at eye-level. The benefits of this are two-fold: a greater sense of perceived safety for people using these streets, and an actual deterrent for would-be criminals.

In spite of these benefits, 'dead' stretches of facades are still a feature of many new developments, largely because of the high demands on plant, refuse and parking. Reducing car use and parking demand is one very simple way to address this issue, but the other challenges still remain. Best practice is generally to locate these away from primary routes and frontages where possible, but demands of refuse collection companies in particular can make this problematic. As Edwin Heathcote has said, however, we should 'design cities around people, not dustbins', and such requests should always be questioned if they will have a negative impact on the quality of a place.[66]

Once we have achieved a largely active facade, we can use other design tools to enhance them further. One such approach is through the integration of colonnades – recessed elements along a building's frontage, creating a shaded area. These have been a feature of architecture since ancient times and can be found in almost all periods of history, yet are sometimes questioned by modern developers due to a loss of valuable floor area.

Nevertheless, they offer a number of wellbeing and comfort benefits, particularly protection from the sun, rain and wind, making it easier and more pleasant for people to walk around urban areas in all weather conditions. A study by Israel's Ministry of Housing discovered that when people know there will be shade on their route, they are more likely to walk or cycle, and less likely to drive, demonstrating their power to make cities healthier, more active places.[67]

With today's towns and cities used by more people than ever before, it is hard to find justification for low-quality streetscapes and frontages. With data showing that we see up to seven times as much activity in front of active facades, they clearly add financial as well as social value, creating a robust case for better ground-floor elevations.[68]

Design tips

1. Maximise active frontages by pushing secondary uses like refuse storage, plant and parking to the rear of buildings where possible.
2. Where true active frontages are difficult to achieve, find other ways to enrich the street scene, through features such as doorways, architectural detailing, art or colour.
3. Consider strategies like colonnades to make street frontages even more pleasant and comfortable regardless of weather conditions.

Community sports facilities and outdoor exercise equipment

> 'Research demonstrates that exercise may be the most reliable happiness booster of all activities.' – SONJA LYUBOMIRSKY, *THE MYTHS OF HAPPINESS*

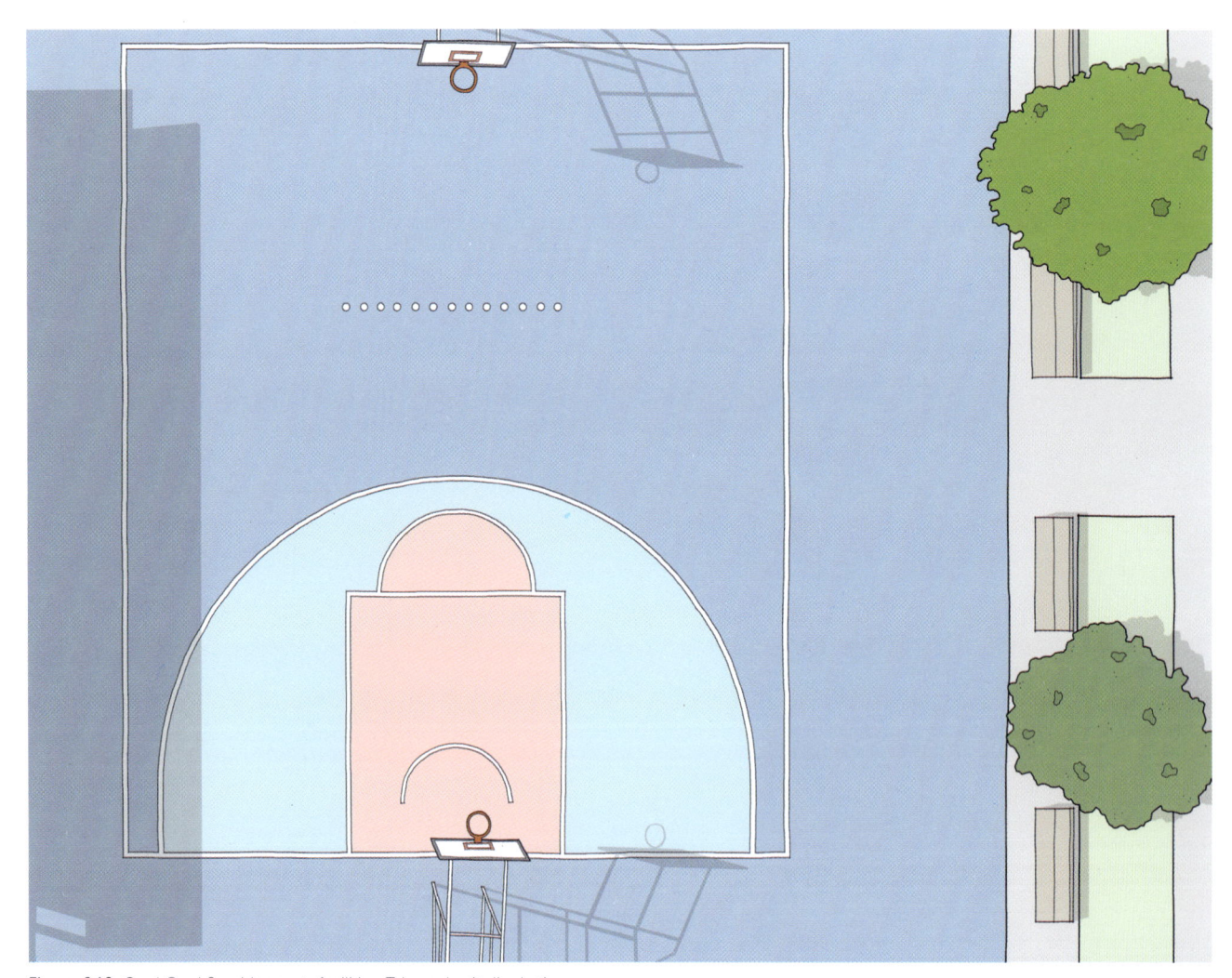

Figure 6.12: Cool Cool Seaside sports facilities, Taiwan, by Atelier Let's

Potential mental wellbeing benefits

- Increased activity
- Physical health improvements
- Social opportunities
- Identity / self-worth
- Feel-good chemical release

Potential issues and considerations

- Space requirements
- Maintenance
- Consultation required

Sport, it seems, is almost as old as mankind itself, with depictions of sprinting, wrestling and swimming found in ancient cave paintings around the world, with team sports such as the Mayan ball game 'pitz' appearing around 3,000 years ago. Today, sport in some form is played in every corner of the globe, and there are believed to be as many as 8,000 different indigenous varieties in existence. One thing seems certain: humans have an innate desire to compete, and we find genuine pleasure in physical challenges and games.

It is therefore important to provide people with the facilities, equipment and space they need to take part in exercise and sport. This can range from a small yard with a few pieces of outdoor gym equipment to a full-sized football pitch or athletics track. A simple example of the former is EVA Studio's Tapis Rouge in Haiti – a small public space incorporating outdoor cardiovascular equipment.[69] The project was funded by the Red Cross in the wake of Haiti's 2010 earthquake to give the community a way to exercise, and it incorporates solar power for night-time lighting. A well provides clean drinking water, which is sold at a low cost, with the money used to fund the maintenance of the project. Interventions like this demonstrate that it is possible to provide place for exercise and play for all, at a minimal cost.

Many companies, such as The Great Outdoor Gym Company, have now started to integrate eco-solutions into outdoor gym equipment, including machines that generate electricity as they are used. Such strategies can be powerful ways to encourage and motivate participation while also creating a sense of altruism and helping to alleviate environmental worries.

Team sports offer potentially even larger benefits to mental wellbeing than exercising alone, with studies showing significant positive impacts to those who exercise in a group. One such study of students aged 16 to 24 showed that over a six-month period those who did group physical activity had better mental health than those who exercised alone, also finding that they felt more connected to people around them.[70] Being part of a team has also been shown to increase motivation and enjoyment of challenges, meaning that we are more likely to stick to exercise as part of a group.[71]

After a decline in UK sporting facilities in the early 2000s, numbers are now generally on the increase, which is largely assumed to be a result of increased awareness around the benefits of sport and exercise, and perhaps a consequence of the success of the 2012 London Olympics.[72] While this is positive, it is important that new facilities continue to emerge to meet this growing demand, particularly as just 21% of children now play outdoors compared to 71% in 1985.[73]

Sport England's 'Active Design' guidance highlights the essential role that open spaces play in supporting informal activity, while also setting out how to create more formal 'sporting hubs'.[74] The document recommends co-location of sporting and recreation facilities so that management can be shared and accessibility improved. It is also recommended that such facilities are located at prominent positions within communities to promote their use and allow them to play a role in local social life.

When designing such facilities, we can also bring in lessons from elsewhere in this book to create high-quality places that are enjoyable to use. This might include elements such as natural materials, a use of colour or art, or places such as a clubhouse or cafe to create opportunities for social interaction before and after participation.

Design tips

1. Provide opportunities for individual and team activities when considering sports or exercise facilities.
2. Locate these in a prominent location to maximise exposure and encourage use.
3. Make these visually or socially appealing by integrating other strategies from this toolkit.

CHAPTER 7
Social interaction, community and sense of place

> 'People ignore design that ignores people.'
> – FRANK CHIMERO, DESIGNER

Figure 7.0: Marmalade Lane co-housing community space, Cambridge, UK, by Mole Architects with TOWN and Trivselhus

While social behaviour is found among most animal species, in humans it plays a particularly important role. In primates, social network size is positively correlated to prefrontal cortex dimensions, leading some experts to believe that our large brains were less important in terms of raw thinking power, but instead allowed us to thrive due to the formation of bigger and more complex social groups.[1]

Living in large groups or 'communities' offers any species a number of advantages.[2] It makes it easier to spot predators or rival groups and gives you better odds of beating them in a fight. It also gives you a better chance of finding or hunting down food. In a larger community, you also have a greater chance of successfully reproducing and rearing the young.

Humans possess one trait that is not found in other animals, however, which enhances all these factors manyfold: complex communication. According to Yuval Noah Harari, author of *Sapiens: A Brief History of Humankind*, the development of nuanced language is one of the key factors in our domination as a species.[3] As a result, scientists have recently discovered that we have evolved to crave human contact much like we crave food.[4]

It may come as little surprise therefore that social interaction and community play an important role in our wellbeing. What has surprised experts in recent years is just how much of an impact a lack of interpersonal interaction can have on our health. Loneliness has been shown to increase the risk of early mortality by 26%, which jumps to 32% for those living alone[5] – roughly equating to the effects of obesity or smoking.[6] This is because isolation affects both our bodies and minds, increasing the chances of coronary heart disease, high blood pressure and stroke, as well as making people more prone to depression, cognitive decline and dementia.

The good news is that the importance of this issue has now been recognised and changes are being made throughout society to combat loneliness. Groups such as the Loneliness Lab have been set up in recent years with the goal of 'tackling loneliness through urban design, placemaking and the built environment'.[7]

The value of such strategies cannot be overstated. In its analysis of the 2016 'World Happiness Report', the What Works Centre for Wellbeing ranked 'social support' as the most important factor in determining where countries and regions were placed, suggesting that improvements in community and social aspects of design could make the most significant difference.[8] This is reflected in markets, too, with a recent survey finding that over two-thirds of people feel the local community is a key factor in choosing where to live.[9]

In spite of this knowledge, and the excellent work by groups such as the Loneliness Lab, modern buildings and cities face numerous challenges in trying to promote social interaction and build communities. Firstly, we now spend more time indoors than ever before – around 22 hours a day – which appears to largely be a result of increasing technology use and work commitments.[10] The first goal of designers must therefore be to find ways to nudge people outdoors or into environments with increased chances of social interaction.

The second challenge the industry faces is a seemingly endless march towards the elimination of any level of risk of danger in society. A good example of this is how challenging it now is to use some healthy (and sustainable) materials like timber in many building types, for fear they should spontaneously combust – despite the fact that we are far more likely to die or have our quality of life impacted as a result of health issues than from a fire.

This has also resulted in growing separation within places and communities. Strategies such as 'Secured by Design' are now mandatory on many UK planning proposals and effectively give the police power over how many aspects of how a scheme is designed.[11] As a result, recommendations are often made for communities to be 'gated off' or for fob systems to be introduced in apartment buildings, which make it challenging for people to even visit their neighbours on the floor above. There is a genuine danger, therefore, that this intense focus on safety is coming at a cost to social interaction and community, which, given the health impacts associated with these issues, may be causing more problems than they are solving.

It is not simply that loneliness is bad for us – doing things for other people has been shown to improve mental health and even promote physiological changes in the brain linked with happiness.[12] Designers must therefore seek to create places which find a balance between safety and sociability, encouraging people to expand their network of friends and engage with community life on a regular basis.

Cluster homes

> 'We create our buildings and then they create us. Likewise, we construct our circle of friends and our communities and then they construct us.'
> – FRANK LLOYD WRIGHT, ARCHITECT

Figure 7.1: 3 Generation House, Amsterdam, the Netherlands, by BETA Office for Architecture and the City

Potential mental wellbeing benefits

- Social opportunities
- Connections to family
- Greater adaptability
- Identity / self-worth
- Greater equity

Potential issues and considerations

- Privacy
- Autonomy reduction

It is easy to think of the current western model of living in individual households as the natural or normal way for people to live. In reality, it has been a relatively recent development. Many mammal species from baboons to elephants live in packs, and historically humans were no different, taking advantage of the abundant benefits of living in a large group. It was not until as late as the thirteenth century in Britain that young couples were expected to move out and establish their own household, and in many examples (particularly the landed gentry), extended families would still live in one large house together. While this may seem strange, in many parts of the world today this is nothing out of the ordinary.[13]

In theory, there are many benefits to the traditional 'community' model of living, provided good levels of privacy can be achieved when desirable. Such models can be highly effective in combating loneliness, as it is far less likely that any member of the household will be left alone for extended periods of time. Residents also enjoy a greatly expanded support network, which research has shown is an important factor in good mental health, particularly for key groups such as the elderly, the unwell and students.[14] Shared space also means shared amenities, which can be of much higher quality when the costs are distributed amongst a larger group.

At its extreme, this model takes the form of living in a commune, but there are also strategies that we can use to align community living or working more closely to our modern lives. A good example of this is student co-housing, which can take a number of forms, some more successful than others. In *Happy City*, Charles Montgomery compares the responses of students who live in a 'corridor block' (double bedrooms along a single long corridor with one shared bathroom and lounge) versus those who lived in clustered 'suites' (two or three bedrooms gathered around a lounge with a small bathroom).[15] The students in the corridor design felt far more stressed as the corridor was exposing and gave little choice about who they bumped into, and friendships were far more likely in the 'cluster' design.

The important factors in this experiment were all psychological concepts – control, exposure and privacy – and are lessons we can take beyond the model of student housing or similar typologies such as co-living. The Dutch Practice, BETA, has designed what it calls the '3 generation house', which as the name suggests provides accommodation for children, their parents and their grandparents.[16] To ensure retention of privacy and control, however, the house has been split into five floors, with only the middle floor as a designated shared space. This also makes the home highly adaptable if any part of the family decides it need more or less space.

The benefits of such a way of living are clear, and while some may baulk at the idea of anything other than the standard nuclear family model, built examples like these demonstrate that it can be achieved successfully and easily. With the challenges of an ageing population ahead of us, it may be that we need to rethink our approach to living in groups or clusters – the key is that we do it well and offer housing that respects the importance of control and privacy while maximising the benefits of community.

Design tips

1. When designing shared housing, privacy and autonomy are of paramount importance. Consider ways to design these in, to help residents achieve a balance of community and independence.

2. Circulation and semi-shared spaces are key to these issues – avoid designing areas such as long corridors where people have little control over who they bump into, as this can result in a feeling of exposure.

3. Explore a range of family models and design homes that can flex as the needs of their inhabitants might change.

(Semi-) open-plan living and working areas

'How anyone imagined that open plan offices would be more efficient is beyond me.'
— PETER GRAINGER, AUTHOR

Figure 7.2: The Italian Building co-living, London, UK, by Mason & Fifth

Potential mental wellbeing benefits

- Social opportunities
- Connections to family
- Increased autonomy
- Learning opportunities
- Increased productivity

Potential issues and considerations

- Comfort issues
- Privacy
- Autonomy reduction
- Productivity reduction

On the surface, open-plan spaces seem like an easy win – we get an increased sense of space and light, places become more adaptable and perhaps most importantly these spaces seem likely to encourage sociability. It is not surprising, therefore, that many estate agents will tell you that 'going open plan' can add value to your home.[17]

Like most things, the situation is slightly more complex in reality, particularly when we look at the places in which people work. As noted in Chapter 2, noise is one of the biggest workplace distractions and is an issue exacerbated by open-plan layouts. These distractions can have a significant impact on our productivity and happiness in the workplace, with one University of California study finding that a typical office worker gets only 11 minutes between each interruption, and for each distraction it takes around 25 minutes to return to full concentration on the original task – unless of course we get distracted again.[18]

We have also seen that labelling open-plan workspaces as 'more sociable' is a misnomer, as in reality they can often decrease face-to-face interaction, with people feeling overexposed in a large open space where everybody can hear what you say.[19] This highlights the other big flaw in the open-plan approach: an almost total lack of privacy.

As a result of these factors, the workplace design industry is now seeing a shift towards flexible work spaces, where people have a choice between working in busier open-plan areas or quieter spaces such as booths or pods. It is important to remember that some people are naturally more extroverted than others, and as Clare Bailey, Director of Savills Commercial Research team explains:

'Some people need noise and chatter to work, and some people need quiet.'[20] It is important that the design of workspaces accommodates both – in what we could perhaps call 'semi open plan'.

In the home these issues are less of a problem generally. We tend to require less privacy around our family and friends than strangers, and we as a rule we don't need quite as high concentration levels at home as we do at work, meaning distractions are slightly less of an issue.

As a result, as well as private residences opening up their ground floors, large open-plan communal spaces are becoming very popular in co-living, build-to-rent and student housing. A good example of this is Mason & Fifth's Italian Building co-living scheme on the adjacent page, which combines cooking, dining, working and living areas into a social hub. Even in this space, however, an occasional need to subdivide spaces was recognised, which the interior designers addressed through the introduction of curtains which could be drawn between spaces to create an extra level of privacy.

Fundamentally, the thinking and intent behind open-plan spaces are honourable: to create more social spaces that promote collaboration or better relationships with those around us. In reality, however, this is tricky to achieve and takes a little more nuance than simply removing dividing walls to create one large space. Taking a more subtle 'semi open-plan' approach can be more successful, particularly when combined with other features in this book such as Flexible Separating Devices (see Chapter 3), Sound Masking Systems (see Chapter 2) or Social Furniture (later in this chapter).

Design tips

1. When contemplating an open-plan design, consider the potential problems as well as the advantages. These may include issues such as sound, privacy or smells.

2. Explore strategies to address these issues through design, rather than through operations or management solutions post-completion.

3. Often some level of separation or partition can be helpful. These may be low level or moveable (see Flexible Separating Devices [Chapter 3] for design ideas on this approach).

4. Ideally, some level of choice and flexibility will be provided in both work and living spaces, giving people greater control over where they spend their time.

Indoor community spaces and spaces for making

'Alone, we can do so little; together, we can do so much.'
– HELEN KELLER, AUTHOR AND DISABILITY RIGHTS ADVOCATE

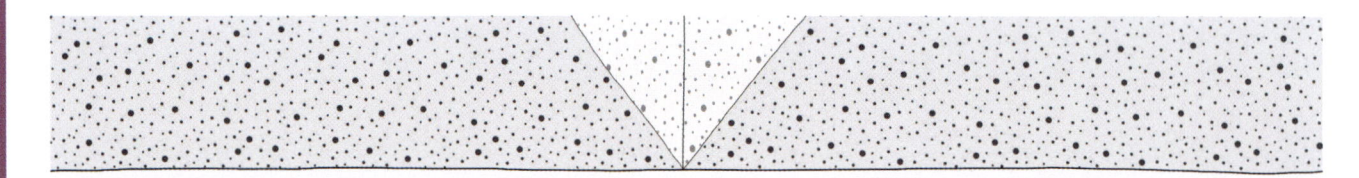

Figure 7.3: Storey's Field Centre, Cambridge, UK, by MUMA Architects

Potential mental wellbeing benefits
- Social opportunities
- Psychological response
- Identity / self-worth
- Greater equity

Potential issues and considerations
- Operational cost
- Maintenance
- Space requirements

Throughout history, societies have had community spaces at the heart of their settlements, from the Viking longhouse to the Anglo-Saxon great hall. In today's society these take a number of forms, be they civic buildings, religious spaces like churches or mosques, or looser community spaces such as village halls or day centres.

One thing is certain: such spaces add value to a community, although as one report explained, this value 'may not always be obvious to outsider or policy-makers'.[21] As such, providing community spaces is not top of every developer's priority list, despite evidence suggesting that, in fact, these could be some of the most important parts of any new scheme. Unfortunately, these are often seen as spaces that are 'given away' for a relatively low value – but again this raises the question of what 'value' means, and whether it's appropriate to think of it simply as a number in a spreadsheet.

In his book *Happiness: Lessons from a New Science*, Richard Layard explores the role that community plays in our mental wellbeing.[22] His conclusions are clear-cut: 'trust and membership in voluntary associations contribute greatly to happiness'. And one of his key recommendations for a happier society is to 'subsidise activities that promote community life'.

Layard's findings are supported by research into churchgoers. Numerous studies show that participating in a religious organisation is associated with greater levels of happiness, although this may be more to do with the social ties this creates than a belief in God.[23] Researchers from the University of Wisconsin–Madison discovered that 33% of people who reported having close friends at church were 'extremely satisfied' with their lives, while only 19% of those who attended church but had no close social connections there reported the same levels of satisfaction. The value in such spaces, it seems, is less about what we do there and more about who we meet and the bonds we form.

Hence, what is perhaps most important is creating adaptable community spaces that can be used for a range of activities from worship to birthday parties or life-drawing classes. Artist Theaster Gates discovered the power of such spaces when he started transforming abandoned buildings in his south Chicago district into community hubs to connect and inspire people who live there, reviving the neighbourhood in the process.[24] Gates is an ardent believer that culture can be a catalyst for social transformation in any city and is a tool to make 'places that are dying beautiful'.

There is evidence that providing spaces for arts and crafts can make people happier too. Charities such as Arts and Minds use art workshops for people experiencing common mental health problems, with a significant impact.[25] An evaluation of the programme discovered that participants had more than a 70% decrease in feelings of anxiety and depression, with 76% saying their wellbeing had increased and 69% feeling more socially included. Creative activities can clearly have a positive impact on people's mental wellbeing, particularly, it seems, when done in a group setting.

It is important therefore that neither developers nor policymakers see community spaces as a 'nice to have' or an add-on bonus use at the end of a project. Instead, they should be a starting point for masterplans: a hub around which all else is built. Research shows they are a powerful tool to generate social ties, with a greater sense of community and the happiness benefits associated with these – and it is vital that we understand their true long-term value.

Design tips

1. Design community spaces that are adaptable and suited to a range of uses. This means flexible spaces and generous storage to allow for numerous community groups to keep equipment on site.
2. Place such spaces at the heart of communities, where they will be clearly visible to encourage use and social interaction. This will also make them easier to access by all.
3. Engage with the local community from an early stage to understand their needs and desires for such a space. Every community is different and their input will likely prove invaluable in creating a strong narrative for the space.

Chance interaction spaces and chatting nooks

> '... chance encounters play a prominent role in shaping the course of human lives.'
> – ALBERT BANDURA, FORMER PRESIDENT OF THE AMERICAN PSYCHOLOGICAL ASSOCIATION

Figure 7.4: Hortsley later-living homes, Seaford, East Sussex, UK, by RCKa and Pegasus

Potential mental wellbeing benefits

- Social opportunities
- Moments of joy / awe
- Engagement with emotions
- Physical comfort

Potential issues and considerations

- Space requirements
- Impact on layouts

In many buildings today, common parts are reduced to their simplest form – a way to get from A to B in an efficient way. We have already touched upon ways to bring joy to these spaces, but it's possible to elevate these even further by creating opportunities for them to become social spaces too. Within the Loneliness Lab's 'Using Design to Connect Us' report, a number of design features are suggested to promote connections between a building's occupants, with many of these centred around increasing the opportunity for 'chance encounters'.[26]

Using such design features is important across all use types, as it is not simply people sitting at home alone who are lonely. According to the report, three in five people feel lonely at work, and this problem costs UK employers £2.5 billion every year. This makes a strong case for employers to create workplaces that allow and encourage social interaction, even if there is a slight increase in build or management cost.

This case is further strengthened by research which demonstrates that for most people talking to a stranger can improve our mood and create a better sense of belonging to a community, boosting feelings of happiness and human connection.[27] Unfortunately, many people are nervous about talking to people they don't know, which has been found to be mostly down to fear that the other person won't enjoy the experience – but the good news is that when we *do* have such interactions, they tend to be more enjoyable than people predict.

Designers of all places therefore need to have a set of tools at their disposal to encourage people to stop, to engage, to meet neighbours and most importantly to encourage conversation. A key question within the RIBA's Social Value Toolkit is 'Does your neighbourhood give you opportunities to stop and communicate with people regularly?', as this was felt to be a key indicator of social value within a development.[28]

As the Loneliness Lab has highlighted, there are many ways in which this can be achieved through the design of buildings. It can start with elements as simple as the corridors, which need only be made a little wider to allow for a bench or have seating nooks built into the walls to encourage people to stop and chat for a little longer. Research has shown that standing meetings are on average 34% shorter than seated ones, which might be useful in the workplace but suggests that if we want people to chat for longer, we should provide the opportunity for them to sit.[29]

While much of modern workplace design is about making people's lives easier by adding more lift cores or additional tea points and kitchens, there is also an argument that these can result in segregated 'clusters' of people, reducing who you interact with at work to those in the immediate vicinity. It may, therefore, be worth providing one or two higher quality scenarios that promote conversation rather than numerous less engaging ones.

Finally, we can encourage chance interactions and conversations in the public realm, be this in parks and streets or in semi-public spaces like front gardens and doorways. The Loneliness Lab recommends pairing front doorways or creating cul-de-sacs to encourage more intimate clusters of neighbours to gather. They also point to the increased likelihood of social interaction in communal gardens or traffic-free streets, with projects such as Marmalade Lane (see Figure 7.0) offering excellent examples of both.

Design tips

1. At an early design stage, review common parts of a building and explore ways in which chance interactions or conversations could be encouraged through design 'nudges'.
2. While elements like wider corridors may increase build cost or reduce saleable area, by understanding the value they add we can properly communicate their importance to clients.
3. Find ways to provide privacy and comfort in these chatting spaces through strategies such as warm lighting, soundproofing strategies, natural materials and comfortable seating that encourages people to stay.

Parenting rooms and crèches

> 'Inclusion is not a matter of political correctness. It is the key to growth.'
> — JESSE JACKSON, POLITICIAN AND CIVIL RIGHTS ACTIVIST

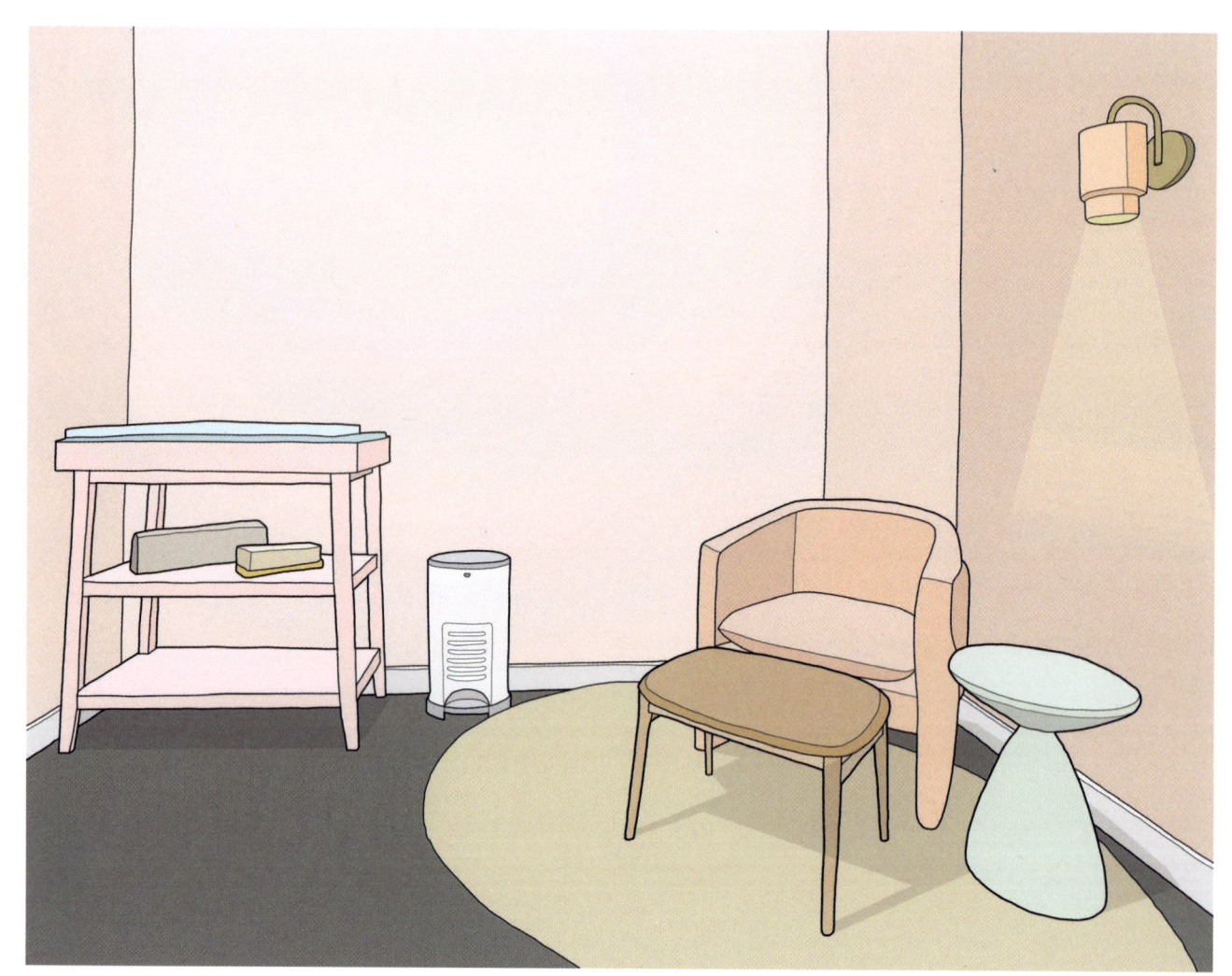

Figure 7.5: 'Mother's room', DUMBO office buildings, Brooklyn, New York City, USA, by The Wing internal design team

Potential mental wellbeing benefits

- Greater equity
- Improved liveability
- Increased productivity
- Social opportunities
- Increased autonomy

Potential issues and considerations

- Operational cost
- Space requirements

The majority of people will, at some point in their lives be a parent to a young child (approximately 81% in the UK[30]). Yet, in spite of this, many buildings are not designed with their needs in mind. While there have been great strides forward in inclusivity and design for equality in recent years, this is one area where much of the design world is lagging behind. The consequences of not supporting new parents are significant: making it more difficult for them to return to work after maternity or paternity leave at what is already a challenging time, affecting workplace happiness and unfortunately having a long-term impact on the trajectory of many careers.

While many parts of the world now thankfully require a space to be made available to new, lactating mothers, these tend not to be designed specifically for this purpose and are often ill-suited to the needs of those who use them. While it might seem like cost saving not to provide such spaces, this turns out to be a false economy, as research shows that employers actually benefit from their provision – allowing employees to breastfeed reduces absenteeism rates, reduces staff turnover and improves staff productivity and loyalty.[31]

The WELL Building Standard recommends providing designated lactation or parenting rooms, which it suggests contain a work surface, a comfortable chair, electrical outlets, a sink with paper towel dispenser and soap, as well as designated storage space for pumping supplies and access to a refrigerator. They should also be lockable to allow for adequate privacy and ideally give parents control over factors such as ambient lighting, thermal comfort and sound. It is also important that these design features are supported by compassionate employment policies, for example paid break times for breastfeeding or pumping.

If designed well, these spaces can also double up as an opportunity for parents of young children to have a moment of comfort and calm, to pause or to have a mindful moment in what is generally a fairly stressful time in people's lives. To support them in this, other lessons from this book could be integrated, from the inclusion of natural materials to the use of calming water features.

Introducing amenities such as crèches can also be a powerful tool in supporting new parents, and again can have significant benefits for employers. Studies have found that nearly half of working parents miss an average of eight days of work each year because of childcare breakdowns, which could be dramatically reduced by having an on-site facility.[32] With UK parents now paying an average of over £7,000 per year for a part-time nursery place, this can also form an incredibly appealing part of any staff benefits package, again increasing loyalty and helping to attract the best staff.[33] Clothing business Patagonia, which is strongly in favour of on-site childcare, has reported that staff turnover rate for parents who use their on-site crèche is 25% lower than other employees.[34]

From the parents' perspective, an on-site crèche offers greater peace of mind, makes the daily schedule easier, and allows parents to return to work sooner should they wish, promoting better gender equality. Ultimately, offering amenities and facilities for new parents is a win-win situation, where both employers and employees benefit, and not designing-in such facilities suggests a short-term approach. With 84% of parents believing that such amenities would make them less stressed and more productive, the real question is whether businesses can afford *not* to provide them.[35]

Design tips

1. Seek to provide a designated parenting room in all workplaces.

2. These should offer privacy and be a calming space. They should also include all the facilities listed above plus any project-specific needs that may need to be catered for.

3. Other facilities, like crèches, can also be a valuable addition to projects and often result in a positive return on investment.

Public squares, marketplaces and village greens

> 'I miss the village green,/ The church, the clock, the steeple./ I miss the morning dew, fresh air and Sunday school.'
> – 'VILLAGE GREEN' BY THE KINKS, LYRICS BY RAYMOND DOUGLAS DAVIES

Figure 7.6: Trinity Square, Hull, UK, by re-form

Potential mental wellbeing benefits

- Social opportunities
- Economic benefits
- Legibility benefits
- Historic / cultural references
- Nature interaction

Potential issues and considerations

- Space requirements
- Maintenance
- Use by all
- Consultation required
- Protection from elements

The earliest public squares tended to be formed where important trade routes met or crossed, with buildings often forming around them to create a marketplace or meeting space.[36] In ancient Greece such spaces were known as *agorae*, while the Romans knew them as forums, and these were a place for politics, trading and social activities. Similar spaces may also have formed as places to safely gather cattle, and these shared grazing areas sometimes evolved into what we might know today as the village green.[37]

Today, the role of such spaces has not changed dramatically from the Greek *agorae*; they remain a place for people to meet, to eat and drink, to shop or to exchange ideas. As the Joseph Rowntree Foundation's 'Social Value of Public Spaces' report puts it: 'they play a vital role in the social and economic life of communities'.

The evidence supports this claim, with research showing that people who live in amenity-dense neighbourhoods are more likely to feel a sense of community and community satisfaction[38] – 45% of those who live in high-amenity neighbourhoods rate their community as an excellent place to live, compared to just 26% of those who live in low-amenity neighbourhoods. Public spaces and town squares can be amenity-rich both around the periphery and within the space itself, particularly if they are designed to be adaptable for use by numerous groups.

Such spaces also frequently become a landmark feature of a village, town or city, improving legibility and contributing to what architect Kevin Lynch called 'scaling' – being a key point or node along a journey which gives people a sense of how far they are along it, especially if used in conjunction with a landmark building.[39] They present an opportunity to contribute to a community's sense of identity, too, and can be an excellent way to celebrate local culture and the history of a place. They therefore add value in an enormous number of ways, creating wealth both literal and less tangible.

There are many successful public squares around the world, in all shapes and sizes, so to some extent what works is highly context-dependent. However, there are some key rules that can be applied to give a new space the best chance of success. In 1889, Camillo Sitte set out his rules for a visually ideal public space, namely: a closed and protected space; a centre that is kept free; monuments on its perimeter; elements of surprise; attractive architectural facades; and aesthetic pavements.

These rules stand firm today, and have been supplemented and supported by numerous other documents, such as the UK's 'National Design Guide', which offers excellent advice on the design of public spaces.[40] It states that well-designed spaces should: support a wide variety of activities; encourage social interaction; create a hierarchy of scale; feel safe, secure and attractive; and have trees and other planting for aesthetic and practical reasons such as shading.

Ultimately, a great architect or urban designer must look at a location and provide a space that is of the correct scale and language for its context. These could be as different in character as the sprawling open marketplace of Marrakesh's Jemaa el-Fnaa and the gentle village greens of Yorkshire, England – but by applying some of the key principles set out above, it is possible to design new public spaces that will offer the most to the wellbeing of residents and visitors alike.

Design tips

1. Good public spaces have a number of key characteristics that should be considered in their design, including enclosure, activity, social elements, safety, attractiveness, and connection to location and history.

2. Scale can vary depending on location and use, but at any scale a space should be modelled and tested to ensure it does not feel overwhelmingly large or claustrophobic. The size of surrounding buildings will also play a significant role in how large or small a space feels.

3. Remember other design tools from this book, particularly the integration of nature and daylight (see Chapter 1).

Places for play for all

❝ Children's playthings are not sports and should be deemed their most serious actions.'
— MICHEL DE MONTAIGNE, PHILOSOPHER

Figure 7.7: Pyramids Playground, Moscow, Russia, by AFA Group

Potential mental wellbeing benefits

- Social opportunities
- Increased activity
- Physical health improvements
- Moments of joy / awe
- Learning opportunities

Potential issues and considerations

- Use by all
- Maintenance
- Safety
- Protection from elements

Play is an essential part of life for animals of all kinds.[41] From ravens 'snowboarding' down Alaskan roofs to dogs play-fighting, scientists have observed play across an enormous range of animal species. Sometimes this is a means of building bonds, while at other times it is a way of practising skills that might be needed in a future survival situation, but occasionally scientists can find 'no obvious utilitarian function' for such play, leading to the conclusion that perhaps these animals are simply doing it because it makes them feel good.

It is of enormous importance to humans too, and like other animals it can serve a wide range of purposes. While children playing may simply seem like a means of having fun, research has shown it is vital to healthy brain development, as it is through play that we first engage and interact with the world around us.[42] It also has a key role in helping us to develop the social skills, confidence and resilience that we will need in later life.

Play is also so important in helping children to express emotions and deal with problems, that 'play therapy' has become one of the primary methods of helping young children with difficult emotional situations, supporting the mental wellbeing of the most vulnerable. And last, but certainly not least, play makes us feel good. According to research, playfulness, humour and a fun-loving attitude are some of the key factors we look for in a partner, and when asked to reflect on how play serves us in relationships the top answer is simple: it makes us feel good.[43]

In spite of this, creating designated places for play seems to be a relatively recent innovation, with the world's first 'formal' playground reportedly built in Manchester, England in 1859.[44] Fortunately, today the inclusion of play space in new developments is mandatory in many parts of the world, although even in the UK this can vary from one area to another.

Like all features in this book, it is vital that we provide spaces for play for people of all backgrounds, abilities and ages. Playground provider HAGS has a number of excellent resources on designing inclusive play areas based around five key principles: elements to address all of our senses; generous accessible spaces; objects and spaces that offer a range of challenges; opportunities for calm; and social environments.[45]

By integrating all of these strategies, it is possible to create play areas that are engaging for children and parents of all ages and needs.

It is also important to consider the elements when designing places for play, be this sun, rain, wind or snow. This is another example of where a small investment can add substantial value to a space. In a school in Israel, for example, $80,000 was invested in shading a 200m^2 outdoor area.[46] As a result, children at the school became around 30% more physically active and showed an improvement in their health worth approximately $25 a year for each of the 1,000 students. As a result, the return on the wellbeing investment was approximately three years.

Finally, it is also important to consider play for adults, from a chess room to a climbing centre. There are opportunities to overlap these with other tools from this book such as 'Parks, large and small (Chapter 4)' or 'Indoor community spaces and spaces for making' (earlier in this chapter). What is important is that we remember the important role that play can have in supporting all of our mental wellbeing.

Design tips

1. Create places for play in every project, be they large or small.

2. Design play spaces that are accessible and interesting to all, regardless of age or ability.

3. Create play areas that people can use in all weathers and conditions, and communicate the potential added value of additional spend on protection from the elements.

Poetry and language

> 'Poetry lifts the veil from the hidden beauty of the world, and makes familiar objects be as if they were not familiar.' – PERCY BYSSHE SHELLEY, POET

Figure 7.8: Wales Millennium Centre, Cardiff, UK, by Jonathan Adams

Potential mental wellbeing benefits
- Historic / cultural references
- Identity / self-worth
- Moments of joy / awe
- Engagement with emotions
- Psychological response

Potential issues and considerations
- Consultation recommended
- Specialist input useful

The earliest forms of writing are believed to have appeared almost 5,550 years ago in Mesopotamia.[47] These took the form of early pictorial signs used initially for counting and recording transactions, which gradually evolved into a system of characters that represented the Sumerian spoken at the time. Since then, writing has played a vital role in our development as a species, allowing us to communicate across time and space, name and record objects and places, and later express complex emotions.[48]

Remarkably, language and how we use it can have an enormous impact on how we behave. Economist Keith Chen discovered in 2012 that people who speak a language without a strong future tense (such as German or Finnish) seem to be more considerate about the future.[49] They are 30% more likely to save money, 24% less likely to smoke and 29% more likely to exercise than those in countries with a 'strong' future tense language. We can also observe that people whose languages have no word for left or right navigate by north, south, east and west instead, and as a result have improved geographical awareness, while those whose languages do not separate orange and yellow actually find it harder to distinguish the two colours.

Language can also have an impact on how we feel, as it provides us with words for the abstract concepts we know as emotions, helping us to make meaning of them.[50] Interestingly, different parts of the world have words for emotions we may not even have considered, such as the Korean word '*han*', meaning to feel simultaneously sad and hopeful.[51]

We have all experienced first hand the emotional power that words can have on us, maybe in the form of a poem, song or book. This ability to share and convey emotions or to transport us to another place or time is perhaps one of language's greatest powers, and as a result writing or reading poetry or stories is now a common form of therapeutic therapy (sometimes known as bibliotherapy).[52] fMRI studies have shown that when people read about an experience, the same parts of their brain display stimulation, as if they were experiencing the emotions themselves, suggesting that reading can indeed have an impact on our mood.[53]

Language doesn't simply have to be confined to books, however. By integrating it into interior design or architecture, it is possible for it to be seen by many more people on a daily basis, and it can even create a small moment of joy for those who read it, lighting up those neurological regions associated with happiness and positivity. Using words and language can also be a tool to enhance a building or a community's connection to their history and place. They can unite us by reminding us of our shared past, our similarities and of the story of an area, making our neighbourhoods culturally richer and enhancing our daily lives.

A number of built projects have explored this concept, such as 'Wall Poems' in the Dutch city of Leiden, in which over 110 poems in various languages were hand-painted on the exteriors of buildings. The poems have been well received by residents and visitors, and as a result wall poems have now been painted in several other Dutch cities, as well as in Paris, Berlin and Sofia.[54] There is even a website helping people to discover the poems and suggesting walking or cycling routes connecting them, nudging people to engage both body and mind.

Design tips

1. At an early stage in a project, explore the opportunities the introduction of language or poetry could play. It may end up being a small moment of joy but could even become a key driver or selling point of the building.
2. Consider working with local communities, poets or authors to ensure any writing has a genuine connection to a place and its history.
3. Explore the possibility of working with other teams or buildings to create a connected network of written artworks, encouraging urban exploration and exercise.

Social furniture

'Good conversation can leave you more exhilarated than alcohol; more refreshed than the theater or a concert. It can bring you entertainment and pleasure; it can help you get ahead, solve problems, spark the imagination of others. It can erase misunderstandings, and bring you closer to those you love.' – DOROTHY SARNOFF, SINGER, ACTOR AND SELF-HELP GURU

Figure 7.9: Parklet, London, UK, by WMB Studio

Potential mental wellbeing benefits

- Social opportunities
- Connections to family
- Increased activity
- Physical comfort

Potential issues and considerations

- Fitout cost
- Design programme / budget
- Use by all

As we have already seen, furniture can serve many positive functions in our daily lives, from making environments more accessible to encouraging interaction with nature or a great view. It also forms the basis of our everyday rituals, whether we are cooking, eating, working or relaxing. It therefore stands to reason that the design and layout of furniture might be able to have an impact on how we behave and even how we feel.

Research shows that furniture can also affect our level of social interaction and has the potential to increase the number of conversations we have or how much we collaborate. Studies into social interaction between care home residents, for example, have shown that furniture angles and separation are significant factors, with extremely low levels of interaction taking place on seating over 2.4m apart, or in back-to-back arrangements.[55] Research also suggests that face-to-face arrangements are selected most for casual conversations, side-by-side for collaborative work, while distant face-to-face can create more competitive situations.[56]

A number of architects and designers are now utilising these strategies in their work to encourage social interaction in a range of scenarios, such as Seray Ozdemir who has created a collection of furniture designed to maximise social exchanges in the common corridors of co-living buildings.[57] These include a ¾ Table which has a quarter cut out to wrap around a 90° corner, with built-in seating below to allow residents to eat or share a coffee together.

We can also use play in furniture design to promote interactions, as with Neulhae Cho's Swingers chairs – public seating which can act almost as a see-saw.[58]

According to the designer, the bend of the bench is intended to move individuals closer to one another, encouraging play and conversation between both friends and strangers in public spaces. We know that play can be a powerful tool in helping overcome awkwardness when people first meet, so introducing ideas of playfulness into the design of furniture may indeed be a prudent strategy when encouraging strangers to connect.

The Social Furniture project by Vienna-based design collective EOOS has taken the concept a step further, designing communal pieces for refugees that are constructed by the end users themselves.[59] Part of a larger project that looks to rehome refugees in disused office buildings, the team created 18 furniture designs, including stools, kitchen shelves, signage and raised-bed garden systems. All the pieces are constructed from three-layer spruce using simple techniques, and by empowering residents to build them themselves, social and community bonds can begin to form amongst the group before the furniture is even in use.

It is also possible to combine this feature with many of the other tools in this book, whether through the use of natural materials or perhaps locating such furniture in semi-shaded spaces to encourage use in a range of weather conditions. As with all tools that look to enhance community, it is vital to consult with end users or stakeholders in the design of such objects to ensure they meet their needs. It is also important to remember, as with many features in this chapter, that people are likely to want furniture that allows for a range of 'sociability' levels, as we don't always want to be sociable and in fact may sometimes prefer furniture that signals to others 'I'd like to be left alone for now.'

Design tips

1. Seek to provide furniture that encourages conversation and collaboration, but also provides some spaces for people to use when they wish to have time alone.

2. Engage with residents, end users or stakeholders to better understand their needs from furniture design.

3. Consider other strategies to promote interaction, such as playfulness or even building or installing pieces of furniture together.

Shared cooking and eating areas

> 'There is something profoundly satisfying about sharing a meal. Eating together, breaking bread together, is one of the oldest and most fundamentally unifying of human experiences.' – BARBARA COLOROSO, AUTHOR AND PARENTING SPECIALIST

Figure 7.10: One Carter Lane offices, London, UK, by Cundall

Potential mental wellbeing benefits

- Social opportunities
- Connections to family
- Physical health improvements
- Improved diet
- Moments of joy / awe

Potential issues and considerations

- Space requirements
- Air quality risks
- Safety (fire)
- Maintenance

Another key tool we might use to promote more cohesive communities and facilitate greater social interaction is the introduction of communal spaces for eating, drinking and cooking. Although a recent piece of research by Oxford University showed that 76% of people think sharing a meal is a good way to bring people closer together, it also found that many of us frequently eat alone.[60]

The average British adult now eats 10 meals out of every 21 on their own each week, largely as a result of being too busy. 69% of people questioned had never shared a meal with neighbours, with nearly a fifth saying that eating an evening meal with others was a 'rare occurrence'.[61]

This may not seem like a big problem, were it not that the same group of researchers also discovered a connection between 'social eating and an individual's happiness, the number of friends they have, their connection to their community, and overall satisfaction with life'. If we can therefore design buildings in such a way that they encourage friends, families or wider communities to cook or eat together, it could have a significant impact on their mental wellbeing.

Sadly, those over the age of 55 are most likely to eat alone, suggesting that in housing designed for older communities the introduction of social cooking and eating spaces could have the largest impact.[62] Studies into older adults have also shown that regularly eating alone can have an impact on dietary choices and create more irregular eating patterns,[63] with ramifications on our physical health and a greater risk of problems like heart disease, stroke and diabetes.[64]

The WELL Building Standard recommends projects provide a dedicated eating space which can accommodate up to 25% of their regular occupants at any given time.[65] It also requires these spaces to be protected from sun, wind and rain, and to provide flexibility by allowing for a variety of seating layouts and group numbers. As a result, many newer buildings are incorporating such spaces from offices such as Cundall's WELL Certified 1 Carter Lane, to numerous co-living and build-to-rent projects pursuing WELL Certification.

While these may sacrifice internal floor space, the social value and sense of community that they add to buildings can be substantial, positively impacting on people's sense of wellbeing, regardless of whether a project is targeting WELL. These spaces needn't be indoors either, with external cooking and eating spaces offering excellent opportunities to make eating more sociable. Further benefits can be enjoyed, such as exposure to daylight and other natural elements, as well as greater opportunities for play.

Unfortunately, this is another area where health and safety may have a negative impact on wellbeing and quality of life, with many buildings being banned from including features such as rooftop barbecues. In such instances, however, it may be possible to provide an internal rooftop amenity space and kitchen that opens out on to a shared external space, providing the best of both worlds, along with protection if the weather takes a turn for the worse.

Any social eating spaces will only be a success, however, if people actually use them, and this relies on enticing, high-quality design. It may therefore be worth bringing in other features from this book to make these spaces feel uplifting and stimulating, whether it is hanging plants, social or adaptable furniture, colour and art for joy, or natural and upcycled materials.

Design tips

1. Across all project types, look to provide spaces where people can sit and eat together, away from screens and in a relaxing setting free from work or other distractions.

2. Target space for at least 25% of overall building users in offices and similar use types, while housing should provide space for all occupants of a dwelling plus additional guests.

3. Ensure required amenities and facilities are also provided, such as storage space, refrigeration, heating devices, utensils and cutlery, and areas for washing up.

Traditional and alternative libraries

> 'Libraries store the energy that fuels the imagination. They open up windows to the world and inspire us to explore and achieve, and contribute to improving our quality of life.'
> – SIDNEY SHELDON, WRITER AND PRODUCER

Figure 7.11: Crystal Palace Library of Things, London, UK

Potential mental wellbeing benefits
- Social opportunities
- Learning opportunities
- Engagement with emotions
- Improved liveability
- Economic benefits

Potential issues and considerations
- Space requirements
- Operational cost
- Maintenance

The library is, by its very nature, a community facility. Libraries were initially created to organise and preserve documents for future generations, but over time evolved into their modern form as a place to borrow books (and in many cases films, movies or software). Traditional libraries such as these certainly add value in both a community and financial sense. Research in Australia has shown that for every dollar invested, $4.30 is generated in benefit through creating more literate, productive and engaged communities.[66]

Modern libraries often provide broad community programmes as well, ranging from poetry slams to manga clubs, coding workshops or conversation cafés to addressing loneliness or mental health issues. This allows them to further tackle social isolation and connect communities more deeply, as well as providing opportunities for making or creativity – meaning a well-run library with a generous set of initiatives has the potential to become the focal point of a neighbourhood.

The idea of a traditional library – as a resource from which to borrow or use things – has now been expanded upon. In recent years, 'Libraries of Things' have emerged as a popular way for people to borrow (or rent at a low cost) useful objects, be they tents, carpet cleaners or pasta makers. These objects tend to be items that local residents may not be able to afford or have space to store.

The financial side seems to add up, with 90% of object borrowers saying they benefit financially from the projects.[67] It also has a perhaps unexpected side-effect, in that people who borrow objects also seem to feel more deeply rooted in their community, with 75% reporting they feel better connected as a result.[68]

The project started small among a group of neighbours but grew to over 1,000 borrowers in the first 18 months. However, its success on a small scale demonstrates that it has the potential to work in one-off projects such as apartment buildings. After all, with 80% of household items used less than once a month, why should a building of 100 apartments need 100 vacuum cleaners?

Another new type of library to emerge in the last few years is the 'Reminiscence Library'.[69] These exist to support people within the community with dementia or memory impairment and consist of a range of materials from throughout the twentieth century. These could include artefacts, books, music, games, flashcards or videos, which are often grouped into themes such as 'seaside' or 'wartime' and can be viewed on site or often borrowed for a few weeks.

The objects are intended to be used in reminiscence therapy – a treatment that helps individuals to remember past events through engaging a range of physical senses. Reminiscence therapy has been shown to reduce the stress and agitation associated with conditions like Alzheimer's,[70] and there is some evidence that it can improve mood, communication, cognition and quality of life for those taking part, although as they are a fairly recent concept further investigation has been recommended.[71]

Perhaps the key benefit of libraries (of any kind) is that they are run by the community for the community. Those involved in running them become naturally embedded in the community and can receive the altruism benefits to mental wellbeing we have already seen, while library users not only have access to an amazing physical resource, they also have the opportunity to meet new people, to take part in events and to generally strengthen their community bonds.

Design tips

1. Explore opportunities to provide library spaces within projects. These can take a number of forms and needn't be a large public space; they could simply be a hard-to-use room turned into a Library of Things, for example.

2. Consider ideas of shared resources more widely in a project. For example, there might be a communal store created for shared gardening tools or a shared cupboard of cleaning equipment.

3. Consider using online tools such as myTurn, which support communities in creating a Library of Things.[72] These platforms can help with tricky issues such as asset tracking and financial aspects of projects.

Equitable and affordable space

> 'Cities have the capability of providing something for everybody, only because, and only when, they are created by everybody.'
> – JANE JACOBS, ARCHITECTURAL AUTHOR AND JOURNALIST

Figure 7.12: New Ground Cohousing, High Barnet, London, UK, by Pollard Thomas Edwards with Hanover Housing Association and the Older Women's Co-housing group

Potential mental wellbeing benefits

- Greater equity
- Social opportunities
- Economic benefits
- Identity / self-worth

Potential issues and considerations

- Build cost
- Maintenance
- Use by all

Despite much progression in recent years, we live in a world where inequality is sadly still prevalent. The same is also unfortunately true of the built environment, particularly in typologies such as housing, where the gap in quality between private and affordable homes can still be significant. This is an issue that the industry still needs to work hard to address, both in terms of the places we are building and the diversity and equality within design teams.

Research shows that in a more equal society we all win, with a correlation existing between equality and happiness. For example, living in a more gender-equal part of the world increases happiness and wellbeing rates for both women and men, regardless of income or class.[73] The same can be seen if we look at income inequality. Data tells us that the higher the share of national income held by the top 1%, the lower the overall wellbeing of the general population.[74]

This tells us that when we work for a fairer society, everybody benefits, and ultimately when we design places that benefit and support everybody, we all benefit too. When seeking to address inequality in the built environment there are a wide range of issues to consider, including (but not limited to): income; race; gender identity; sexuality; age; physical ability and neurodiversity – many of which overlap and intersect one another. Tackling inequality in any of these areas of design could justify a book in itself, but what is key is that designers consider such issues from the outset of every project and create a design philosophy based around inclusion, fairness and empathy.

However, a key starting point that can be applied to most projects is the inclusion of affordable housing or workspace within every scheme. There is a correlation between low incomes and mental health problems, with people in the 20% lowest income brackets between two and three times as likely to develop issues than those in the highest, making the provision of high-quality affordable space even more important.[75]

This is something that London has historically done fairly well. In the words of the 2015 Superdensity report, 'unlike other global cities, London's residential neighbourhoods have evolved by successfully integrating diverse people of different income, age and household size'.[76] Other cities can certainly learn from the approach London has taken. Walking through almost any part of the city, one can find expensive townhouses within a stone's throw of affordable housing. This is still an important part of the city's philosophy on housing, with the London Plan 2021 targeting 50% of all new homes to be 'genuinely affordable'.[77]

There are areas of concern, however. Changes to the planning system in recent years have threatened the levels of affordable housing required by new projects, which could potentially exacerbate the existing nationwide shortfall.[78] It is therefore important for planners, architects and developers to understand the importance of diverse communities and providing equitable places, while seeking to maximise the provision of affordable housing and workspaces.

The other perennial challenge in affordable housing is the potential for a shortfall in quality between different tenures. Affordable housing should always be designed 'tenure blind', meaning that it isn't possible to tell different tenures apart from the outside. As we have already seen, our home plays a fundamental role in our sense of self-identity and self-worth, making it vital that we provide places of high quality for people from all parts of society.

Design tips

1. Provide housing and workspace at a range of tenures wherever possible. This may also include a mix of rented and 'for sale' property to improve accessibility to all.

2. Ensure this is at a range of sizes and house types too, from studio flats to family houses.

3. There are often funds or grants available for those seeking to provide affordable elements such as co-working spaces – explore what may be available in your area and utilise such schemes to ensure high-quality spaces are delivered.

Temporary infill projects

> 'Now and then, someone is able to look at an empty space, conclude it would be a great place to start a revolution, and bravely go forward.'
> — HENRY ROLLINS, SINGER AND ACTIVIST

Figure 7.13: Glossier Pop-up Store, London, UK, by Glossier in-house design team

Potential mental wellbeing benefits
- Aesthetic benefits
- Psychological response
- Economic benefits
- Identity / self-worth

Potential issues and considerations
- Environmental impacts
- Consultation recommended

Wherever you go in the world, you are likely to find empty or disused plots of land. Sometimes these are simply in between uses or owners, while some have been abandoned altogether. What is clear is that they play a negative role in the cityscape and in how people feel. Research carried out in Scotland has shown that derelict sites can affect almost every element of a community, including its health, the local economy, environmental markers and the overall sense of social cohesion.[79]

There are numerous reasons for this phenomenon. The first is simple: such sites can quickly become visually unpleasant as a result of vandalism such as graffiti or broken elements, and as the 'Living with Beauty' report tells us, there is a connection between the aesthetics of a place and the happiness of people who live there.[80] Secondly, such sites have an impact on how we perceive a neighbourhood. They suggest that an area has little worth and does not justify investment or maintenance, and data supports this: the same study found that in Scotland under a third of the population lives within 500m of a derelict site but that this rises to 58% in deprived communities.[81] This therefore becomes an issue connected back to inequality.

While many people are aware of the impact of derelict sites on them personally, having the data to understand the impact they can have on places urges us to act and address such health inequalities. This is a particularly prescient issue today, with the current crisis in empty storefronts and town centre sites. Fortunately, there are many strategies and successful case studies that can help us bring these sites back to life, even if only temporarily until another use can be found.

Temporary structures or 'pop-ups' are not a new phenomenon, dating back to at least Roman times in the form of temporary stages constructed for festivals called *Ludi*.[82] Today they encompass a wide range of uses and programmes as diverse as restaurants, retail spaces, art installations, hotels, play spaces or even classrooms. These can also take the form of standalone objects if a site is empty, make use of existing forms and structures, or even sit entirely within an empty building. Ultimately, the use and form of a building like this is not important; the key thing is to reactivate empty sites, allowing them to provide valuable amenity to a community and create a sense that this is a neighbourhood that is cared for and worthy of investment.

Some pop-up structures are so successful that they end up becoming permanent features, making a lasting contribution to a location. Perhaps the best-known example of this is the Eiffel Tower, which was initially intended to be a temporary exhibition for the 1889 Exposition Universelle. More recently, many retail pop-ups have continued this trend, such as Shoreditch's Boxpark, which was intended to open for five years initially – at time of writing it has been open for ten and has spawned two sister sites elsewhere in London.

However, there is no guarantee that any temporary or infill project will have this success, and as such their life cycle and use of materials should be a key consideration in their design. Consider using materials that have already been upcycled and create a plan for the project's disassembly and re-use. Such strategies may also help to make such a project more affordable and potentially more attractive to local planning departments.

Design tips

1. Pop-up projects can present a great opportunity for young designers, architects or artists. It may be worth approaching landowners of empty sites with any ideas for such spaces.
2. Consider the ethical issues around constructing a temporary building, particularly around use (and ideally re-use) of materials.
3. A pop-up space is more likely to be successful if it provides a much-needed amenity for the local community. Carry out a 'community needs' study to understand what programme might best benefit the neighbourhood.

Stakeholder engagement and post-occupancy evaluation

'A diverse mix of voices leads to better discussions, decisions, and outcomes for everyone.' – SUNDAR PICHAI, CEO OF GOOGLE

Figure 7.14: Colville Estate, London, UK, by Karakusevic Carson Architects, led by active community engagement

Potential mental wellbeing benefits

- Increased autonomy
- Historic / cultural references
- Improved liveability
- Identity / self-worth

Potential issues and considerations

- Local opposition
- Cost of initiatives
- Resistance from owner

Henri Lefebvre argued that the people who live in a city and use it every day have far more of a right to participate in decisions about its future and design than people who simply arrive and purchase land.[83] Yet in today's world those people do not always have a voice. In Chapter 3 we saw the role that a sense of self-determination can play in people's mental wellbeing and happiness, and as The Glass-House Community Led Design charity explains, design is 'not only a tool for creating great places, but also a way to connect people and empower them with enhanced confidence, skills and a greater sense of agency'.[84]

Discussing the goals and strategies behind a project from an early stage in a project can be a highly effective way of offering this agency, not only helping to get local communities 'on board' but also allowing the client and design team to fully understand the challenges and opportunities a project might present. On smaller projects for a private client, such as a one-off house, engagement with the end user begins the moment they first pick up the phone to the architect. In larger projects, though, such as residential apartment buildings or offices, such interactions may take place very late in the design process, or in some cases may never occur at all. Most local authorities in the UK require some level of consultation with local people or politicians, but this is unfortunately seen as a formality by many developers and often occurs once the majority of design work is completed.

Thankfully, however, attitudes around this important process do seem to be changing, with the RIBA arguing that there has been a 'genuine shift in the perceived value of providing residents with more ownership of the design process in recent years'.[85] Unfortunately, data on the benefits of such engagement is still scarce, but case studies such as the work of Levitt Bernstein or Karakusevic Carson Architects demonstrate the enormous impact that early, high-quality community engagement can have.

It is also important that designers analyse the success of projects after their completion, to allow them to understand what worked well and what didn't, and to avoid similar mistakes in future projects. This is commonplace in the design of almost all other products, and yet recent research by the *Architects' Journal* revealed that just 4% of large practices 'always' carry out post-occupancy evaluation studies, with another 22% undertaking it 'frequently'.[86] This means that almost three-quarters of larger architectural practices often have little to no idea of the success of their projects, or whether residents felt they improved their quality of life.

There are thankfully many tools available to design teams and developers supporting them in this process, such as the RIBA's Social Value Toolkit, which was developed specifically to make it simple to evaluate and demonstrate the social impact of design on people and communities.[87] The toolkit asks occupants of new schemes to compare their quality of life before and after moving in, to gain an understanding of where and how the project has added social value.

Fundamentally, this book is focused on creating places that improve people's happiness, mental wellbeing and quality of life. Without consulting on what is important to them in a place, a building or a home, we are vastly decreasing our chances of creating somewhere that does so successfully.

Design tips

1. Consider setting up a non-hierarchical steering group early in a project's life, including key stakeholders such as community representatives, local groups, the client, operators and members of the design team.
2. Avoid unnecessary design jargon and run an explanatory session early in the process to give stakeholders a better understanding of terms and issues they need to understand.
3. Explore alternatives to dialogue-based sessions. This could include co-design workshops, site visits or ways to tap into stakeholders' emotions, such as making sessions.

Conclusions and further thoughts

' We need to center design on people. What's the good in sustainable materials if you're using them to make a prison?' – TOMMY JOSHUA, COMMUNITY ACTIVIST AND EDUCATOR

Figure 8.0: Maggie's Oldham, UK, by dRMM

Over the last decade, we have seen attitudes and understanding towards mental health and wellbeing take great strides forward, in both the construction industry and the wider society within which we all live. What was once a taboo subject is now discussed openly in boardrooms and schools. Groups like 'Mates in Mind' are doing incredible work to tackle this issue in construction, and I have personally seen a seismic shift in the way that many clients and consultants are prepared to think about designing buildings with wellbeing at their core.

This has been echoed in my journey through architecture, which started with burning myself out and overcoming my own mental health challenges, sending me down a path specialising in an area of design I was almost entirely unaware of as a university student. It is fantastic to see more specialists emerging in the area of design for wellbeing, whether focusing on physical or mental health aspects – I believe these people have an important role to play in helping to make our buildings and cities better.

However, there is still a long way to go. Too often design suggestions that would improve end users' quality of life are seen as luxuries and are prone to being designed out of the project through the process known as 'value engineering'. This attitude seems outdated, given that we now have clear scientific proof that the built environment and places where we live our lives have an impact on our state of mind, behaviour and, ultimately, our happiness. Sadly, this philosophy of value engineering often hits the most disadvantaged people in society hardest and might therefore even be viewed as a form of discrimination. As we would encourage people to speak out against discrimination in any form, I strongly believe that we should be doing everything we can to champion design for wellbeing, regardless of who the end-user may be.

The other challenge we face is that architecture is a slow process: if we start designing healthier buildings today, we may not see the results for three or four years. As the first wave of WELL Certified buildings has emerged in the UK, there appears to have been a realisation among many developers that any buildings which are not focused on health and wellbeing (existing or proposed) may already be behind the curve. This risks them being left with potentially outdated building stock that will be, at best, harder to market, and at worst obsolete. The time to think about designing healthier buildings is not, therefore, on the next project or the one after that, but on the buildings that we are designing right now.

I have a number of hopes for our industry moving forward. The first of these is that in decades' time, wellbeing in buildings will be viewed in the same way as sustainability is now: not as something optional or that is used to make a building stand out from the crowd, but as an essential part of every project. Sustainability is no longer a USP for most building typologies and this is a clear illustration that while we still have some way to go, real progress is being made in this area.

We live in a world where the health impact of every man-made product is now under incredible scrutiny, yet there is a sense that buildings are perhaps lagging behind. However, as the general public's understanding of mental health improves alongside a greater acceptance that the built environment can affect our broader wellbeing, it seems unlikely that this will be the case forever. The value that people are increasingly placing on healthy buildings ultimately can only be a positive thing, which I believe will lead to an improvement in the quality of our homes, schools, workplaces and public spaces.

My biggest hope, however, is that this book will help you to create healthier places, whether you are a designer, developer, funder, planner or simply someone looking to improve your own mental health in your home or workplace. We all have our part to play in improving the built environment, and trends are created through many small actions coming together to change the way people think and act, until the unimaginable becomes normality.

I am extremely grateful to anybody who has bought and read this book, but if I may I would like to ask one more thing of you: please join me as an advocate for healthier places and better buildings. Champion good design and quality materials. Speak out against cost-cutting if it will have a negative impact on the quality of people using those places. And spread the word. Only by working together can we create buildings and cities that allow people to thrive by making their lives better, more enjoyable and happier.

References

Introduction

1. 'BNP Paribas Securities Services ESG Global Survey 2019: trends and key figures', April 2019, https://group.bnpparibas/en/news/bnp-paribas-securities-services-esg-global-survey-2019-trends-key-figures (accessed 4 October 2021).
2. 'How London Lives', *Foxtons Report*, October 2018, https://page-assets.foxtons.co.uk/img/press/pr/2018/foxtons_how_london_lives_report.pdf (accessed 4 October 2021).
3. 'RIBA Homeowner Survey – Happiness Through Design: Executive Summary', October 2020, https://www.architecture.com/knowledge-and-resources/knowledge-landing-page/riba-homeowner-survey-happiness-through-design-executive-summary (accessed 4 October 2021).
4. Flora Samuel, 'Impact of housing design and placemaking on social value and wellbeing in the pandemic: Interim Report', *UK Collaborative Centre for Housing Evidence*, October 2020, https://housingevidence.ac.uk/publications/impact-of-housing-design-and-placemaking-on-social-value-and-wellbeing-in-the-pandemic-interim-report (accessed 4 October 2021).
5. Mark Wheeler, 'Be happy: Your genes may thank you for it', *Science Daily*, July 2013, https://www.sciencedaily.com/releases/2013/07/130729192548.htm (accessed 4 October 2021).
6. Richard Layard, *Happiness: Lessons from a New Science*, Penguin, 2011.
7. Shawn Achor, *The Happiness Advantage: The Seven Principles of Positive Psychology that Fuel Success and Performance at Work*, Ebury, 2011.
8. David R. Topor, 'If you are happy and you know it... you may live longer', *Harvard Health Blog*, October 2019, https://www.health.harvard.edu/blog/if-you-are-happy-and-you-know-it-you-may-live-longer-2019101618020 (accessed 4 October 2021).
9. 'Mental Health Problems – An Introduction', *Mind*, October 2017, https://www.mind.org.uk/information-support/types-of-mental-health-problems/mental-health-problems-introduction/causes (accessed 4 October 2021).

Chapter 1

1. Bill Bryson, *At Home: A Short History of Private Life*, Doubleday, 2010.
2. 'Circadian Rhythms', *National Institute of General Medical Sciences*, https://www.nigms.nih.gov/education/fact-sheets/Pages/circadian-rhythms.aspx (accessed 4 October 2021).
3. 'Sleep Drive and your Body Clock', *The Sleep Foundation*, https://www.sleepfoundation.org/circadian-rhythm/sleep-drive-and-your-body-clock (accessed 4 October 2021).
4. Matthew Walker, *Why We Sleep: The New Science of Sleep and Dreams*, Penguin, 2018.
5. Dr G.W. Lambert, C. Reid, D.M. Kaye, G.L. Jennings and M.D. Esler, 'Effect of sunlight and season on serotonin turnover in the brain', *The Lancet*, Research Letters, vol. 360, issue 9348, pp. 1840–42, December 2002, https://doi.org/10.1016/S0140-6736(02)11737-5 (accessed 4 October 2021).
6. Le Corbusier, *Toward an Architecture* (trans. by John Goodman), Getty Publications, 2007. Original work published 1923.
7. Alice Park, 'Why Sunlight is so Good for You?', *Time*, https://time.com/collection/guide-to-happiness/4888327/why-sunlight-is-so-good-for-you/ (accessed 4 October 2021).
8. '14 Patterns of Biophilic Design: Improving Health & Well-Being in the Built Environment', *Terrapin Bright Green*, https://www.terrapinbrightgreen.com/reports/14-patterns/ (accessed 4 October 2021).
9. 'History of Windows', Architecture & Design, https://www.architectureanddesign.com.au/suppliers/paarhammer-windows-doors/history-of-windows (accessed 4 October 2021).
10. 'What was used in windows before glass was invented?', *Windows & More*, https://www.windowsonlineuk.co.uk/blog/used-windows-glass-invented/ (accessed 4 October 2021).
11. 'Windows, glass, glazing – a brief history', *NBS*, https://www.thenbs.com/knowledge/windows-glass-glazing-a-brief-history (accessed 4 October 2021).
12. How architects have tried to create "streets in the sky"', The Financial Times, https://www.ft.com/content/8f2bab62-2b32-11e7-bc4b-5528796fe35c (accessed on 9 December 2021).
13. Andrew McKay, 'Viking Longhouses: A Glimpse of Everyday Viking Life', Life in Norway, https://www.lifeinnorway.net/viking-longhouses/ (accessed on 9 December 2021).
14. https://www.velux.com/what-we-do/research-and-knowledge/deic-basic-book/daylight/daylight-with-roof-windows-flat-roof-windows-and-modular-skylights (accessed 4 October 2021).
15. Ben Channon, *Happy by Design: A Guide to Architecture and Mental Wellbeing*, RIBA Publishing, 2018.
16. Nick Baker and Koen Steemers, *Healthy Homes: Designing with light and air for sustainability and wellbeing*, RIBA Publishing, 2019.
17. Op. cit., Walker, *Why We Sleep*.
18. Ibid.
19. Ibid.
20. 'Effects of sleep deprivation on serum cortisol level and mental health in servicemen', *International Journal of Psychophysiology*, vol. 96, issue 3, June 2015, pp 169–75, https://doi.org/10.1016/j.ijpsycho.2015.04.008 (accessed 4 October 2021).
21. 'Sleep and mental health: Sleep deprivation can affect your mental health', Harvard Mental Health Letter, https://www.health.harvard.edu/newsletter_article/sleep-and-mental-health (accessed 4 October 2021).
22. https://www.sleephealth.org/sleep-health/the-state-of-sleephealth-in-america/ (accessed 4 October 2021).
23. 'Circadian Lighting Design', https://v2.wellcertified.com/wellv2/en/light (accessed 4 October 2021).
24. https://v2.wellcertified.com/wellv2/en/light/feature/3 (accessed 4 October 2021).
25. Johnathan Rush, 'The Ultimate Guide to Circadian Lighting: The Science of Light and Health', Hoare Lea, https://hoarelea.com/2019/01/15/the-ultimate-guide-to-circadian-lighting/ (accessed 4 October 2021).
26. Op. cit., Channon, *Happy by Design*.
27. Summer Allen, 'Eight Reasons Why Awe Makes Your Life Better', *Greater Good Magazine*, https://greatergood.berkeley.edu/article/item/eight_reasons_why_awe_makes_your_life_better (accessed 4 October 2021).

28. 'Definition of *Cloister*', *Dictionary by Merriam-Webster*, https://www.merriam-webster.com/dictionary/cloister (accessed 4 October 2021).
29. 'Philosophy and the Tradition of Architectural Theory', *Stanford Encyclopedia of Philosophy*, https://plato.stanford.edu/entries/architecture/tradition.html (accessed 4 October 2021).
30. Simon Aldous, 'Government issues design code for "beautiful" new housing', *RIBA Journal*, February 2021, https://www.ribaj.com/intelligence/news-catch-up-government-design-code-bbbbc-permitted-development-rights-fire-safety-training-grenfell-pompidou-centre (accessed 4 October 2021).
31. 'The value of WELL', *WELL*, https://www.wellcertified.com/certification/v1/ (accessed 4 October 2021).
32. Op. cit., Channon, *Happy by Design*.
33. https://en.wikipedia.org/wiki/Agriculture_in_the_United_Kingdom (accessed 4 October 2021).
34. Amy J. Lloyd, 'Education, Literacy and the Reading Public', *British Library Newspapers*, Gale, Detroit, https://www.gale.com/binaries/content/assets/gale-us-en/primary-sources/intl-gps/intl-gps-essays/full-ghn-contextual-essays/ghn_essay_bln_lloyd3_website.pdf, 2007, p.2.
35. 'Employment and Employment Types', *Office for National Statistics*, https://www.ons.gov.uk/employmentandlabourmarket/peopleinwork/employmentandemployeetypes (accessed 1 January 2021).
36. https://v2.wellcertified.com/wellv2/en/light (accessed 4 October 2021).
37. Michael Feeley, 'Screen time survey reveals consumers spend 50 days a year on smartphones', *The Drum Network*, May 2019, https://www.thedrum.com/news/2019/05/02/screen-time-survey-reveals-consumers-spend-50-days-year-smartphones (accessed 4 October 2021).
38. 'How to tell if you could be addicted to your phone', *Healthline*, https://www.healthline.com/health/mental-health/cell-phone-addiction#dopamine-connection (accessed 4 October 2021).
39. 'Why it's time to ditch the phone before bed', *SCL Health*, https://www.sclhealth.org/blog/2019/09/why-it-is-time-to-ditch-the-phone-before-bed/ (accessed 4 October 2021).
40. Good Homes Alliance, https://kb.goodhomes.org.uk/ (accessed 4 October 2021).
41. https://signaturemaids.com/our-blog/how-much-time-does-the-average-person-spend-cleaning-house/ (accessed 4 October 2021).
42. 'Percentage of households with dishwashers in the United Kingdom (UK) from 1994 to 2018', *Statista*, https://www.statista.com/statistics/289151/household-dishwashing-in-the-uk/ (accessed 4 October 2021).
43. Ishani Nath, 'Washing The Dishes Can Be A Good Mindfulness Tool: Scrubbing pots and pans can help slow things down', *The Huffington Post*, March 2020, https://www.huffingtonpost.ca/entry/dishwashing-mindfulness (accessed 4 October 2021).
44. FPJ Bureau, 'Washing the Dishes: Thich Nhat Hanh', *Free Press Journal*, May 2017, https://www.freepressjournal.in/cmcm/washing-the-dishes-thich-nhat-hanh (accessed 4 October 2021).

Chapter 2

1. AECOM, 'Research into overheating in new homes', *Ministry of Housing, Communities and Local Government*, 2019, https://assets.publishing.service.gov.uk/government/uploads/system/uploads/attachment_data/file/835240/Research_into_overheating_in_new_homes_-_phase_1.pdf (accessed 4 October 2021).
2. R.E. Cooney, J. Joormann, F. Eugène, et al., 'Neural correlates of rumination in depression', *Cognitive, Affective and Behavioral Neuroscience*, vol. 10, pp 470–78, December 2010, https://doi.org/10.3758/CABN.10.4.470 (accessed 4 October 2021).
3. J.M. Burg and J. Michalak, 'The Healthy Quality of Mindful Breathing: Associations with Rumination and Depression', *Cognitive Therapy Research*, vol. 35, pp 179–85, April 2011, https://doi.org/10.1007/s10608-010-9343-x (accessed 4 October 2021).
4. Mia Hansson, 'NHS recognises that mindfulness meditation is good for depression', *The Guardian*, 26 February 2013, https://www.theguardian.com/society/2013/feb/26/mindfulness-meditation-depression-nhs (accessed 4 October 2021).
5. https://www.mentalhealth.org.uk/a-to-z/m/mindfulness-based-cognitive-therapy-mbct (accessed 4 October 2021).
6. Juhani Pallasmaa, *The Eyes of the Skin: Architecture and the Senses*, Wiley, 2012.
7. http://naturalhomes.org/vernacular.htm (accessed 4 October 2021).
8. 'UK Brick Makers are Failing to meet demand', *The Construction Index*, March 2018, https://www.theconstructionindex.co.uk/news/view/uk-brick-makers-are-failing-to-meet-demand (accessed 4 October 2021).
9. https://www.modlar.com/news/219/materials-changing-the-future-of-architecture/ (accessed 4 October 2021).
10. Sally Augustin, 'Wood as a Restorative Material in Healthcare Environments', *Forestry Innovation Investment* Ltd, February 2015, www.woodworks.org/wp-content/uploads/Wood-Restorative-Material-Healthcare-Environments.pdf (accessed 4 October 2021).
11. Tom Ireland, 'What Does Mindfulness Meditation Do to Your Brain?', *Scientific American*, June 2014, https://blogs.scientificamerican.com/guest-blog/what-does-mindfulness-meditation-do-to-your-brain/ (accessed 4 October 2021).
12. 'Air pollution', *World Health Organization*, https://www.who.int/health-topics/air-pollution (accessed (accessed 4 October 2021).
13. Atif Khan, Oleguer Plana-Ripoll, Sussie Antonsen, Jørgen Brandt, Camilla Geels, Hannah Landecker, et al., 'Environmental pollution is associated with increased risk of psychiatric disorders in the US and Denmark', *PLOS Biology* 17(8): e3000353, 2019, https://doi.org/10.1371/journal.pbio.3000353 (accessed 4 October 2021).
14. Naureen A. Ali and Adeel Khoja, 'Growing Evidence for the Impact of Air Pollution on Depression', *Ochsner Journal*, vol. 19(1), Spring 2019, doi: 10.31486/toj.19.0011. https://www.ncbi.nlm.nih.gov/pmc/articles/PMC6447209/
15. https://v2.wellcertified.com/wellv2/en/materials (accessed 4 October 2021).
16. Wood for Good conference, 2018.
17. Jennifer Huizen, medically reviewed by Timothy J. Legg, 'What to Know about Eco Anxiety', *Medical News Today*, https://www.medicalnewstoday.com/articles/327354 (accessed 4 October 2021).
18. Zing Tsjeng, 'The Climate Change Paper So Depressing It's Sending People to Therapy', *Vice*, February 2019, https://www.vice.com/en/article/vbwpdb/the-climate-change-paper-so-depressing-its-sending-people-to-therapy (accessed 4 October 2021).
19. Lizzie Crook, 'Pretty Plastic shingles made from recycled PVC windows and gutters are "first 100 per cent recycled cladding material"', *Dezeen*, March 2020, https://www.dezeen.com/2020/03/03/pretty-plastic-overtreders-w-bureau-sla-upcycled-products (accessed 4 October 2021).

20. Dr Meera Joshi, 'How does mindfulness affect the brain?', *BUPA*, November 2017, https://www.bupa.co.uk/newsroom/ourviews/mindfulness-my-brain (accessed 4 October 2021).
21. 'Are you sitting too much?', *Heat Matters Magazine*, https://www.bhf.org.uk/informationsupport/heart-matters-magazine/activity/sitting-down (accessed 4 October 2021).
22. https://v2.wellcertified.com/wellv2/en/movement/feature/2 (accessed 4 October 2021).
23. Els van Bronckhorst, Ed Bouterse and Jordy Kleemans, 'What Workers Want – Working remotely: make a virtue of necessity', *Savills*, April 2020, https://www.savills.com/research_articles/255800/299480-0 (accessed 4 October 2021).
24. Linda Wasmer Andrews, 'Why warm weather and hot tubs make us happy', *Psychology Today*, April 2015, https://www.psychologytoday.com/us/blog/minding-the-body/201504/why-warm-weather-and-hot-tubs-make-us-happy (accessed 4 October 2021).
25. https://www.nu-heat.co.uk/blog/does-underfloor-heating-increase-property-value (accessed 4 October 2021).
26. Chris Reardon 'Thermal Mass', *Your Home: Australia's Guide to Environmentally Sustainable Homes*, 2013, https://www.yourhome.gov.au/passive-design/thermal-mass (accessed 4 October 2021).
27. World Health Organization, https://www.euro.who.int/en/health-topics/environment-and-health/noise/data-and-statistics (accessed 4 October 2021).
28. Eleanor Crossley, Tim Biggs, Phillip Brown and Tahwinder Singh, 'The Accuracy of iPhone Applications to Monitor Environmental Noise Levels', *Laryngoscope*, 131(1):E59-E62, doi: 10.1002/lary.28590, 2020
29. 'What is the Ideal Sleep Environment?', *Everyday Health*, https://www.everydayhealth.com/sleep/experts-whats-the-ideal-sleep-environment.aspx (accessed 4 October 2021).
30. Tom de Castella, 'The Plague of Light in our Bedrooms', *BBC News Magazine*, June 2014, https://www.bbc.co.uk/news/magazine-27661394 (accessed 4 October 2021).
31. 'Environmental Noise Guidelines for the European Region', *World Health Organization*, 2018, http://www.euro.who.int/__data/assets/pdf_file/0008/383921/noise-guidelines-eng.pdf?ua=1 (accessed 4 October 2021).
32. Ibid.
33. Nick Baker and Koen Steemers, *Healthy Homes: Designing with light and air for sustainability and wellbeing*, RIBA Publishing, 2019, p 62.
34. Fran Williams, 'Beep Studio creates noise-blocking road barrier in London's East End', *Architects' Journal*, December 2020, https://www.architectsjournal.co.uk/news/beep-studio-creates-noise-blocking-road-barrier-in-londons-east-end (accessed 4 October 2021).
35. Ravi Mehta, Rui (Juliet) Zhu and Amar Cheema, 'Is Noise Always Bad? Exploring the Effects of Ambient Noise on Creative Cognition', *Journal of Consumer Research*, vol. 39, no. 4, December 2012, pp 784–99, https://doi.org/10.1086/665048 (accessed 4 October 2021).
36. https://v2.wellcertified.com/wellv2/en/sound/feature/1 (accessed 4 October 2021).
37. Katharine Schwab, 'Everyone hates open plan offices. Here's why they still exist', *Fast Company*, January 2019, https://www.fastcompany.com/90285582/everyone-hates-open-plan-offices-heres-why-they-still-exist (accessed 4 October 2021).
38. Els van Bronckhorst, Ed Bouterse and Jordy Kleemans, 'What Workers Want – Working remotely: make a virtue of necessity', *Savills*, April 2020, https://www.savills.com/research_articles/255800/299480-0 (accessed 4 October 2021).
39. 'How Sound Masking Works', *CIE*, https://cie-group.com/how-to-av/videos-and-blogs/sound-masking-works (accessed 4 October 2021).
40. '"Too much glass" risks overheating modern buildings', *The Financial Times*, https://www.ft.com/content/91857d8e-5bf7-11e7-9bc8-8055f264aa8b (accessed 4 October 2021).
41. 'How Building regulations have changed over time', *The Green Age*, https://www.thegreenage.co.uk/building-regulations-changed-time (accessed 4 October 2021).
42. Kathryn Brown 'The Hidden Problem of Overheating', *The Climate Change Committee*, August 2017, https://www.theccc.org.uk/2017/08/08/hidden-problem-overheating (accessed 4 October 2021).
43. Mare Lõhmus, 'Possible Biological Mechanisms Linking Mental Health and Heat – A Contemplative Review', *International Journal of Environmental Research for Public Health*, vol. 15, July 2018, doi: 10.3390/ijerph15071515.
44. Thomas Lane, 'London homes to have smaller windows than rest of UK', *Building*, January 2021, https://www.building.co.uk/news/london-homes-to-have-smaller-windows-than-rest-of-uk/5110052.article (accessed 4 October 2021).
45. Christopher Ingraham, 'People who spend more time outdoors live more fulfilling lives', *The Washington Post*, June 2019, https://www.washingtonpost.com%2fbusiness%2f2019%2f06%2f19%2fpeople-who-spend-more-time-outdoors-lead-more-fulfilling-lives-new-research-shows%2f (accessed 4 October 2021).
46. Stephanie Walden, 'The "Indoor Generation" and the health risks of spending more time inside', *USA Today*, May 2018, https://eu.usatoday.com/story/sponsor-story/velux/2018/05/15/indoor-generation-and-health-risks-spending-more-time-inside/610289002/ (accessed 4 October 2021).
47. 'The History of Awnings & Shade Structures', *Awning Resources*, https://www.awningresources.com/the-history-of-awnings-shade-structures (accessed 4 October 2021).
48. 'Studies link air pollution to mental health issues in children', *Health Europa*, September 2019, https://www.healtheuropa.eu/air-pollution-to-mental-health-children/93569/ (accessed 4 October 2021).
49. Sofie Pelsmakers, *Environmental Design Pocketbook*, RIBA Publishing, 2015.
50. Claire Bennie, 'London needs a million new homes – but how do we get there?', *Inside Housing*, August 2019, https://www.insidehousing.co.uk/comment/comment/london-needs-a-million-new-homes--but-how-do-we-get-there-62775 (accessed 4 October 2021).
51. M. van der Tempel, Ine Wouters, Filip Descamps and Dorien Aerts, 'Ventilation techniques in the 19th century: learning from the past', *Conference Paper*, 2011, doi 10.2495/STR110231.
52. https://www.iea.org/reports/cooling (accessed 4 October 2021).
53. Tim Heffernan, 'Can HEPA Air Purifiers Capture the Coronavirus?', *Wirecutter, New York Times*, November 2020, https://www.nytimes.com/wirecutter/blog/can-hepa-air-purifiers-capture-coronavirus (accessed 4 October 2021).
54. J.L. Perry Marshall, J.H. Agui Glenn and R. Vijayakumar, 'Submicron and Nanoparticulate Matter Removal by HEPA-Rated Media Filters and Packed Beds of Granular Materials', *NASA Technical Reports*, https://ntrs.nasa.gov/citations/20170005166 (accessed 4 October 2021).
55. https://v2.wellcertified.com/v/en/air (accessed 4 October 2021).
56. 'Ventilation Rates and Absences in Offices and Schools', *Indoor Air Quality Scientific Resource Bank, Berkley Lab*, https://iaqscience.lbl.gov/ventilation-rates-and-absences-offices-and-schools (accessed 4 October 2021).

57 John M. Grohol, 'Weather can change your mood', *Psych Central*, November 2008, https://psychcentral.com/blog/weather-can-change-your-mood (accessed 4 October 2021).
58 '2020 Greenest Year for UK Electricity', *RENEWS.BIZ*, December 2020, https://renews.biz/65483/2020-greenest-year-for-uk-electricity/#:~:text=This%20year%20is%20set%20to,2013's%20figure%20of%20529CO2%20KWh (accessed 4 October 2021).

Chapter 3

1 Nancy Hey, 'World Happiness Report 2016 summary findings', *What Works Wellbeing*, March 2016, https://whatworkswellbeing.org/blog/world-happiness-report-2016-summary-findings (accessed 4 October 2021).
2 Richard Layard, *Happiness: Lessons from a New Science*, Penguin, 2011.
3 Ibid., p 70.
4 'How happy is your home?', https://resi.co.uk/happy_homes (accessed 4 October 2021).
5 Stephanie Timm, 'Can architects solve employee burnout?', *Well*, September 2019, https://resources.wellcertified.com/articles/can-architects-solve-employee-burnout-/ (accessed 4 October 2021).
6 R. Nicholas Carleton, 'Fear of the unknown: One fear to rule them all?', *Journal of Anxiety Disorders*, vol. 41, June 2016, pp 5–21, https://doi.org/10.1016/j.janxdis.2016.03.011 (accessed 4 October 2021).
7 'How happy is your home?', https://resi.co.uk/happy_homes (accessed 4 October 2021).
8 John Spacey, '17 Classic Features of Japanese Homes', Japan Talk, April 2015, https://www.japan-talk.com/jt/new/japanese-houses (accessed 4 October 2021).
9 Pieter Singelenberg, 'Space, light and art', *Rietveld Paviljoen*, http://rietveldpaviljoen.com/file/download_articoli/48/1311066725pieter-singelenberg.pdf (accessed 4 October 2021).
10 Flora Samuel, 'Impact of Housing Design and Placemaking on Social Value and Wellbeing in the Pandemic – Interim Report', *UK Collaborative Centre for Housing Evidence*, October 2020, https://housingevidence.ac.uk/publications/impact-of-housing-design-and-placemaking-on-social-value-and-wellbeing-in-the-pandemic-interim-report (accessed 4 October 2021).
11 'What Workers Want: Europe 2019', *Savills*, https://www.savills.co.uk/research_articles/229130/283562-0/what-workers-want-europe-2019 (accessed 4 October 2021).
12 Graham Kendall, 'Apollo 11 anniversary: Could an iPhone fly me to the moon?' *The Independent*, July 2019, https://www.independent.co.uk/news/science/apollo-11-moon-landing-mobile-phones-smartphone-iphone-a8988351.html (accessed 4 October 2021).
13 Mark Swilling, 'The curse of urban sprawl: how cities grow, and why this has to change', *The Guardian*, July 2016, https://www.theguardian.com/cities/2016/jul/12/urban-sprawl-how-cities-grow-change-sustainability-urban-age (accessed 4 October 2021).
14 Patrick Collinson, 'UK living rooms have shrunk by a third', *The Guardian*, April 2018, https://www.theguardian.com/business/2018/apr/08/uk-living-rooms-have-shrunk-by-a-third-survey-finds (accessed 1 February 2021).
15 https://globalworkplaceanalytics.com/telecommuting-statistics (accessed 4 October 2021).
16 'Switching off from work', *Employee Benefits*, March 2019, https://employeebenefits.co.uk/switching-off-from-work (accessed 4 October 2021).
17 Zaria Gorvett, 'This is why you can't switch off at the weekend', *BBC Worklife*, July 2016, https://www.bbc.com/worklife/article/20160728-this-is-why-you-cant-switch-off-at-the-weekend (accessed 4 October 2021).
18 Michael Graziano, *The Spaces Between Us: A Story of Neuroscience, Evolution and Human Nature*, OUP, 2018.
19 Simon Worrall, 'You Need Your Personal Space – Here's the Science Why', January 2018, updated November 2020, *National Geographic*, https://www.nationalgeographic.co.uk/science/2018/01/you-need-your-personal-space-heres-science-why (accessed 4 October 2021).
20 'A tight squeeze: How dense is too dense?', *BOMA Magazine*, July/August 2018, https://www.boma.org/BOMA/Research-Resources/News/Tenant_Experience/A_Tight_Squeeze_How_Dense_Is_Too_Dense.aspx (accessed 4 October 2021).
21 Lily Bernheimer, Rachel O'Brien and Richard Barnes, 'Wellbeing in prison design: A guide', *Matter Architecture*, 2017, http://www.matterarchitecture.uk/wp-content/uploads/2018/05/421-op-02_Design-toolkit-report-online.pdf (accessed 4 October 2021).
22 'Densification: How dense is too dense?', *BOMA Resources*, https://www.boma.org/BOMA/Research-Resources/Trends/Densification.aspx (accessed 4 October 2021).
23 Ibid.
24 Darby E, Saxbe and Rena Repetti, 'No place like home: home tours correlate with daily patterns of mood and cortisol', *Personality and Social Psychology Bulletin: SAGE Journals*, November 2009, doi: 10.1177/0146167209352864.
25 Mary MacVean, 'For many people, gathering possessions is just the stuff of life', *LA Times*, March 2014, https://www.latimes.com/health/la-xpm-2014-mar-21-la-he-keeping-stuff-20140322-story.html (accessed 4 October 2021).
26 'Ten-year-old's have £7,000 worth of toys to play with, but play with just £300 worth', *The Telegraph*, October 2010, https://www.telegraph.co.uk/finance/newsbysector/retailandconsumer/8074156/Ten-year-olds-have-7000-worth-of-toys-but-play-with-just-330.html (accessed 4 October 2021).
27 Emma Johnson, 'The Real Cost of Your Shopping Habits', *Forbes*, January 2015, https://www.forbes.com/sites/emmajohnson/2015/01/15/the-real-cost-of-your-shopping-habits/?sh=d580ee91452d (accessed 4 October 2021).
28 https://www.homequalitymark.com/professionals/standard/ (accessed 4 October 2021).
29 Amanina Abdur Rahman and Ruut Veenhoven, 'Freedom and Happiness in Nations: A Research Synthesis', *Applied Research Quality Life*, vol. 13, pp 435–56, June 2018, https://doi.org/10.1007/s11482-017-9543-6 (accessed 4 October 2021).
30 Sheena Iyengar, *The Art of Choosing: The Decisions We Make Everyday of our Lives, What They Say About Us*, Abacus, 2011.
31 Henry Ford in collaboration with Samuel Crowther, *My Life and Work*, 1922, p 72, cited in 'The truth about "any color so long as it is black"', *OpLaunch*, April 2015, http://oplaunch.com/blog/2015/04/30/the-truth-about-any-color-so-long-as-it-is-black/ (accessed 4 October 2021).
32 Laura Bright, 'Consumer control and customization in online environments: an investigation into the psychology of consumer choice and its impact on media enjoyment, attitude, and behavioural intention', *The University of Texas at Austin, Dissertations and theses*, http://hdl.handle.net/2152/18054 (accessed 4 October 2021).
33 Ingrid Fetell Lee, *Joyful: The Surprising Power of Ordinary Things to Create Extraordinary Happiness*, Rider, 2018.

34. Hilary Ribons, 'New Poll Suggests Millennials Lack Basic Survival Skills', *Field and Stream*, January 2017, https://www.fieldandstream.com/new-poll-suggests-millennials-survival-skills-are-sorely-lacking (accessed 4 October 2021).
35. Bradley Garrett, *Bunker: Building for the End Times*, Allen Lane, 2020.
36. Mirele Mann, '7 Scientific Facts About the Benefit of Doing Good', *Good Net*, January 2017, https://www.goodnet.org/articles/7-scientific-facts-about-benefit-doing-good (accessed 4 October 2021).
37. Space 10, *The Ideal City: Exploring Urban Futures*, Gestalten, 2021.
38. P.S. Burge, 'Sick building syndrome', *Occupational and Environmental Medicine*, vol. 61, pp 18–190, 2004, http://dx.doi.org/10.1136/oem.2003.008813 (accessed 4 October 2021).
39. Gail S. Brager, 'Benefits of Improving Occupant Comfort and Well-being in Buildings', 2013, https://src.lafargeholcim-foundation.org/dnl/93603859-d59e-498a-b056-405d16e39171/F13_OrangeWS_Brager.pdf (accessed 4 October 2021).
40. Imogen Calderina, 'New schools and homes in Britain must have windows that won't open because fresh air is so polluted', *Mail Online*, December 2015, https://www.dailymail.co.uk/news/article-3348096/New-schools-homes-Britain-windows-won-t-open-fresh-air-polluted.html (accessed 4 October 2021).
41. Ron Frederick, 'Why your brain is on the lookout for danger', *The Centre for Courageous Living*, https://www.cfcliving.com/brain-threat-detector (accessed 4 October 2021).
42. 'What would a city designed by women look like?', *The Financial Times*, 2020, https://www.ft.com/content/406d5748-564c-48da-ab8e-55578b93def6 (accessed 4 October 2021).
43. Ibid.
44. Rory Fitzgerald, 'Survey shows 32% of British women don't feel safe walking alone at night – compared to just 13% of men', *The Conversation*, March 2021, https://theconversation.com/survey-shows-32-of-british-women-dont-feel-safe-walking-alone-at-night-compared-to-just-13-of-men-157446 (accessed 4 October 2021).
45. 'Creating Safe Places to Live through Design', *Design Council*, https://www.designcouncil.org.uk/sites/default/files/asset/document/creating-safe-places-to-live.pdf (accessed 4 October 2021).
46. Tony Lawson, Robert Rogerson and Malcolm Barnacle, 'A comparison between the cost effectiveness of CCTV and improved street lighting as a means of crime reduction', *Computers, Environment and Urban Systems*, vol. 68, March 2018, pp 17–25, https://doi.org/10.1016/j.compenvurbsys.2017.09.008 (accessed 4 October 2021).
47. Anne East, 'How do gardens add value to your house price?' *Property Price Advice*, February 2019, https://www.propertypriceadvice.co.uk/home-improvements/how-do-gardens-affect-house-price (accessed 4 October 2021).
48. 'One in eight British households has no garden', *Office for National Statistics*, May 2020, https://www.ons.gov.uk/economy/environmentalaccounts/articles/oneineightbritishhouseholdshasnogarden/2020-05-14 (accessed 4 October 2021).
49. Linda Poon, 'A Lesson from Social Distancing: Build Better Balconies', *Bloomberg CityLab*, April 2020, https://www.bloomberg.com/news/articles/2020-04-20/lesson-from-coronavirus-build-better-balconies (accessed 4 October 2021).
50. J. B. Greenough, 'The Fauces of the Roman House', *Harvard Studies in Classical Philology*, vol. 1, 1890, pp 1–12, https://doi.org/10.2307/310454 (accessed 4 October 2021).
51. https://v2.wellcertified.com/v/en/air/feature/9 (accessed 4 October 2021).
52. Flora Samuel, 'Impact of Housing Design and Placemaking on Social Value and Wellbeing in the Pandemic – Interim Report', *UK Collaborative Centre for Housing Evidence*, October 2020, https://housingevidence.ac.uk/publications/impact-of-housing-design-and-placemaking-on-social-value-and-wellbeing-in-the-pandemic-interim-report (accessed 4 October 2021).
53. https://v2.wellcertified.com/wellv2/en/mind/feature/6 (accessed 4 October 2021).
54. Catherine E, Milner and Kimberly A. Cote, 'Benefits of napping in healthy adults: impact of nap length, time of day, age, and experience with napping', *Journal of Sleep Research*, May 2009, https://onlinelibrary.wiley.com/doi/full/10.1111/j.1365-2869.2008.00718.x (accessed 4 October 2021).
55. Reviewed by Carol DerSarkissian, 'Health Benefits of Napping', *WebMD*, June 2020, https://www.webmd.com/a-to-z-guides/ss/slideshow-health-benefits-of-napping (accessed 4 October 2021).
56. Dr Travis Bradberry, 'There's an optimal way to structure your day – and it's not the 8-hour workday', *Quartz at Work*, March 2019, https://qz.com/work/1561830/why-the-eight-hour-workday-doesnt-work (accessed 4 October 2021).
57. https://v2.wellcertified.com/wellv2/en/mind (accessed 4 October 2021).
58. Madhav Goyal, Sonal Singh, Erica M.S. Sibinga, Neda F. Gould, Anastasia Rowland-Seymour, Ritu Sharma, Zackary Berger, Dana Sleicher, David D. Maron, Hasan M. Shihab, Padmini D Ranasinghe, Shauna Linn, Shonali Saha, Eric B. Bass and Jennifer A. Haythornthwaite, 'Meditation Programs for Psychological Stress and Well-being: A Systematic Review and Meta-analysis', *JAMA Intern Med.*, vol. 174, pp 357–68, March 2014, doi: 10.1001/jamainternmed.2013.13018.
59. https://v2.wellcertified.com/wellv2/en/mind/feature/7 (accessed 4 October 2021).
60. Shawn Achor, *The Happiness Advantage: The Seven Principles of Positive Psychology that Fuel Success and Performance at Work*, Virgin Books, 2011.

Chapter 4

1. Edward O. Wilson, *Biophilia: The Human Bond with Other Species*, Harvard University Press, 1984.
2. 'House plants: to support human health' *RHS*, https://www.rhs.org.uk/advice/profile?PID=949 (accessed 4 October 2021).
3. 'Greener Gardens Promote Healthier Residents', *RHS*, October 2020, https://www.rhs.org.uk/advice/health-and-wellbeing/articles/greener-gardens-promote-healthier-residents (accessed 4 October 2021).
4. Michael Marshall, 'The Secret of how Life on Earth Began', *BBC Earth*, October 2016, http://www.bbc.com/earth/story/20161026-the-secret-of-how-life-on-earth-began (accessed 4 October 2021).
5. Simon Worrall, 'Building walls may have allowed civilization to flourish', *National Geographic*, April 2019, updated November 2020, https://www.nationalgeographic.co.uk/2018/10/building-walls-may-have-allowed-civilization-flourish (accessed 4 October 2021).
6. 'How Green is your View? Benefits of Exterior Living Walls', *Biotecture*, https://www.biotecture.uk.com/benefits/benefits-of-exterior-living-walls (accessed 4 October 2021).
7. R.S. Ulrich, 'View through a window may influence recovery from surgery', *Science*, vol. 224, issue 4647, April 1984, pp 420–21, DOI: 10.1126/science.6143402.

8. Russell Barnett, 'British Trees in Folklore', *BBC Wildlife*, https://www.discoverwildlife.com/plant-facts/trees/trees-in-folklore (accessed 4 October 2021).
9. Julia Falconer and Carla R. S. Koppell (ed.), 'The Major Significance of "Minor" Forest Products: The Local Use and Value of Forests in the West African Humid Forest Zone', *Food and Agriculture Organization of the United Nations*, 1990, http://www.fao.org/3/t9450e/t9450e00.htm#Contents (accessed 4 October 2021).
10. Jill Suttie, 'Why Trees Can Make You Happier', *Greater Good Magazine*, April 2019, https://greatergood.berkeley.edu/article/item/why_trees_can_make_you_happier (accessed 4 October 2021).
11. Jill Suttie, 'How Nature Can Make You Kinder, Happier, and More Creative', *Greater Good Magazine*, March 2016, https://greatergood.berkeley.edu/article/item/how_nature_makes_you_kinder_happier_more_creative (accessed 4 October 2021).
12. Oliver Heath Design, 'Creating Positive Spaces Using Biophilic Design', Global Wellness Institute, June 2018.
13. Tania Schusler, Leah Weiss, David Treering and Earvin Balderamab 'Research note: Examining the association between tree canopy, parks and crime in Chicago', *Landscape and Urban Planning*, vol. 170, February 2018, pp 309–13, https://doi.org/10.1016/j.landurbplan.2017.07.012 (accessed 4 October 2021).
14. 'There's A Convincing New Theory That Water Shaped Human Evolution', Business Insider, *The Economist*, July 2014, https://www.businessinsider.com/water-may-have-shaped-human-evolution-2014-7?r=US&IR=T (accessed 4 October 2021).
15. Joanne K. Garrett, Theodore J. Clitherow, Mathew P. White, Benedict W. Wheeler and Lora E. Fleming, 'Coastal proximity and mental health among urban adults in England: The moderating effect of household income', *Health & Place*, vol. 59, September 2019, https://doi.org/10.1016/j.healthplace.2019.102200 (accessed 4 October 2021).
16. Wallace J. Nichols, *Blue Mind How Water Makes You Happier, More Connected and Better at What You Do*, Abacus, 2018.
17. Alissa M. Clouse, 'Human Psychological Response to and Benefits of Interior Water Features', *Honors Thesis, The University of Southern Mississippi*, Spring 2016, https://aquila.usm.edu/cgi/viewcontent.cgi?article=1363&context=honors_theses (accessed 4 October 2021).
18. National Geographic Society, 'The Development of Agriculture', *National Geographic*, August 2019, https://www.nationalgeographic.org/article/development-agriculture (accessed 4 October 2021).
19. Carolyn Steel, *Hungry City: How Food Shapes Our Lives*, Vintage, 2013.
20. https://www.statista.com/statistics/301486/trend-in-british-adults-growing-their-own-produce-uk-great-britain (accessed 4 October 2021).
21. 'The benefits of gardening and food growing for health and wellbeing', *Sustain*, 2014, https://www.sustainweb.org/publications/the_benefits_of_gardening_and_food_growing (accessed 4 October 2021).
22. 'Why gardening is good for your mental wellbeing', *Thrive*, https://www.thrive.org.uk/how-we-help/what-we-do/why-gardening-is-good-for-our-health/why-gardening-is-good-for-your-mental-wellbeing (accessed 4 October 2021).
23. J.J. Richardson and L.M. Moskal, 'Urban food crop production capacity and competition with the urban forest', *Urban Forestry & Urban Greening*, vol. 15, 2016, pp 58–64, DOI: 10.1016/j.ufug.2015.10.006.
24. University of Exeter, 'Why plants in the office make us more productive', *Science Daily*, September 2014, www.sciencedaily.com/releases/2014/09/140901090735.htm (accessed 4 October 2021).
25. Adrienne Katz Kennedy, 'London's Urban Farms Move Underground', *Modern Farmer*, November 2019, https://modernfarmer.com/2019/11/londons-urban-farms-move-underground (accessed 4 October 2021).
26. See 'Vertical Future' website, https://verticalfuture.co.uk (accessed 4 October 2021).
27. WHO, 'Household air pollution and health', *World Health Organization*, May 2018, https://www.who.int/news-room/fact-sheets/detail/household-air-pollution-and-health (accessed 4 October 2021).
28. 'Indoor Air Quality', *United States Environmental Protection Agency*, https://www.epa.gov/indoor-air-quality-iaq/introduction-indoor-air-quality (accessed 4 October 2021).
29. B. Geerts, 'How long can we survive in a sealed enclosure?', *University of Wyoming Department of Atmospheric Science*, 1997, http://www-das.uwyo.edu/~geerts/cwx/notes/chap01/ox_exer.html (accessed 4 October 2021).
30. Robinson Meyer, 'A Popular Benefit of Houseplants Is a Myth: The science is clear: Indoor vegetation doesn't significantly remove pollutants from the air', *The Atlantic*, March 2019, https://www.theatlantic.com/science/archive/2019/03/indoor-plants-clean-air-best-none-them/584509 (accessed 4 October 2021).
31. Majbrit Dela Cruz, Jan H. Christensen, Jane Dyrhauge Thomsen and Renate Müller, 'Can ornamental potted plants remove volatile organic compounds from indoor air?', *Springer*, 2014, DOI 10.1007/s11356-014-3240-x.
32. 'Houseplants: to support human health', *RHS*, https://www.rhs.org.uk/advice/profile?PID=949 (accessed 4 October 2021).
33. Mohd Mahathir Suhaimi, A.M Leman, Azizi Afandi, Azian Hariri, Ahmad Fu'ad Idris, S.N. Mohd Dzulkifli and Paran Gani, 'Effectiveness of Indoor Plant to Reduce CO_2 in Indoor Environment', *MATEC Web of Conferences 103*, 2017, DOI: 10.1051/matecconf/20171030.
34. Deborah Franklin, 'How Hospital Gardens Help Patients Heal', *Scientific American*, March 2012, https://www.scientificamerican.com/article/nature-that-nurtures (accessed 4 October 2021).
35. 'Awe Story', *Greater Good Magazine*, https://ggia.berkeley.edu/practice/awe_story?_ga=2.104022851.2127766267.1609352500-1954117105.1609155060 (accessed 4 October 2021).
36. Deborah Franklin, 'How Hospital Gardens Help Patients Heal', *Scientific American*, March 2012, https://www.scientificamerican.com/article/nature-that-nurtures (accessed 4 October 2021).
37. See Misha Semenov 'Framing the View to Nature: Windows as Empathic Mediators between Indoor and Outdoor Ecology', *Eco-Empathy Project*, December 2017, https://ecoempathyproject.wordpress.com/2017/12/17/framing-the-view-to-nature-windows-as-empathic-mediators-between-indoor-and-outdoor-ecology (accessed 4 October 2021).
38. 'Windows and their meaning in Japanese Architecture', *Tsunagu Japan*, July 2014, https://www.tsunagujapan.com/windows-and-their-meanings-in-japanese-architecture (accessed 1 March 2021).
39. Sofia Lekka Angelopoulou, 'Windowology' exhibition at Japan House, London explores windows as cultural objects', *Design Boom*, February 2020, https://www.designboom.com/architecture/windowology-exhibition-japan-house-london-windows-02-01-2020 (accessed 4 October 2021).
40. Manuel Lima, 'Why do we find circles so beautiful?', *Science Focus*, August 2017, https://www.sciencefocus.com/science/why-do-we-find-circles-so-beautiful (accessed 4 October 2021).

41. Ibid.
42. 'Parks and Improved Mental Health and Quality of Life', *Park and Recreation Fact Sheet, National Recreation and Park Association*, https://www.nrpa.org/contentassets/9c491783f73a45f89abb0443b1a3e977/parks-improved-mental-health-quality-life.pdf (accessed 4 October 2021).
43. Ibid.
44. Deborah A. Cohen, Thomas L. McKenzie, Amber Sehgal, Stephanie Williamson, Daniela Golinelli and Nicole Lurie, 'Contribution of Public Parks to Physical Activity', *American Journal of Public Health*, vol. 97, March 2007, pp 509–14, doi: 10.2105/AJPH.2005.072447.
45. 'Improving access to greenspace: A new review for 2020', *Public Health England*, March 2020, https://assets.publishing.service.gov.uk/government/uploads/system/uploads/attachment_data/file/904439/Improving_access_to_greenspace_2020_review.pdf (accessed 4 October 2021).
46. Ibid.
47. '68% of the world population projected to live in urban areas by 2050', *United Nations, Department of Economic and Social Affairs*, May 2018, https://www.un.org/development/desa/en/news/population/2018-revision-of-world-urbanization-prospects.html (accessed 4 October 2021).
48. Deborah Orr, 'Humans are losing touch with nature – it's a tragedy with no quick fix', *The Guardian*, July 2017, https://www.theguardian.com/commentisfree/2017/jul/24/humans-losing-touch-nature-alcoholism-gambling (accessed 4 October 2021).
49. Selin Kesebir and Pelin Kesebir, 'How Modern Life Became Disconnected from Nature', *Greater Good Magazine*, September 2017, https://greatergood.berkeley.edu/article/item/how_modern_life_became_disconnected_from_nature (accessed 4 October 2021).
50. Miles Richardson, 'Connecting Children with Nature: By Nature Trails and Learning or through Art?', *Finding Nature*, September 2015, https://findingnature.org.uk/2015/09/06/connecting-children-with-nature-by-nature-trails-and-learning-or-through-art (accessed 4 October 2021).
51. Louise Delagran, 'How does nature impact our wellbeing?', *Earl E. Bakken Center for Spirituality & Healing, University of Minnesota*, https://www.takingcharge.csh.umn.edu/how-does-nature-impact-our-wellbeing (accessed 4 October 2021).
52. Robin Mazumder, 'Build A City I Can Be Proud Of: How Urban Design Impacts Civic Pride', August 2017, https://robinmazumderdotcom.wordpress.com/2017/08/02/build-a-city-i-can-be-proud-of-how-urban-design-impacts-civic-pride/ (4 October 2021).
53. Mandy Oaklander, 'Science Says Your Pet Is Good for Your Mental Health', *Time*, https://time.com/collection/guide-to-happiness/4728315/science-says-pet-good-for-mental-health (accessed 4 October 2021).
54. Jon Johnson, reviewed by Vincent J. Tavella, 'What to know about animal therapy', *Medical News Today*, July 2020, https://www.medicalnewstoday.com/articles/animal-therapy (accessed 4 October 2021).
55. 'Empirical Support for Therapy Animal Interventions', *Pet Partners*, https://petpartners.org/wp-content/uploads/2020/02/Benefits-of-the-Human-Animal-Bond-final.pdf (accessed 4 October 2021).
56. H.J. Ko, C.H. Youn, S.H. Kim, S.Y. Kim, 'Effect of Pet Insects on the Psychological Health of Community-Dwelling Elderly People: A Single-Blinded, Randomized, Controlled Trial', *Gerontology*, vol. 62, 2016, pp 200–09. doi: 10.1159/000439129.
57. John F. Helliwell, Richard Layard, Jeffrey D. Sachs and Jan-Emmanuel De Neve (eds), 'World Happiness Report 2020', https://happiness-report.s3.amazonaws.com/2020/WHR20.pdf (accessed 4 October 2021).
58. See for example https://www.rospa.com/leisure-safety/water/advice/signs.aspx (accessed 4 October 2021).
59. Paul Talling, *London's Lost Rivers*, Random House, 2011.
60. Oliver Wainwright, 'Smartphone use blamed as water feature is bricked up', *The Guardian*, June 2018, https://www.theguardian.com/artanddesign/2018/jun/20/smartphones-blamed-the-rill-water-feature-london-bridge-bricked-up (accessed 4 October 2021).
61. '10 Key Benefits of Roof Gardens', *Urban Rooftop and Terrace, Outdoor Space and Design*, January 2017, https://www.toddhaimanlandscapedesign.com/gardening-resources/10-key-benefits-of-roof-gardens (accessed 4 October 2021).
62. Lizzie Crook, 'Barcelona to convert a third of central streets into car-free green spaces', *Dezeen*, November 2020, https://www.dezeen.com/2020/11/19/barcelona-eixample-masterplan-streets-green-space (accessed 4 October 2021).
63. https://v2.wellcertified.com/wellv2/en/movement/feature/5 (accessed 4 October 2021).
64. National Association of City Transportation Officials, *Global Street Design Guide*, Island Press, 2016.
65. P. Prolo, 'A sensory garden in dementia care: from design to practice Balerna Diurnal Therapeutic Centre', *Alzheimers Dement Cogn Neurol*, 2017, DOI: 10.15761/ADCN.1000116
66. See for example https://www.rotterdam.nl/wonen-leven/geveltuinen (accessed 4 October 2021).

Chapter 5

1. 'Living with Beauty: Promoting health, well-being and sustainable growth', *The report of the Building Better, Building Beautiful Commission*, January 2020, https://www.stcuthbertout-pc.gov.uk/uploads/living-with-beauty-bbbbc-report.pdf (accessed 4 October 2021).
2. Simon Aldous, 'Government issues design code for "beautiful" new housing', *RIBA Journal*, February 2021, https://www.ribaj.com/intelligence/news-catch-up-government-design-code-bbbbc-permitted-development-rights-fire-safety-training-grenfell-pompidou-centre (accessed 4 October 2021).
3. Elina Grigoriou, *Wellbeing in Interiors: Philosophy, design and value in practice*, RIBA Publishing, 2019.
4. Michael Bond, 'The hidden ways that architecture affects how you feel', *BBC Future*, June 2017, https://www.bbc.com/future/article/20170605-the-psychology-behind-your-citys-design (accessed 4 October 2021).
5. Ibid.
6. Charles Montgomery, *Happy City: Transforming Our Lives Through Urban Design*, Penguin, 2015.
7. Jose Caivano, 'The research on color in architecture: Brief history, current developments, and possible future', *Color Research & Application*, vol. 31, 2006, pp 350–63, doi 10.1002/col.20224.
8. Ingrid Fettell Lee, *Joyful: The surprising power of ordinary things to create extraordinary happiness*, Rider, 2018.
9. Mariam Adawiah Dzulkifli and Muhammad Faiz Mustafar, 'The influence of colour on memory performance: a review', *The Malaysian Journal of Medical Sciences*, vol. 20, 2013, pp 3–9, https://www.ncbi.nlm.nih.gov/pmc/articles/PMC3743993 (accessed 4 October 2021).

10   Sarah Cascone, 'Archaeologists Have Discovered a Pristine 45,000-Year-Old Cave Painting of a Pig That May Be the Oldest Artwork in the World', *Art Net*, January 2021, https://news.artnet.com/art-world/indonesia-pig-art-oldest-painting-1937110 (accessed 4 October 2021).
11   Jonathan Jones, 'God, sex or evolution – why did humans start making art?', *The Guardian*, November 2016, https://www.theguardian.com/artanddesign/jonathanjonesblog/2016/nov/03/on-the-origins-of-art-exhibition-tasmania-why-did-humans-start-making-art-comment (accessed 4 October 2021).
12   Meera Lee Sethi, 'Does Art Heal?', *Greater Good Magazine*, December 2008, https://greatergood.berkeley.edu/article/item/does_art_heal (accessed 4 October 2021).
13   Richard Alleyne, 'Viewing Art Gives the same Pleasure as Being in Love', *The Telegraph*, May 2011, https://www.telegraph.co.uk/culture/art/8501024/Viewing-art-gives-same-pleasure-as-being-in-love.html (accessed 4 October 2021).
14   Tomas Chamorro-Premuzic, Adrian Furnham and Stian Reimers, 'Personality and art', *The British Phycological Society*, vol. 20, February 2007, pp. 84–87, https://thepsychologist.bps.org.uk/volume-20/edition-2/personality-and-art (accessed 4 October 2021).
15   Jeroen Koolhaas and Dre Urhahn, 'How Painting can transform communities', *TEDGlobal*, 2014, https://www.ted.com/talks/haas_hahn_how_painting_can_transform_communities?referrer=playlist-street_art&language=en (accessed 4 October 2021).
16   https://v2.wellcertified.com/community/en/community/feature/17 (accessed 4 October 2021).
17   'Optical illusion: Dress colour debate goes global', *BBC News*, February 2015 https://www.bbc.co.uk/news/uk-scotland-highlands-islands-31656935 (accessed 4 October 2021).
18   'Color vision problems become more common with age, study shows', *Science Daily*, February 2014, https://www.sciencedaily.com/releases/2014/02/140220102614.htm (accessed 4 October 2021).
19   Randy Dotinga, 'Color vision tends to fade with age', *WebMD*, March 2014, https://www.webmd.com/healthy-aging/news/20140318/color-vision-tends-to-fade-with-age-study#1 (accessed 4 October 2021).
20   'The importance of colour and contrast', *DSDC The Dementia Centre*, https://dementia.stir.ac.uk/design/virtual-environments/importance-colour-and-contrast (accessed 4 October 2021).
21   Jonathan Docksey, 'Accessibility & Legibility in Wayfinding Design', *Design JD*, https://designjd.co.uk/accessibility-legibility-in-wayfinding-design (accessed 4 October 2021).
22   Edward Allen and Patrick Rand, *Architectural Detailing: Function, Constructibility, Aesthetics*, Wiley, 2016.
23   Mayor of London, 'The London Plan: The Spatial Development Strategy for Greater London', March 2021, p 111, https://www.london.gov.uk/sites/default/files/the_london_plan_2021.pdf (accessed 4 October 2021).
24   Toby Israel, *Some Place Like Home: Using Design Psychology to Create Ideal Places*, Design Psychology Press, 2010.
25   James D. Wright (ed.), *International Encyclopedia of the Social and Behavioral Sciences*, Second Edition, Elsevier Ltd., 2015.
26   'The cost of importing the materials you specify', *RIBA Journal*, August 2017, https://www.ribaj.com/intelligence/material-concerns-in-a-post-brexit-world-market-analysis (accessed 4 October 2021).
27   Michael Bond, 'The hidden ways that architecture affects how you feel', *BBC*, June 2017, https://www.bbc.com/future/article/20170605-the-psychology-behind-your-citys-design (accessed 4 October 2021).
28   Elizabeth Quinn Brown, '15 of the World's Most Historically Significant Doors', *Architectural Digest*, July 2019, https://www.architecturaldigest.com/story/worlds-most-historically-significant-doors (accessed 4 October 2021).
29   Zarah Hussain, 'Islamic art', *BBC Religion*, June 2009, https://www.bbc.co.uk/religion/religions/islam/art/art_1.shtml (accessed 4 October 2021).
30   Philip Ball, *Patterns in Nature: Why the Natural World Looks the Way It Does*, University of Chicago Press, 2016.
31   Lily Bernheimer, *The Shaping of Us: How Everyday Spaces Structure Our Lives, Behaviour and Well-Being*, Trinity University Press, 2019.
32   American Marketing Association (AMA), 'Consumers value handmade products: What's love got to do with it?', *Science Daily*, March 2015, https://www.sciencedaily.com/releases/2015/03/150324111544.htm (accessed 4 October 2021).
33   Leonard Koren, *Wabi-sabi: For Artists, Designers, Poets & Philosophers*, Imperfect Publishing, 2008.
34   Yi Hsu and Anh Nguyen Ngoc, 'The Handmade Effect: What is Special about Buying Handmade?', *International Review of Management and Business Research*, vol. 5, June 2016, https://irmbrjournal.com/papers/1466711111.pdf (accessed 4 October 2021).
35   'What are the health benefits of altruism?', *Mental Health Foundation*, https://www.mentalhealth.org.uk/publications/doing-good-does-you-good/health-benefits-altruism (accessed 4 October 2021).
36   Diana Cepsyte, 'How Colors Affect You: What Science Reveals', *Medium*, November 2018, https://diana-cepsyte.medium.com/how-colors-affect-you-what-science-reveals-c904d918d440 (accessed 4 October 2021).
37   Alison Lurie, *The Language of Houses: How Buildings Speak to Us*, Delphinium Books, 2015.
38   Op. cit., Bernheimer, *The Shaping of Us*.
39   Marc Shoffman, 'From building a conservatory to getting a new kitchen – which home improvements deliver the best return?', *This Is Money*, November 2014, https://www.thisismoney.co.uk/money/mortgageshome/article-2834756/Which-home-improvements-add-house-prices-investment.html (accessed 4 October 2021).
40   See http://www.fashionarchitecturetaste.com (accessed 4 October 2021).
41   Michael Bond, 'The hidden ways that architecture affects how you feel', *BBC Future*, June 2017, https://www.bbc.com/future/article/20170605-the-psychology-behind-your-citys-design (accessed 4 October 2021).
42   Edgar Chan, Oliver Baumann, Mark A. Bellgrove and Jason B. Mattingley, 'From objects to landmarks: the function of visual location information in spatial navigation', *Frontiers in Psychology*, August 2012, https://doi.org/10.3389/fpsyg.2012.00304 (accessed 4 October 2021).

Chapter 6

1   Herman Pontzer, 'Humans Evolved to Exercise', *Scientific American*, January 2019, https://www.scientificamerican.com/article/humans-evolved-to-exercise (accessed 4 October 2021).
2   Lito Howse, 'Humans have not evolved to exercise', *The Current*, February 2021, https://www.cbc.ca/radio/thecurrent/the-current-for-feb-9-2021-1.5906730/humans-have-not-evolved-to-exercise-says-harvard-prof-1.5907580 (accessed 4 October 2021).

3. Herman Pontzer, 'The Exercise Paradox', *Scientific American*, February 2017, https://exss.unc.edu/wp-content/uploads/sites/779/2018/09/Exercise-paradox-Pontzer-2017.pdf (accessed 4 October 2021).
4. https://v2.wellcertified.com/wellv2/en/movement (accessed 4 October 2021).
5. David Lock Associates, Sports England and Public Health England, 'Active Design: Planning for health and wellbeing through sport and physical activity', *Sports England*, October 2015, https://sportengland-production-files.s3.eu-west-2.amazonaws.com/s3fs-public/spe003-active-design-published-october-2015-high-quality-for-web-2.pdf?uCz_r6UyApzAZlaiEVaNt69DAaOCmklQ (accessed 4 October 2021).
6. David J. Linden, 'The Truth Behind 'Runner's High' and Other Mental Benefits of Running', *Hopkins Medicine*, https://www.hopkinsmedicine.org/health/wellness-and-prevention/the-truth-behind-runners-high-and-other-mental-benefits-of-running (accessed 4 October 2021).
7. Ashish Sharma, Vishal Madaan, and Frederick D. Petty, 'Exercise for Mental Health', *Primary Care Companion to the Journal for Clinical Psychiatry*, vol. 8, 2006, p 106, doi: 10.4088/pcc.v08n0208a.
8. Duck-chul Lee, Angelique G. Brellenthin, Paul D. Thompson, Xuemei Sui, I-Min Lee and Carl J. Lavie, 'Running as a Key Lifestyle Medicine for Longevity', *Progress in Cardiovascular Diseases*, vol. 60, 2017, pp 45–55, https://doi.org/10.1016/j.pcad.2017.03.005 (accessed 4 October 2021).
9. A. Dietrich and W. F. McDaniel, 'Endocannabinoids and exercise', *British Journal of Sports Medicine*, 2004, vol. 38, pp 536–41, http://dx.doi.org/10.1136/bjsm.2004.011718 (accessed 4 October 2021).
10. Christopher McDougall, *Born to Run: The Hidden Tribe, the Ultra-Runners, and the Greatest Race the World Has Never Seen*, Profile Books, 2010.
11. Mattias Qviström, 'The nature of running: On embedded landscape ideals in leisure planning', *Urban Forestry & Urban Greening*, vol. 17, 2016, pp 202–10, https://doi.org/10.1016/j.ufug.2016.04.012 (accessed 4 October 2021).
12. See https://www.nationalparkcity.london (accessed 4 October 2021).
13. Deborah A. Cohen, Thomas L. McKenzie, Amber Sehgal, Stephanie Williamson, Daniela Golinelli and Nicole Lurie, 'Contribution of Public Parks to Physical Activity', *American Journal of Public Health*, March 2007, vol. 97, pp 509–14, doi: 10.2105/AJPH.2005.072447.
14. See https://dsrny.com/project/the-high-line (accessed 4 October 2021).
15. 'Living with Beauty: Promoting health, well-being and sustainable growth', *The report of the Building Better, Building Beautiful Commission*, January 2020, https://www.stcuthbertout-pc.gov.uk/uploads/living-with-beauty-bbbbc-report.pdf (accessed 4 October 2021).
16. Iain Roberts, @slowbikeiain, Twitter, 13 November 2020, https://twitter.com/slowbikeiain/status/1327169679224418304 (accessed 4 October 2021).
17. Fiona Rajé and Andrew Saffrey, 'The value of cycling', *Department of Transport, Phil Jones Associates and Birmingham University*, https://assets.publishing.service.gov.uk/government/uploads/system/uploads/attachment_data/file/509587/value-of-cycling.pdf (accessed 4 October 2021).
18. Mayor of London, 'London Infrastructure Plan 2050: Transport Supporting Paper', https://www.london.gov.uk/sites/default/files/Transport%20Supporting%20Paper_3.pdf (accessed 4 October 2021).
19. Op. cit., Rajé and Saffrey, 'The value of cycling'.
20. See https://www.sharedmobilityprinciples.org (accessed 4 October 2021).
21. https://www.theguardian.com/commentisfree/2021/mar/13/men-curfew-sarah-everard-women-adapt-violence (accessed 4 October 2021).
22. Gareth Owen, '50 Million Global Street Lights Expected to Be Connected by 2023', *Counterpoint*, March 2019, https://www.counterpointresearch.com/50-million-global-street-lights-expected-connected-2023 (accessed 4 October 2021).
23. UCL Jill Dando Institute and was co-funded by the College of Policing and the Economic and Social Research Council (ESRC), 'Street Lighting', *What Works Network, College of Policing*, February 2015, https://whatworks.college.police.uk/toolkit/Pages/Intervention.aspx?InterventionID=3 (accessed 4 October 2021).
24. C.M. Lenhart, A. Wiemken, A. Hanlon, et. al., 'Perceived neighborhood safety related to physical activity but not recreational screen-based sedentary behavior in adolescents', *BMC Public Health*, vol. 17, p 722, 2017, https://doi.org/10.1186/s12889-017-4756-z (accessed 4 October 2021).
25. https://v2.wellcertified.com/community/en/light/feature/4 (accessed 4 October 2021).
26. See 'Smart Streetlights', https://tvilight.com (accessed 4 October 2021).
27. Op. cit., Owen, '50 Million Global Street Lights Expected to Be Connected by 2023'.
28. 'Transport Statistics Great Britain 2017', *Department for Transport*, November 2017, https://assets.publishing.service.gov.uk/government/uploads/system/uploads/attachment_data/file/661933/tsgb-2017-report-summaries.pdf (accessed 4 October 2021).
29. YouGov, 'Just 9% of working Brits Cycle to Work', *YouGov Poll*, November 2016, https://yougov.co.uk/topics/politics/articles-reports/2016/02/25/just-9-working-brits-cycle-work (accessed 4 October 2021).
30. https://v2.wellcertified.com/wellv2/en/movement/feature/4 (accessed 4 October 2021).
31. https://www.scientificamerican.com/article/why-do-you-think-better-after-walk-exercise/ (accessed 4 October 2021).
32. Op. cit., Rajé and Saffrey, 'The value of cycling' (accessed 4 October 2021).
33. Adam Shaw, 'How to save the UK's crisis-hit High Streets', *BBC News*, January 2020, https://www.bbc.co.uk/news/business-51094109 (accessed 4 October 2021).
34. See http://www.stirlingactivetravelhub.org/about-us (accessed 4 October 2021).
35. Op. cit., Rajé and Saffrey, 'The value of cycling'.
36. 'Why Do People Act Differently in Groups Than They Do Alone?', *Walden University*, https://www.waldenu.edu/online-masters-programs/ms-in-psychology/resource/why-do-people-act-differently-in-groups-than-they-do-alone (accessed 4 October 2021).
37. Helen Woolley, Sian Rose, Matthew Carmona and Jonathan Freedman, 'The Value of Public Space', *Design Council*, https://www.designcouncil.org.uk/sites/default/files/asset/document/the-value-of-public-space1.pdf (accessed 4 October 2021).
38. Lizzie Ward, Marian Barnes and Beatrice Gahagan, 'Well-being in old age: findings from participatory research', *University of Brighton and Age Concern Brighton, Hove and Portslade*, 2012, https://www.brighton.ac.uk/_pdf/research/ssparc/wellbeing-in-oldage-executive-summary.pdf (accessed 4 October 2021).

39 Radhika Bynon and Clare Rishbeth, 'Benches for everyone: Solitude in public, sociability for free', *The Young Foundations*, October 2015, https://youngfoundation.org/wp-content/uploads/2015/11/The-Bench-Project_single-pages.pdf (accessed 4 October 2021).

40 'What Makes a Successful Place?', *Project for Public Spaces*, https://www.pps.org/article/grplacefeat (accessed 4 October 2021).

41 'National Design Guide: Planning practice guidance for beautiful, enduring and successful places', *Ministry of Housing, Communities and Local Government*, January 2021, https://assets.publishing.service.gov.uk/government/uploads/system/uploads/attachment_data/file/962113/National_design_guide.pdf (accessed 4 October 2021).

42 Nathan Massey, 'The History of Lifts', *Designing Buildings Wiki*, July 2017, edited October 2020, https://www.designingbuildings.co.uk/wiki/The_history_of_lifts (accessed 4 October 2021).

43 S. Shah, M. O'Byrne, M. Wilson and T. Wilson, 'Research of a Holiday kind: elevators or stairs?', *Canadian Medical Association Journal*, vol. 183, December 2011, https://doi.org/10.1503/cmaj.110961 (accessed 4 October 2021).

44 M.J. Kinsey, E.R. Galea and P.J. Lawrence, 'Stairs or Lifts? A Study of Human Factors associated with Lift/Elevator usage during Evacuations using an online Survey', *Fire Safety Engineering Group (FSEG)*, University of Greenwich, London, Paper presented at PED 2010, NIST, Maryland USA, March 2010, https://fseg.gre.ac.uk/fire/fseg_ped2010_liftstairchoice_paper_distrib_final_final.pdf (accessed 4 October 2021).

45 J. Rezmovitz, Jack Taunton, E. Rhodes and B. Zumbo, 'The effects of a lower body resistance training programme on static balance and well-being in older adult women', *BC Medical Journal*, vol. 45, no. 9, November 2003, pp 449–55, https://bcmj.org/articles/effects-lower-body-resistance-training-program-static-balance-and-well-being-older-adult (accessed 4 October 2021).

46 Shaunacy Ferro, 'People Really, Really Don't Like Taking the Stairs', *Mental Floss*, July 2015, https://www.mentalfloss.com/article/66071/people-really-really-dont-taking-stairs (accessed 4 October 2021).

47 Michael R. Bloomberg, David Burney, Thomas Farley, Janette Sadik-Khan and Amanda Burden, 'Active Design Guidelines: Promoting Physical Activity and Health in Design', *City of New York*, 2010, https://www1.nyc.gov/assets/planning/download/pdf/plans-studies/active-design-guidelines/adguidelines.pdf (accessed 4 October 2021).

48 Lily Bernheimer, *The Shaping of Us: How Everyday Spaces Structure Our Lives, Behaviour and Well-Being*, Trinity University Press, 2019.

49 Murat Z. Memluk, 'Designing Urban Squares', *Advances in Landscape Architecture*, 2013, DOI: 10.5772/55826.

50 Charles Montgomery, *Happy City: Transforming Our Lives Through Urban Design*, Penguin, 2015.

51 Josh Gabbatiss, 'The strange experiments that revealed most mammals can swim', *BBC Earth*, March 2017, http://www.bbc.com/earth/story/20170320-the-cruel-experiments-that-revealed-most-mammals-can-swim (accessed 4 October 2021).

52 Eric Chaline, 'How Europe Leant to Swim', *History Today*, July 2018, https://www.historytoday.com/miscellanies/how-europe-learnt-swim (accessed 4 October 2021).

53 Statistics from Swim England https://www.swimming.org/swimengland/key-swimming-statistics (accessed 4 October 2021).

54 'The Mental Health and Wellbeing Benefits of Swimming', *Everyone Active*, https://www.everyoneactive.com/content-hub/swimming/mental-health-and-well-being-benefits-of-swimming (accessed 4 October 2021).

55 Gina Shaw, 'Water Tips for Efficient Exercise', *WebMD*, July 2009, https://www.webmd.com/fitness-exercise/features/water-for-exercise-fitness (accessed 4 October 2021).

56 Paul McArdle (expert reviewer), 'Keeping hydrated for exercise', *BUPA*, September 2020, https://www.bupa.co.uk/health-information/exercise-fitness/hydration-exercise (accessed 4 October 2021).

57 'The Importance of Hydration', *Harvard School of Public Health*, https://www.hsph.harvard.edu/news/hsph-in-the-news/the-importance-of-hydration (accessed 4 October 2021).

58 E.L. Kenney, M.W. Long, A.L. Cradock and S.L. Gortmaker, 'Prevalence of Inadequate Hydration Among US Children and Disparities by Gender and Race/Ethnicity: National Health and Nutrition Examination Survey, 2009–2012', *American Journal of Public Health*, vol. 105, 2015, https://doi.org/10.2105/AJPH.2015.302572 (accessed 4 October 2021).

59 Erica L. Kenney, James G. Daly, Rebekka M. Lee, Rebecca S. Mozaffarian, Katherine Walsh, Jill Carter and Steven L. Gortmaker, 'Providing Students with Adequate School Drinking Water Access in an Era of Aging Infrastructure: A Mixed Methods Investigation', *International Journal of Environmental Research and Public Health*, December 2019, https://pubmed.ncbi.nlm.nih.gov/31861778/(accessed 4 October 2021).

60 Eleanor Beardsley, 'To Burst The Bottle Bubble, Fountains In Paris Now Flow With Sparkling Water', *The Salt*, December 2017, https://www.npr.org/sections/thesalt/2017/12/01/567294632/to-burst-the-bottle-bubble-fountains-in-paris-now-flow-with-sparkling-water?t=1617460970659&t=1619523410963 (accessed 4 October 2021).

61 https://v2.wellcertified.com/wellv2/en/water/feature/4 (accessed 4 October 2021).

62 Melissa Denchak, 'Flint Water Crisis: Everything You Need to Know', *NRC*, November 2018, https://www.nrdc.org/stories/flint-water-crisis-everything-you-need-know (accessed 4 October 2021).

63 Daniel A. Cox, 'The importance of place: Neighborhood amenities as a source of social connection and trust', *American Enterprise Institute*, May 2019, https://www.aei.org/research-products/report/the-importance-of-place-neighborhood-amenities-as-a-source-of-social-connection-and-trust (accessed 4 October 2021).

64 Michael Bond, 'The hidden ways that architecture affects how you feel', *BBC*, June 2017, https://www.bbc.com/future/article/20170605-the-psychology-behind-your-citys-design (accessed 4 October 2021).

65 Op. cit. Charles Montgomery, *Happy City*.

66 Edwin Heathcote, 'Design cities around people, not dustbins', *Financial Times*, https://www.ft.com/content/e121c1a3-b083-4971-adce-028ba9c0a464 (accessed 4 October 2021).

67 Miriam Kresh, 'Surprising Reasons Why Cities Need More Shade', *Green Prophet*, August 2019, https://www.greenprophet.com/2019/08/surprising-reasons-why-cities-need-more-shade (accessed 4 October 2021).

68 Nicolas Boys Smith, 'Can High-rise homes make you ill?', *EG Magazine*, May 2017, https://www.egi.co.uk/news/can-high-rise-homes-make-you-ill (accessed 4 October 2021).

69 See http://www.evastudio.co.uk/tapis-rouge (accessed 4 October 2021).

70 Laura Healy, 'Mental health: which is better – team sports or solo exercise?', *The Conversation*, December 2019, https://theconversation.com/mental-health-which-is-better-team-sports-or-solo-exercise-126462 (accessed 4 October 2021).

71. P.B. Carr and G.M. Walton, 'Cues of working together fuel intrinsic motivation', *Journal of Experimental Social Psychology*, vol. 53, 2014, pp 169–84. doi:10.1016/j.jesp.2014.03.015.
72. 'Number of fitness facilities in the United Kingdom (UK) from 2008 to 2018', *Statista*, https://www.statista.com/statistics/433786/fitness-facilities-enterprises-uk-united-kingdom (accessed 4 October 2021).
73. 'Active Design', Sports England, https://www.sportengland.org/how-we-can-help/facilities-and-planning/design-and-cost-guidance/active-design (accessed 4 October 2021).
74. Ibid.

Chapter 7

1. Michael Harré, 'Social Network Size Linked to Brain Size: How and why the volume of the orbital prefrontal cortex is related to the size of social networks', *Scientific American*, August 2012, https://www.scientificamerican.com/article/social-network-size-linked-brain-size (accessed 4 October 2021).
2. Isabelle Catherine Winder and Vivien Shaw, 'Coronavirus: experts in evolution explain why social distancing feels so unnatural', *The Conversation*, March 2020, https://theconversation.com/coronavirus-experts-in-evolution-explain-why-social-distancing-feels-so-unnatural-134271 (accessed 4 October 2021).
3. Yuval Noah Harari, *Sapiens: A Brief History of Humankind*, Vintage, 2015.
4. Anne Trafton, 'A hunger for social contact: Neuroscientists find that isolation provokes brain activity similar to that seen during hunger cravings', *Science Daily*, November 2020, https://www.sciencedaily.com/releases/2020/11/201123120724.htm (accessed 4 October 2021).
5. J. Holt-Lunstad, T.B. Smith, M. Baker, T. Harris and D. Stephenson, 'Loneliness and social isolation as risk factors for mortality: a meta-analytic review', *Perspective Psychology Science*, vol. 10, March 2015, pp 227–37, doi: 10.1177/1745691614568352. PMID: 25910392.
6. See Campaign to End Loneliness, https://www.campaigntoendloneliness.org/threat-to-health (accessed 4 October 2021).
7. See Loneliness Lab, https://www.lonelinesslab.org (accessed 4 October 2021).
8. Nancy Hey, 'World Happiness Report 2016 summary findings', What Works Wellbeing, March 2016, https://whatworkswellbeing.org/blog/world-happiness-report-2016-summary-findings (accessed 4 October 2021).
9. 'How Does Your Community Make You Proud?', *Lifestyle*, 2018, https://lifestyle.co.uk/homes/guides/how-does-your-community-make-you-proud.htm (accessed 4 October 2021).
10. 'Brits spend 90% of their time indoors', *Opinium*, October 2018, https://www.opinium.com/brits-spend-90-of-their-time-indoors (accessed 4 October 2021).
11. Secured by Design, https://www.securedbydesign.com/ (accessed 4 October 2021).
12. 'What are the health benefits of altruism?', *Mental Health Foundation*, https://www.mentalhealth.org.uk/publications/doing-good-does-you-good/health-benefits-altruism (accessed 4 October 2021).
13. Kay Hymowitz, 'The Real Roots of the Nuclear Family', *Institute for Family Studies*, December 2013, https://ifstudies.org/blog/the-real-roots-of-the-nuclear-family (accessed 4 October 2021).
14. T.F. Harandi, M.M. Taghinasab and T.D. Nayeri, 'The correlation of social support with mental health: A meta-analysis', *Electronic physician*, vol. 9(9), 2017, pp 5212–222, https://doi.org/10.19082/5212 (accessed 4 October 2021).
15. Charles Montgomery, *Happy City: Transforming Our Lives Through Urban Design*, Penguin, 2015.
16. See https://beta-office.com/project/3-generation-house (accessed 4 October 2021).
17. 'Building projects adding most value', *My Home Extension*, https://www.myhomeextension.co.uk/building-projects-adding-most-value (accessed 4 October 2021).
18. Bob Sullivan and Hugh Thompson, 'Brain, Interrupted', *The New York Times*, May 2013, https://www.nytimes.com/2013/05/05/opinion/sunday/a-focus-on-distraction.html (accessed 4 October 2021).
19. Katharine Schwab, 'Everyone hates open offices. Here's why they still exist', *Fast Company*, January 2019, https://www.fastcompany.com/90285582/everyone-hates-open-plan-offices-heres-why-they-still-exist (accessed 4 October 2021).
20. Clare Bailey, 'The office soundscape: How to get the right balance of noise in the workplace', *Work in Mind*, 2020, https://workinmind.org/2020/04/15/the-office-soundscape-how-to-get-the-right-balance-of-noise-in-the-workplace (accessed 4 October 2021).
21. Ken Worpole and Katharine Knox, 'The social value of public spaces', *Joseph Rowntree Foundation*, https://www.jrf.org.uk/sites/default/files/jrf/migrated/files/2050-public-space-community.pdf (accessed 4 October 2021).
22. Richard Layard, *Happiness: Lessons from a New Science*, Penguin, 2011.
23. Bryan Walsh, 'Does Spirituality Make You Happy?', *Time*, https://time.com/collection/guide-to-happiness/4856978/spirituality-religion-happiness (accessed 4 October 2021).
24. Theaster Gates, 'How to revive a neighbourhood with imagination, beauty and art', *TED*, March 2015, https://www.ted.com/talks/theaster_gates_how_to_revive_a_neighborhood_with_imagination_beauty_and_art (accessed 4 October 2021).
25. Nicola Slawson, 'It's time to recognise the contribution arts can make to health and wellbeing', *The Guardian*, October 2017, https://www.theguardian.com/healthcare-network/2017/oct/11/contribution-arts-make-health-wellbeing (accessed 4 October 2021).
26. 'Using Design to Connect Us', *The Loneliness Lab*, Autumn 2020, https://www.lonelinesslab.org/knowledge-hub/using-design-to-connect-us (accessed 4 October 2021).
27. Paul Nicolaus, 'Want to Feel Happier Today? Try Talking to a Stranger', *NPR*, July 2019, https://www.npr.org/sections/health-shots/2019/07/26/744267015/want-to-feel-happier-today-try-talking-to-a-stranger (accessed 4 October 2021).
28. 'Social Value Toolkit for Architecture', *RIBA*, June 2020, https://www.architecture.com/knowledge-and-resources/resources-landing-page/social-value-toolkit-for-architecture (accessed 4 October 2021).
29. Melissa Dahl, 'Work Smarter: Meetings Are 34 Percent Shorter If You're Standing Up', *The Cut*, May 2014, https://www.thecut.com/2014/05/work-smarter-for-shorter-meetings-stand-up.html (accessed 4 October 2021).
30. 'Childbearing for women born in different years, England and Wales: 2018', *Office for National Statistics*, December 2019, https://www.ons.gov.uk/peoplepopulationandcommunity/birthsdeathsandmarriages/conceptionandfertilityrates/bulletins/childbearingforwomenbornindifferentyearsenglandandwales/2018 (accessed 4 October 2021).
31. 'What are the benefits to employers?', *US Breastfeeding Committee*, http://www.usbreastfeeding.org/p/cm/ld/fid=234 (accessed 4 October 2021).

32 Daniele Chicca, 'The Many Advantages of Workplace Daycare', *Ampersand*, November 2019, https://magazine.ampersand-world.com/advantages-workplace-daycare (accessed 4 October 2021).
33 'Average Childcare Costs', *Money Advice Service*, https://www.moneyadviceservice.org.uk/en/articles/childcare-costs (accessed 4 October 2021).
34 Rose Marcario, 'Patagonia's CEO Explains How To Make On-Site Child Care Pay For Itself', *Fast Company*, August 2016, https://www.fastcompany.com/3062792/patagonias-ceo-explains-how-to-make-onsite-child-care-pay-for-itself (accessed 4 October 2021).
35 Op. cit., Chicca, 'The Many Advantages of Workplace Daycare'.
36 Murat Z. Memluk, 'Designing Urban Squares', in *Advances in Landscape Architecture*, Murat Ozyavuz (ed.), 2013, DOI: 10.5772/55826.
37 Rob Shirley, 'Village greens of England: a study in historical geography', *Doctoral thesis, Durham University*, 1994, http://etheses.dur.ac.uk/6120/ (accessed 4 October 2021).
38 Félicie Krikler and Ben Channon, 'Myth busting: Density and Wellbeing', *Assael Architecture*, October 2020, https://assael.co.uk/news/2020/myth-busting-density-and-wellbeing (accessed 4 October 2021).
39 Kevin Lynch, *The Image of the City*, MIT Press, 1960, https://www.miguelangelmartinez.net/IMG/pdf/1960_Kevin_Lynch_The_Image_of_The_City_book.pdf (accessed 4 October 2021).
40 'National Design Guide: Planning practice guidance for beautiful, enduring and successful places', *Ministries of Housing, Communities and Local Government*, January 2021, https://assets.publishing.service.gov.uk/government/uploads/system/uploads/attachment_data/file/962113/National_design_guide.pdf (accessed 4 October 2021).
41 Jason G. Goldman, 'Why do animals like to play?', *BBC Future*, January 2013, https://www.bbc.com/future/article/20130109-why-do-animals-like-to-play (accessed 4 October 2021).
42 Kenneth R. Ginsburg, 'The Importance of Play in Promoting Healthy Child Development and Maintaining Strong Parent-Child Bonds', *Pediatrics*, January 2007, 119 (1) 182-191, DOI: https://doi.org/10.1542/peds.2006-2697 (accessed 4 October 2021).
43 Kira M. Newman, 'What Playfulness Can Do for Your Relationship: Being silly with your partner may have some serious benefits', *Greater Good Magazine*, February 2020, https://greatergood.berkeley.edu/article/item/what_playfulness_can_do_for_your_relationship (accessed 4 October 2021).
44 Kin Hart, 'History of Playgrounds', *AAA State of Play*, https://www.aaastateofplay.com/history-of-playgrounds (accessed 4 October 2021).
45 'Guide to designing inclusive playgrounds', *HAGS*, https://www.hags.com/en-us/designing-inclusive-playgrounds (accessed 4 October 2021).
46 Miriam Kresh, 'Surprising Reasons Why Cities Need More Shade', *Green Prophet*, August 2019.
47 Ewan Clayton, 'A history of Writing: Where did writing begin?', *British Library*, 2019, https://www.bl.uk/history-of-writing/articles/where-did-writing-begin (accessed 4 October 2021).
48 Ibid.
49 Derek Thompson, 'Can Your Language Influence Your Spending, Eating, and Smoking Habits? An absurd-sounding claim leads to a surprising finding', *The Atlantic*, September 2013, https://www.theatlantic.com/business/archive/2013/09/can-your-language-influence-your-spending-eating-and-smoking-habits/279484 (accessed 4 October 2021).
50 Kristen A. Lindquist, et al., 'The role of language in emotion: predictions from psychological constructionism', *Frontiers in Psychology*, vol. 6, April 2015, doi:10.3389/fpsyg.2015.00444.
51 Tiffany Watt Smith, *The Book of Human Emotions: From Ambiguphobia to Umpty – 154 Words for Around the World for How We Feel*, Little, Brown, 2016.
52 Joanna Moorhead, 'How poetry can light up our darker moments', *The Guardian*, September 2018, https://www.theguardian.com/lifeandstyle/2018/sep/30/how-poetry-can-light-up-our-darker-moments-mental-illness (accessed 4 October 2021).
53 Ceridwen Dovey, 'Can Reading Make You Happier?', *The New Yorker*, June 2015, https://www.newyorker.com/culture/cultural-comment/can-reading-make-you-happier (accessed 4 October 2021).
54 Daniel Salinas, 'The poetry on Leiden's walls', *The Leidener*, February 2019, https://theleidener.com/2019/02/07/the-poetry-on-leidens-walls (accessed 4 October 2021).
55 Lisa Joan Kinch, 'The Effect of Furniture Arrangements on the Social Interaction of Institutionalised Elderly', *Dissertation for the degree of Master of Science in Clothing, Textiles, and Related Arts*, November 1982, https://ir.library.oregonstate.edu/downloads/v979v643s?locale=en (accessed 4 October 2021).
56 Robert Sommer, *Personal Space: The Behavioral Basis of Design*, Bosko Books, 1969.
57 Simone Reynolds, 'Into co-living? This furniture can increase social interaction in shared housing', *Frame*, May 2019, https://www.frameweb.com/article/into-co-living-this-furniture-can-increase-social-interaction-in-shared-housing (accessed 4 October 2021).
58 Samuel Medina, '"Playing Seesaw" in Public Space', *Architizer*, https://architizer.com/blog/inspiration/industry/playing-seesaw-in-public-space (accessed 4 October 2021).
59 Joann Plockova, 'Social Furniture: For Austria's entry in the Venice Architecture Biennale, Vienna-based EOOS offers a problem-solving design to help Europe's refugee crisis', *WHY Magazine*, 2016, https://www.hermanmiller.com/en_gb/stories/why-magazine/social-furniture (accessed 4 October 2021).
60 R.I.M. Dunbar, 'Breaking Bread: The Functions of Social Eating', *Adaptive Human Behavior and Physiology*, vol. 3, 2017, pp 198–211, https://doi.org/10.1007/s40750-017-0061-4
61 'Social eating connects communities', *University of Oxford*, March 2017, https://www.ox.ac.uk/news/2017-03-16-social-eating-connects-communities (accessed 4 October 2021).
62 Op. cit., Dunbar, 'Breaking Bread'.
63 A.I. Conklin, N.G. Forouhi, P. Surtees, K.T. Khaw, N.J. Wareham and P. Monsivais, 'Social relationships and healthful dietary behaviour: Evidence from over-50s in the EPIC cohort, UK', *Social Science Medicine*, vol. 100 January 2014, pp 167–75. doi: 10.1016/j.socscimed.2013.08.018.
64 A.R. Kwon, Y.S. Yoon, K.P. Min, Y.K. Lee and J.H. Jeon, 'Eating alone and metabolic syndrome: A population-based Korean National Health and Nutrition Examination Survey 2013–2014', *Obesity Research Clinic Practice*, vol. 12, March– April 2018, pp 146–57, doi: 10.1016/j.orcp.2017.09.002.
65 https://v2.wellcertified.com/wellv2/en/nourishment/feature/8 (accessed 4 October 2021).
66 See 'Libraries Change Lives', https://librarieschangelives.org.au/learn-more (accessed 4 October 2021).
67 See 'Library of Things', https://www.libraryofthings.co.uk/why (accessed 4 October 2021).
68 Ibid.

69. See for example 'Reminiscence Collection', *Surrey County Council*, https://www.surreycc.gov.uk/libraries/borrow-or-renew/collections-and-reading-lists/reminiscence-collection (accessed 4 October 2021).
70. Heather Geller, 'Benefits of Reminiscence Therapy', *Elder Care Alliance*, October 2017, https://eldercarealliance.org/blog/benefits-reminiscence-therapy (accessed 4 October 2021).
71. Fiona Macleod, Lesley Storey, Teresa Rushe and Katrina McLaughlin, 'Towards an increased understanding of reminiscence therapy for people with dementia: A narrative analysis', *Dementia*, August 2020, https://doi.org/10.1177/1471301220941275 (accessed 4 October 2021).
72. See https://myturn.com (accessed 4 October 2021).
73. 'Does Equality Really Make Us Happier?', *Equality Check*, May 2020, https://www.equalitycheck.it/blog/does-equality-really-make-us-happier (accessed 4 October 2021).
74. Jan-Emmanuel De Neve and Nattavudh Powdthavee, 'Income Inequality Makes Whole Countries Less Happy', *Harvard Business Review*, January 2016, https://hbr.org/2016/01/income-inequality-makes-whole-countries-less-happy (accessed 4 October 2021).
75. 'Mental Health Statistics: Poverty', *Mental Health Foundation*, https://www.mentalhealth.org.uk/statistics/mental-health-statistics-poverty (accessed 4 October 2021).
76. 'Superdensity: The Sequel', 2015, http://www.pollardthomasedwards.co.uk/download/SUPERDENSITY_2015_download.pdf (accessed 4 October 2021).
77. 'The London Plan: The Spatial Development Strategy for Greater London', *Greater London Authority*, March 2021, https://www.london.gov.uk/sites/default/files/the_london_plan_2021.pdf (accessed 4 October 2021).
78. Ben Quinn, 'Affordable housing "will diminish due to UK planning changes"', *The Guardian*, August 2020, https://www.theguardian.com/politics/2020/aug/06/affordable-housing-will-diminish-due-to-uk-planning-changes (accessed 4 October 2021).
79. 'Negative impact of vacant land on communities', *Greenspace, Scotland*, https://www.greenspacescotland.org.uk/news/derelict-sites-contribute-to-perceptions-of-urban-decline (accessed 4 October 2021).
80. 'Living with Beauty: Promoting health, well-being and sustainable growth', *Report of the Building Better*, Building Beautiful Commission, https://assets.publishing.service.gov.uk/government/uploads/system/uploads/attachment_data/file/861832/Living_with_beauty_BBBBC_report.pdf (accessed 4 October 2021).
81. 'The Impact of Vacant and Derelict Land', *The Scottish Land Commission*, December 2019, https://www.landcommission.gov.scot/news-events/news/the-impact-of-vacant-and-derelict-land (accessed 4 October 2021).
82. Eric Baldwin, 'Tiny Pop-Ups: Delivering New Experiences in Small Packages', *Arch Daily*, September 2020, https://www.archdaily.com/947429/tiny-pop-ups-delivering-new-experiences-in-small-packages (accessed 4 October 2021).
83. Richard Brown, Kat Hanna and Rachel Holdsworth (eds), 'Making good – shaping places for people: A Centre for London Collection', *Centre for London*, March 2017, https://www.centreforlondon.org/wp-content/uploads/2017/02/CFLJ5081_collection_essay_placemaking_0217_WEB-1.pdf (accessed 4 October 2021).
84. See 'The Glass House', https://theglasshouse.org.uk/about-us (accessed 4 October 2021).
85. 'Good community engagement leads to successful projects', *RIBA*, https://www.architecture.com/knowledge-and-resources/knowledge-landing-page/good-community-engagement-leads-to-successful-projects (accessed 4 October 2021).
86. Philip Watson, 'The uncomfortable truth about post-occupancy evaluation', *Architects' Journal*, July 2020, https://www.architectsjournal.co.uk/news/opinion/the-uncomfortable-truth-about-post-occupancy-evaluation (accessed 4 October 2021).
87. Op. cit., 'Social Value Toolkit for Architecture', *RIBA*.

Index

A

acoustics *see* noise
activity *see* exercise and activity
aesthetics 130–131
    architectural detailing 138–139
    architectural patterns 144–145
    artworks 134–135
    colour 132–133
    entrances 142–143
    handmade furniture 146–147
    nooks and crannies 148–149
    pitched roofs 150–151
    playful typologies 150–151
affordable housing 204–205
air pollution 34–35, 55, 59, 79
    houseplants and 104–105
allotments 100–101
animals 116–117
artworks 134–135
atria 16–17, 19
autonomy and control 60–61
    adaptable work spaces 66–67
    entrance spaces 84–85
    flexible separating devices 62–63
    laundry spaces 86–87
    meditation spaces 90–91
    openable windows 78–79
    personal space bubbles 68–69
    personalisation of spaces 74–75, 149
    private outdoor space 82–83
    safety 80–81, 160–161, 171
    self-sufficiency 76–77
    sense of choice 72–73
    sleep and rest spaces 88–89
    smart control systems 64–65
    storage 70–71
awnings 52–53

B

balconies 26–27, 54–55, 83
bedrooms 42–43
benches *see* seating, public
biophilia *see* nature and biophilia

C

chatting spaces 188–189
choice, sense of 72–73
circadian lighting 14–15
circadian rhythms 5, 15
circulation spaces
    chance interaction spaces 188–189
    characterful 171
    cloisters 18–19
    daylit 18–19
    deck access 10–11
climate change 37, 51, 77, 117, 129
cloisters 18–19
cluster homes 182–183
colonnades 177
colour 132–133

comfort 30–31
    acoustic baffles and panels 46–47
    acoustic buffers 44–45
    dual-aspect spaces 56–57
    ergonomic furniture 38–39
    mechanical ventilation 58–59, 79
    openable windows 78–79
    overheating 5, 9, 11, 31, 51
    shading 50–53, 177
    sleeping environments 42–43
    sound-masking systems 48–49
    thermal mass 40–41
    underfloor heating 40–41
    winter gardens 54–55
community *see* social interaction and community
control *see* autonomy and control
cooling
    dual-aspect spaces 56–57
    mechanical ventilation 58–59, 79
    openable windows 78–79
    roof lights 13
    sleep and 43
corkboards 74–75
corridors *see* circulation spaces
courtyards 16–17, 19
COVID-19 pandemic 2, 59, 67, 69, 71, 77, 83, 93, 125
crèches 190–191
cycling 155, 156–159, 162–165

D

daylight/sunlight 4–5, 53
    atria and courtyards 16–17, 19
    circulation spaces 18–19
    deck access 10–11
    dual-aspect spaces 56–57
    roof lights 12–13
    shading 50–53, 177
    staggered balconies 26–27
    window seats 6–7
    see also windows
deck access 10–11
detailing, architectural 138–139
doorways 142–143

E

eco-anxiety 37
emotive learning trails 112–113
entrances 84–85, 142–143
equitable spaces 204–205
exercise and activity 154–155
    active commuting facilities 162–163
    active facades and colonnades 176–177
    active transport hubs 164–165
    cycle-friendly streets 158–159
    filtered water dispensers 174–175
    green routes and spaces 111, 156–157
    intriguing routes 170–171
    lakes and 119

    outdoor exercise equipment 178–179
    public seating and 166–167
    running trails 156–157
    sports facilities 178–179
    stairs 168–169
    street lighting and 160–161
    swimming pools and lidos 172–173
    walkable neighbourhoods 158–159

F

facades
    active 176–177
    gardens 128–129
    green 94–95
food growing 100–103
furniture
    ergonomic 38–39
    handmade 146–147
    planter 114–115
    social 198–199
    window seats 6–7
    see also street furniture
fusuma 63

G

garden streets 124–125
gardens 82–83, 100–101
    facade 128–129
    indoor 102–103
    rooftop 101, 122–123
    sensory 126–127
    wildlife 116–117
    winter 54–55
geveltuin 128–129
green routes 156–157
green spaces 110–111, 157
green walls and facades 94–95
growing areas 100–103

H

heating 40–41
homeworking 66–67
houseplants 104–105

L

lakes 118–119
landmarks 152–153
language 196–197
laundry spaces 86–87
legibility 130–131
    colour for wayfinding 132–133
    entrances 142–143
    signage 136–137
    urban landmarks 152–153
    visual identities 140–141
libraries 202–203
lidos 172–173
light tubes 12–13

lighting 4–5
    circadian 14–15
    street 160–161
    task 22–23
    see also daylight/sunlight
loneliness 181
low traffic neighbourhoods 124–125

M

materials 32–33
    natural 33
    thermal mass 40–41
    upcycling 36–37
    Volatile Organic Compounds (VOCs) 34–35, 37, 59, 105, 147
meditation spaces 90–91
mindfulness 29, 31, 39, 91, 119, 127, 173
mobile phones 24–25, 89, 91, 121
murals 134–135

N

napping 88–89
nature and biophilia 92–93
    biophilic patterns 144–145
    curved and organic forms 108–109
    facade gardens 128–129
    garden streets 124–125
    green routes 156–157
    green walls and facades 94–95
    growing areas 100–103
    houseplants 104–105
    indoor water features 98–99
    materials and 33
    nature trails 112–113
    parks and green spaces 110–111, 157
    planter furniture 114–115
    ponds and lakes 118–119
    roof gardens 101, 122–123
    sensory gardens 126–127
    trees 96–97
    views of nature 106–107
    water channels 120–121
    wildlife 116–117
navigation see wayfinding
noise
    acoustic baffles and panels 46–47
    acoustic buffers 44–45
    background sounds 89, 99
    open-plan spaces and 185
    sleep and 43
    sound-masking systems 48–49
    winter gardens and 55
nooks and crannies 148–149

O

off-grid living 77
open-plan spaces 47, 49, 85, 184–185
overheating 5, 9, 11, 31, 51

P

parenting rooms 190–191
parking, cycle 162–163, 165
parks 110–111, 157
patterns, architectural 144–145
personal space bubbles 68–69
personalisation of spaces 74–75, 149
phone lockers 24–25, 89
plants see nature and biophilia
play areas 194–195
poetry 196–197
pollution see air pollution
ponds 118–119
pop-up projects 206–207
post-occupancy evaluation 208–209
prospect and refuge theory 43, 107, 123
public spaces 192–193

Q

quality, sense of 138–139, 144–145

R

roof gardens 101, 122–123
roof lights 12–13
roofs
    pitched 150–151
    sawtooth 12–13
rumination 31
running trails 156–157

S

safety 80–81, 160–161, 171
sculptures 134–135
seating, public 114–115, 166–167, 198–199
self-sufficiency 76–77
sensory gardens 126–127
shading 50–53, 177
signage 136–137
sinks 28–29
sleep 5, 15, 25, 42–43, 88–89
smart control systems 64–65
social interaction and community 180–181
    affordable spaces 204–205
    chance interaction spaces 188–189
    cluster homes 182–183
    crèches 190–191
    indoor community spaces 186–187
    libraries 202–203
    open-plan spaces 184–185
    parenting rooms 190–191
    play areas 194–195
    poetry and language 196–197
    post-occupancy evaluation 208–209
    public spaces 192–193
    shared cooking and eating areas 200–201
    social furniture 198–199
    stakeholder engagement 208–209
    temporary infill projects 206–207
sound-masking systems 48–49
sports facilities 178–179
stairs 168–169
stakeholder engagement 208–209
storage 70–71
street furniture 114–115, 125, 166–167, 198–199
streets
    cycle-friendly 158–159
    garden streets 124–125
    intriguing routes 170–171
    lighting 160–161
    public squares and village greens 192–193
    walkable neighbourhoods 158–159
    water channels 120–121
    see also facades
sunlight see daylight/sunlight
swimming pools 172–173

T

temporary infill projects 206–207
thermal mass 40–41
trees 96–97

U

underfloor heating 40–41
upcycling 36–37

V

ventilation
    dual-aspect spaces 56–57
    mechanical 58–59, 79
    openable windows 78–79
    roof lights 13
    sleep and 43
    urban landmarks 152–153
village greens 192–193
visual identities 140–141
Volatile Organic Compounds (VOCs) 34–35, 37, 59, 105, 147

W

wabi-sabi 147
walkable neighbourhoods 158–159
walking see exercise and activity
walls, green 94–95
washing-up 28–29
water
    filtered water dispensers 174–175
    indoor water features 98–99
    ponds and lakes 118–119
    water channels 120–121
wayfinding
    colour for 132–133
    signage 136–137
    visual identities 140–141
    water channels 121
wildlife 116–117
windows
    dual-aspect spaces 56–57
    openable 78–79
    positioning of 20–21
    raised sills 8–9
    roof lights 12–13
    shading devices 50–51
    sinks next to 28–29
    views of nature 106–107
    window seats 6–7
winter gardens 54–55
woonerfs 124–125